Gundolf S. Freyermuth
Games | Game Design | Game Studies

Media Studies

Gundolf S. Freyermuth (PhD) is Professor of Media and Game Studies and a founding director of the Cologne Game Lab at TH Köln–University of Applied Sciences in Cologne, Germany. He also teaches Comparative Media Studies at the ifs international film school Cologne. His research interests include video games, audiovisuality, transmediality, and network culture.

GUNDOLF S. FREYERMUTH
Games | Game Design | Game Studies
An Introduction

With Contributions by André Czauderna,
Nathalie Pozzi and Eric Zimmerman

[transcript]

Bibliographic Information published by the Deutsche Nationalbibliothek
The Deutsche Nationalbibliothek lists this publication in the Deutsche Nationalbibliografie; detailed bibliographic data are available in the Internet at http://dnb.d-nb.de

© 2015 transcript Verlag, Bielefeld

All rights reserved. No part of this book may be reprinted or reproduced or utilized in any form or by any electronic, mechanical, or other means, now known or hereafter invented, including photocopying and recording, or in any information storage or retrieval system, without permission in writing from the publisher.

Cover layout: Kordula Röckenhaus, Bielefeld
Printed and bound in Great Britain by Marston Book Services Ltd, Oxfordshire
Print-ISBN 978-3-8376-2983-5
PDF-ISBN 978-3-8394-2983-9

Contents

PROLOG

Playing, Making, Thinking Games | 11
Playing—Games | Making Games—Game Design |
Thinking Games—Game Studies | Acknowledgments

I GAMES

Introduction | 33

1 What is a Game? Systematic and Historical Approaches | 35
Attempts at Systematic Definitions | Failure of Systematic
Definitions | Historical Definition: The Alterity of Digital Games

2 Games in the Modern Era. A Short Media History | 43
Games | Primary, Secondary, and Tertiary Mediality | Case Study:
Soccer—A Game's Journey Through Medialities | Quaternary Mediality:
From Spectator to Player

3 Procedural Turn (since the 1950s) | 59
Quadruplicate Origin of Digital Games | Digital Technology | Artificial
Intelligence | Flight Simulation | Virtualization of Analog Games | Playful
Use of Digital Technology | Procedurality

4 Hyperepic Turn (since the 1970s) | 69
Game Economics | From Mainframe and Arcade Games to Console and PC
Games | The Innovative Genre of Text-Adventures | The Evolution of
Audiovisual Storytelling | The Hyperepic

5 Hyperrealistic Turn (since the 1990s) | 81
Digital Technology | From the Model of the Novel to the Model of the
Film | Hyperrealism | Authenticity and Operativity | The Innovative Genre
of the First-Person Shooter

6 The Double Alterity of Digital Games | 91
The Evolution of Games into an Audiovisual Medium | Digital Games vs. Analog Games and Linear Audiovisions | The Defining Medium of Digital Culture

7 A Look Ahead: Hyperimmersive Turn? | 97
The Evolution of Digital Games | Lifelike Agency in Games | Utopia Holodeck | Gamelike Agency in Real Life | Potential for Hyperimmersive Turn

INTERMEZZO: GAME // FILM

Introduction | 111

1 Game and Film | 115
Competition | Collaboration | Convergence

2 Audiovisual Rivalries | 125
Media History | Media Theory

3 Modes of Audiovisual Storytelling | 131
Storytelling in Space and Time | Pre-Industrial Audiovisions: Theater | Industrial Audiovisions: Film and Television | Digital Audiovisions: Games | Complementarity | Summary: The Four Cs

II GAME DESIGN

Introduction | 143

1 Analog Design | 147
The Evolution of Industrial Design Practices | The Evolution of Industrial Design Thinking

2 Digital Design | 153
The Digitalization of Design Practice | The Digitalization of Design Thinking

3 A Short History of Game Design | 161
The First 40 Years | Present and Future

4 Areas of Game Design | 165
The Role of the Game Designer | Triad, Tetrad, and the Function of Narration

5 Practices of Game Design | 171
The Process of Game Development | The Principle of Worldbuilding | Authorship in Game Design | Don't Follow These Rules! A Primer for Playtesting *by Nathalie Pozzi and Eric Zimmerman*

III GAME STUDIES

Introduction | 187

1 Theories of Analog Games vs. Theories of Digital Games | 191
Pre-Industrial Theories of Playing and Games | Industrial Theories of Playing and Games

2 The Schisms of Game Studies | 201
Sedimentative Approaches: Game Design Theories | Exaptative Approaches 1: Theories from Social Sciences | Exaptative Approaches 2: Theories from the Humanities

3 Desideratum: Overcoming the Schisms | 209
Longing for Synthesis | Adaptative Approaches

4 Perspectives of Research 1: Digital Games | 217
Mechanics | Story | Aesthetics | Technology | Transmedia

5 Perspectives of Research 2: Serious Games | 225
Mechanics, Story, Aesthetics, Technology, Transmedia | Gamification | Opposition to Industrialism

EPILOG

Academization and Aesthetic Production | 235
The Cultural Rise of Games | Game Studies and Digital Game Design Education in Germany | International Higher Game Design Education: Six Examples from Five Countries *by André Czauderna* | Structure of an Undergraduate Program for Game Design | Consequences of Academization

Sources | 263

Prolog

Playing, Making, Thinking Games

In the early 21st century we are now experiencing—as witnesses and as protagonists—the aesthetic development and cultural rise of a new audiovisual form of expression and narration. Like earlier forms of defining audiovisual media, such as theater, film, and television, digital games are shaping our self-perception as well as our perception of the world around us. Parallel to this development, two new practices and fields of research are emerging:

- For one, new practices in the field of software development—part handicraft, part art—are coming about, organized under the headings "Media Design" and "Game Design." Just as games differentiate themselves from movies through dramatic composition and means of representation—by tending towards nonlinearity and iterative experiences—, so does game design differentiate itself from the traditional practices of analog film production through iterative and less-linear tendencies.
- Second, a new academic discipline is forming: the analytical and critical interpretation of digital games. Just as we speak of literary studies, film studies, or design studies, so may we speak of Game Studies.

Consequently, the goal of this book is to offer a part-historical, part-theoretical introduction to address three aspects of digital games: 1) the origin and history of the new medium digital games, 2) the innovative processes of their production, and 3) the emerging discipline of their academic investigation. The following questions lie at the center of this study:

- How did digital games come to be and how did they rise to become the central audiovisual form of expression and storytelling in digital culture?
- How did the procedures of their technical-artistic production develop and what are the current practices of game design?

- How did the academic analysis of the social effects and cultural meaning of digital games form?
- Where is Game Studies today and in what direction is it developing?

In three chapters I will outline the stages of the media-historical development of analog and digital games (*I Games*), the history and artistic practices of their production in the context of analog and digital design (*II Game Design*), as well as the most important approaches and research questions of their analysis from the different perspectives of game design theory, social sciences and humanities (*III Game Studies*). Particular attention will be placed on the mutual relationship between game design and Game Studies in artistic-academic education and research.

First, two terms—which this volume already carries in its title—require clarification: *games* and *game design*. In Game Studies there has been some debate over which term best describes their object of scholarly focus—*computer game, videogame, digital game*. *Computer game* connotes games played on PCs and hardly those played on consoles, tablets or smartphones. *Videogame* connotes games that use moving pictures, meaning also pre-digital games like TENNIS FOR TWO (1958) or analog arcade games of the 1960s and 1970s. Corresponding thoughts can be found, for example, by Jesper Juul and Tristan Donovan.[1] Both authors have, for different reasons, nonetheless decided on the term *videogame*. However, in order to place the emphasis on games with a basis in digital technology, in this book I will primarily speak of *digital games* and will use *games* as a synonym to refer to the same concept. Older forms of games I will specifically reference as *analog games*.[2]

---

1 Juul, Jesper: *Half-Real: Video Games Between Real Rules and Fictional Worlds*, Cambridge, Mass.: MIT Press (Kindle edition) 2005, loc. 26 and Donovan, Tristan: *Replay: The History of Video Games*, Lewes, East Sussex: Yellow Ant (Kindle edition) 2010, loc. 74.

2 Social and technological changes effect semantic change. The use of the word *computer* demonstrates that. According to the Oxford English Dictionary, *computer* was first used in 1613 as a designation for humans who were making calculations or computations (http://www.oed.com/view/Entry/37975?redirectedFrom=computer#eid). In 1869 *computer* was used for non-human calculators for the first time (ibid.; see also OED, ibid.). In everyday live, however, *computer* continued to denote "a *person* who solved equations; it was only around 1945 that the name was carried over to machinery." (Ceruzzi, Paul E. *A History of Modern Computing*, Cambridge Mass.: MIT Press 1998, p. 1) At that point it came to mean analog computing machines. If you were dis-

The term 'game design' is no less undefined. An important reason for this is the lack of codification with regard to the different roles involved in the production of digital games. So far a clear division of labor, as witnessed in theater, film and television, does not exist in game production. Game design is, therefore, often used to mean two different things: either to designate the entire process of game development or to designate a specific field of work in this production process along with the likes of game arts or game informatics.[3]

The title of this introduction uses the term clearly in the first, synecdochic sense: This book concerns itself with digital games, their production and their analysis. A central aspect of this process of production is, of course, game design in the second, narrower sense, which will be a central topic in chapter *II Game Design*.

PLAYING—GAMES

In his "Manifesto for a Ludic Century"[4] the game designer and game design theoretician Eric Zimmerman presents the thesis that a structural affinity exists between the fundamental characteristics of digital technology and the fundamental characteristics of games, analog as well as digital: "Games like Chess, Go, and Parcheesi are much like digital computers, machines for creating and storing numerical states. In this sense, computers didn't create games; games created computers."[5] Beyond that, digital networking would promote evermore-complex information systems. For a digital culture shaped by such systems, games would be the ideal medium thanks to their systematicity: "[G]ames are dynamic systems [...] While every poem or every song is certainly a system, games are dynamic systems in a much more literal sense. From Poker to Pac-Man to War-

---

cussing one of the few existing digital computers, you had to explicitly emphasize this. Within a decade, however, this relation reversed: By the end of the 1950s, computer meant digital computer. If you were discussing analog computers, you had to explicitly emphasize this.—The cultural rise of digital games seems to effect a similar change: The word "game" has come to mean digital game. If we are discussing analog games, we soon might have to explicitly emphasize this.

3 Compare for a definition of these fields of work below. p. 140.
4 Zimmerman, Eric: "Manifesto for a Ludic Century," *Kotaku*, September 9, 2013; http://kotaku.com/manifesto-the-21st-century-will-be-defined-by-games-1275355204.
5 Ibid.

craft, games are machines of inputs and outputs that are inhabited, manipulated, and explored."[6]

Film and television, the defining media of the 20th century, corresponded—with the linearity of their passively received audivisions—to the information and entertainment needs of industrial work and culture. Digitalization, however, writes Zimmerman, initiated a categorical metamorphosis: "In the last few decades, information has taken a playful turn. [...] When information is put at play, game-like experiences replace linear media."[7] Games would, therefore, become the most important medium of the ludic 21st century: "Increasingly, the ways that people spend their leisure time and consume art, design, and entertainment will be games—or experiences very much like games."[8]

Zimmerman's "ludic manifesto" can be understood as a concise depiction of perspectives and opinions that are circulating in contemporary culture. Indeed, before our eyes a lasting medial upheaval is taking place that targets audiovisual forms of expression and representation. Their transformation is the product of technological progress—a development which has already occurred twice in modern times.[9]

Between the Renaissance and the Enlightenment, mechanization brought about the theater of illusion with its proscenium or picture-frame stage, outfitted with the most modern technical means available. For example, equipment and procedures used in shipbuilding to quickly move heavy objects were put into practice in theaters to move sets and even actors. Thanks to its mechanical means for manipulating space and time, the theater of illusion and its most important genre, the drama, became the genuine audiovisual form of storytelling in the pre-industrial period.

With the next technological push brought about between the Enlightenment and postmodern times through industrialization, photography was introduced, followed by film and, finally, television; the last two, of course, were based on the technology first developed for and by photography. Through means of stored, edited and "made to move" pictures and sounds, time and space could be manipulated as never before and new kinds of stories could be told audiovisually. This categorical performance increase over the theater—the potential for a successive development of epicness of audiovisual representation—film and television owe to evermore-advanced industrial recording, storing, editing,

---

6 Ibid.
7 Ibid.
8 Ibid.
9 Compare for this in more detail below p. 128ff.

distribution and transfer techniques. In the medium of linear audiovisuality, feature films and television series emerged as genuine and dominant storytelling methods of industrial culture. Thus, since the early 20th century, first silent movies, then talkies, and finally television influenced the audiovisual construction of reality and its perception.

Against this media-historical background it should be no surprise that aesthetic consequences are also tied to the current technological push: digitalization. Digital software allows the recording, generation, storing, editing, distribution and interactive manipulation of texts and sounds, as well as still and moving pictures. Through two unique characteristics, software thereby distinguishes itself from all analog media as a means of production and storage. First, software is transmedial. In the universal medium of stored bits and the software programs with which they can be edited, the analog diversity of specific media and tools—paper and typewriter, celluloid, camera and cutting room, vinyl, magnetic tape, microphone and mixing board etc.—is unified. Second, the digital transmedium possesses a 'fluidity' that, together with feedback systems, to a large extent eliminates the primacy of chronology that characterizes analog mediality.[10] In this quality lies the principal interactivity of the transmedium known as software.

This potential for transmediality and fluidity is aesthetically realized above all in digital games. Earlier, movies simultaneously expressed the experiences of, and impacted, industrial culture—not least in the industrial work environments of hierarchical and linear processes. The experiences of digital culture are expressed similarly today in digital games, which are now also impacting the postindustrial work environment that is characterized by knowledge-work, i.e., networked manipulation of digital symbols. The machine as central metaphor for industrial culture is replaced by the game as a central metaphor for digital culture.[11]

Society, said Niklas Luhmann, creates media for the purpose of self-observation.[12] Digital games are the youngest means—medium—for such reality construction and, thereby, also for perceiving the world as well as for self-perception. As Noah Wardrop-Fruin writes, games allow us—more so than linear audiovisual media do—"to understand our evolving society, in which (often hidden)

---

10 Compare below chapter II, part *2 Digital Design*, p 149ff.
11 See Chaplin, Heather: "Will The 21st Century Be Defined By Games?," *Kotaku*, September 12, 2013; http://www.kotaku.com.au/2013/09/will-the-21st-century-be-defined-by-games/
12 Luhmann, Niklas. *The Reality of the Mass Media*, Stanford, Calif.: Stanford University Press 2000, p. 97.

software models structure much of how we live now."[13] In the interactive mirror of digital games we experience ourselves and search for an understanding of what is under development in our everyday lives—a digital society and culture just as different from the industrial culture of the 19th and 20th centuries as that culture was distinct from the society and culture of the preindustrial period.

The first part of this book (*I Games*) describes how digital games went from their—audiovisually as well as narratively restricted—beginnings in the middle of the past century to the equally narrative and hyperrealistic medium of today that is able to compete with film and television. The starting point is formed by an analysis of the diverse attempts to define analog as well as digital games (*I-1 What is a game? Systematic and Historical Approaches*). The overview leads to the understanding that, like all media and arts, digital games can only be understood in their historical development. The second chapter, therefore, outlines the history of games in the context of modern media and the arts (*I-2 Games in the Modern Era: A Short Media History*). The broader focus then lies on the three artistic-technical pushes in which digital games have evolved since the middle of the 20th century (*I-3 Procedural Turn, since the 1950s; I-4 Hyperepic Turn, since the 1970s; I-5 Hyperrealistic Turn, since the 1990s*). At the preliminary end of this development, digital games characterize themselves in their otherness in relation to both analog games and linear audiovisions.[14] I seek to define this otherness in the sixth chapter (*I-6 The Double Alterity of Digital Games*). A further turn that has been transpiring for several years now has led to the proliferation of natural user interfaces (NUIs) and 'natural' ways of interacting with virtual worlds and non-player characters (NPCs). This turn should further strength-

---

13 Wardrip-Fruin, Noah: *Expressive Processing: Digital Fictions, Computer Games, and Software Studies*, Cambridge, MA: The MIT Press 2009, p. 19.
14 For the term "audiovisions" see Zielinski, Siegfried: *Audiovisions: Cinema and Television as Entr'actes in History*, Amsterdam: Amsterdam University Press 1999: "Audiovision has become an amalgam of many media communication forms that used to be separate and is thus, for the interim, the fulfillment of that project to occupy the minds and hearts with culture-industrial commodities, which was begun in the nineteenth century." (p. 14) Zielinsky distinguishes four "dispositif arrangements" that exist so far: (1) the mostly pre-cinematic "production of illusions of motion in space with the aid of a heterogeneous ensemble of picture machines"; (2) cinema; (3) television; (4) digital "audiovisions, as a complex construction kit of machines, storage devices, and programmes for the reproduction, simulation, and blending of what can be seen and heard …" (p. 19).

en the categorical otherness of digital games (*I-7 A Look Ahead: Hyperimmersive Turn?*).

In the development of digital games, their relation to film has carried a special meaning. Since the 1980s both of these forms of audiovisual media have been engaged in a close technical, economic and aesthetic exchange, while at the same time they have been competing for both consumers and talent. More than a few artists and theoreticians have even envisaged a merging of the two audiovisual media. The *Intermezzo: Game // Film* first takes stock (*Intermezzo-1 Game and Film*), only to then look back on the earlier audiovisual rivalries between theater and film as well as between film and television and to discuss which of the two historical models the relationship between games and film will most closely come to resemble (*Intermezzo-2 Audiovisual Rivalries*). Foundational for the aesthetic relationship between audiovisual media in general and between games and film in particular proves to be their highly different affordances for the manipulation of time and space in the representation of narrative processes (*Intermezzo-3 Modes of Audiovisual Storytelling*).

MAKING GAMES—GAME DESIGN

Whoever develops digital games today is historically privileged: they are confronted with the opportunity, as only very few generations before them, to actively help shape the important beginnings and to set the course of a radically new medium. Contributing to this opportunity is the fact that since the turn of the century no other medium has made progress that was as speedy—both in an economic as well as a technical-aesthetic respect.

In 2014 digital gaming made up an approximately 86 billion-dollar industry, up from 23.3 billion in 2003 and 52.5 billion in 2009.[15] The seven countries with the highest game revenues were the US (22 billion), China (18 billion), Japan (12 billion), South Korea (3.8 billion), Germany (3.6 billion), the UK (3.5 billion) and France (2.7 billion).[16] However, there exists a huge international imbalance between production and consumption. Germany, for example, is the largest market in Europe, but non-German companies produced 75% of German

---

15 N. N.: "Global Revenues of the Video Game Industry from 2003 to 2014," http://www.statista.com/statistics/269744/global-revenues-of-the-video-game-industry-since-2003/, as of Aug 6, 2015.

16 N. N.: "Top 100 Countries by Game Revenues," http://www.newzoo.com/free/rankings/top-100-countries-by-game-revenues/

revenue. Furthermore, German games make up only three percent of the world market, which is dominated by American productions, followed by games made in Japan, Canada and the United Kingdom.[17]

In 2013 the worldwide most successful game was GRAND THEFT AUTO V. On its first day alone it brought in 800 million dollars: "...more money than any movie—*Titanic* or *Avatar* or *The Avengers*—has made in its entire run in North American theaters. And given the game's $270 million budget, it may also have cost more than any movie."[18] AAA games—meaning digital games that are produced with a large budget and promoted with a great deal of marketing—are even bigger global phenomena than literary bestsellers and movie blockbusters.

Cultural differences among the bestselling games can be seen most clearly in popular sports. In 2013 in the US, for example, MADDEN NFL 25 belonged to the top-five bestselling games with 2.7 million copies sold.[19] In Germany, the soccer-simulator FIFA 14 took the top spot in place of the football-simulator with around 870,000 copies sold.[20] Certain differences also show themselves in the

---

[17] N. N.: "Hintergrund: Computer- und Videospiele in Deutschland: Kreativbranche mit Wachstum- und Innovationspotential," *BIU—Bundesverband Interaktive Unterhaltungssoftware*, 2014; http://www.biu-online.de/de/presse/newsroom/themendossier-computer-und-videospiele-in-deutschland.html; Quillen, Dustin: "Canada Overtakes U.K. as Third Largest Game Maker. Canada now sits behind the U.S. and Japan in the ranks of top game developing nations," *1Up.com*, April 6, 2010; http://www.1up.com/news/canada-overtakes-largest-game-maker.—This situation is somewhat similar to the film business where Anglo-Saxon productions dominate the global market as well: In 2013, Hollywood film productions "held a share of nearly 70% of the EU market, while European productions represented only 26%." (European Parliament Think Tank: "An Overview of Europe's Film Industry," December 16, 2014; http://www.europarl.europa.eu/thinktank/en/document.html?reference=EPRS_BRI(2014)545705)— In 2014, German movies had a German market share of only 26.7 percent. (N. N., "The German Film Scene Production – Subsidies – Contacts A Comprehensive Overview," June 25, 2015; http://www.german-films.de/fileadmin/mediapool/pdf/Marktanalyse/THE_GERMAN_FILM_SCENE_2014_25June2015.pdf)

[18] Corliss, Richard: "Prisoners Wins the Weekend, but It's No 'Grand Theft Auto V'," *Time*, September 22, 2013; http://entertainment.time.com/2013/09/22/prisoners-wins-the-weekend-but-its-no-grand-theft-auto-v/

[19] N. N.: "USA Yearly Chart: The Year's Top-Selling Game at Retail Ranked by Unit Sales—2013," *VGChartz* 2014; http://www.vgchartz.com/yearly/2013/USA/

[20] N. N.: "Germany Yearly Chart: The Year's Top-Selling Game at Retail Ranked by Unit Sales—2013," *VGChartz* 2014; http://www.vgchartz.com/yearly/2013/Germany/

popularity of platforms and genres. In the US, games played on computers make up only a fraction of total revenue—220 million of the 15.4 billion dollars total brought in by game software in 2013.[21] In contrast, in Germany 76% of all gamers sit at a computer.[22] However, smartphones enjoy the same amount of popularity in both countries (44% in the US as well as Germany).[23]

The demographic data also converge over time if one adopts a long-term perspective. In 2013 59% of Americans played digital games; 52% of these gamers were men and 48% women.[24] 29% were under 18 years old and 39% over 36. In Germany almost every other person played regularly—the numbers fluctuate between 34.2 million and 39.8 million German gamers.[25] The percentage of female gamers in Germany was at 44%. 29% of German gamers were under the age of 18 and 20% over 50.[26]

The constant growth—more gamers, more games, higher revenue—, which has characterized the cultural assertion of digital games since the 1970s, occurred in the context of constant change in the requirements of production, distribution, and use. The foundation for this ongoing radical transition was laid with the establishment of first stationary and then also mobile broadband networking. Since the 1990s, the distribution and use of AAA console and PC titles has been virtualized and novel distribution platforms have emerged (*Steam* as well as app stores from Apple and Android, among others). In the USA the share of digital distribution rose between 2010 and 2014 from 29% to 52%.[27] The in-

---

21 ESA, Entertainment Software Association: "Essential Facts about the Computer and Video Game Industry 2013," April 2014, p. 12 http://www.theesa.com/facts/pdfs/ESA_EF_2014.pdf
22 Illek, Christian P.: "Gaming in Deutschland," *Bitkom*, August 13, 2013; http://www.bitkom.org/files/documents/BITKOM_Praesentation_Gaming_PK_130813(1).pdf
23 ESA: "Essential Facts about the Computer and Video Game Industry 2013," p. 5; Illek: "Gaming in Deutschland."
24 ESA: "Essential Facts about the Computer and Video Game Industry 2013," pp. 2-3.
25 N. N.: "Infographic: The German Games Market," *Newzoo: Games Market Research*, January 6, 2014; http://www.newzoo.com/infographics/infographic-german-games-market/
26 BIU, Bundesverband Interaktive Unterhaltungssoftware: "Altersverteilung," 2014; http://www.biu-online.de/de/fakten/reichweiten/altersverteilung.html
27 ESA: "Essential Facts about the Computer and Video Game Industry 2014," p. 13.— In most other countries, the virtualization of distribution is lagging behind. For example, in Germany the market share of downloaded PC and console games grew from 7% in 2010 to 32% in 2014. (BIU, Bundesverband Interaktive Unterhaltungssoftware:

troduction of smartphones, starting in 2007 with Apple's iPhone, and of touchtablets, starting in 2010 with Apples's iPad, popularized the new genre of mobile and casual games.

In the last decade, the extreme development of distribution channels for digital games has correlated with equally strong changes in how they are financed. Promoted as well through ubiquitous digital networking, a variety of alternative economic approaches, processes, and funding models came about. Disruptive were, for one, Free-to-Play (F2P) and freemium models, based on micropayments in games that started off free, and for another pre-financing through so-called crowdfunding, i.e., the collecting of a large number of small contributions by future users of technical or medial products that had yet to be produced.

Among the currently most successful F2P online games are LEAGUE OF LEGENDS, which brought in almost a billion dollars worldwide in 2014, as well as CROSSFIRE and DUNGEON FIGHTER ONLINE—both sitting at about 900 million dollars each.[28] In the field of F2P casual games, three count as the most important measuring sticks for all others: (1) FARMVILLE (2009), which had, at one point, over 80 million monthly users on Facebook[29], stayed the most popular game for two years, despite attacks from critics[30] and brought in more than a billion dollars in revenue;[31] (2) ANGRY BIRDS (since 2009), which in 2014 had been downloaded more than 2 billion times in its various incarnations,[32] and (3) CAN-

---

"Kauf digitaler Spiele per Download," 2014; http://www.biu-online.de/fileadmin/ user_upload/bilder/marktzahlen/2014/Marktzahlen_-_2014_gesamt/Infografik_-_Kauf _per_Download/BIU_Infografik-4_Kauf_per_Download.PNG)

28 Campbell, Colin: "How League of Legends is Upending the Video Game Business," October 24, 2014; http://www.polygon.com/2014/10/24/7061573/how-league-of-lege nds-is-upending-the-video-game-business

29 Cashmore, Pete: "FarmVille Surpasses 80 Million Users," *Mashable*, February 20, 2010; http://mashable.com/2010/02/20/farmville-80-million-users/

30 On the controversy around FARMVILLE and Ian Bogost's satire game COW CLICKER (2010) see Tanz, Jason: "The Curse of Cow Clicker: How a Cheeky Satire Became a Videogame Hit," *Wired*, December 20, 2011; http://archive.wired.com/magazine/20 11/12/ff_cowclicker/all/

31 See Ha, Anthony: "Zynga's Pincus Says FarmVille Has Passed $1B In Total Player Purchases," *TechCrunch*, February 4, 2013; http://techcrunch.com/2013/02/05/farmvil le-1-billion/

32 Long, Neil: "Two Billion Downloads? We're Just Getting Started, Says Angry Birds Creator Rovio," January 23, 2014; http://www.edge-online.com/features/two-billion-downloads-were-just-getting-started-says-angry-birds-creator-rovio/

DY CRUSH SAGA (2012), which in 2013 was played daily by 93 million people for more than a billion plays, while around 4% of players made in-game purchases[33]. Analyzing the MMO Game Marketplace, Cameron Koch states: "Free-to-play works because it eliminates any barrier for entry, and allows developers to penetrate markets that otherwise might be unable to play traditional console video games. [...] By having millions upon millions of players, even a small percentage of players paying money regularly can add up big time."[34]

As influential for the development of games was the establishment of virtualized and globalized subscription models, as they existed in principle during the early modern era at the beginning of the production of printed books. Games, which cannot find funding through traditional channels, can be financed on platforms like Indiegogo (founded 2008), Kickstarter (2009), or the German Startnext (2010). By its own account, Kickstarter alone had collected 1.5 billion dollars for 75,000 projects across 220 countries by the end of 2014, among which was a quarter-billion dollars for more than 4,000 digital games.[35] So far, the most successful game projects on Kickstarter have been TORMENT: TIDES OF NUMENERA, which raised 4.2 million dollars in 2013, PROJECT ETERNITY (later titled: PILLARS OF ETERNITY), which reached 4 million in 2012, as well as MIGHT NO. 9, which made 3.8 million in 2013.[36] The "upcoming space trading and combat simulator"[37] STAR CITIZEN, by the game design veteran Chris Roberts (WING COMMANDER, 1990) has managed, through a combination of traditional Kickstarter campaign and a self-run crowdfunding website, to accumulate over 85 million dollars between 2012 and 2015.[38]

Just as with the older audiovisual media of theater, film, and television, the economic potentials of digital games are based on the requirement that products

---

33 Grubb, Jeff: "King: 93M Daily Candy Crush Saga Players, 500M installs, and $568M Profit in 2013," *VentureBeat*, February 18, 2014; http://venturebeat.com/2014/02/18/candy-crush-saga-publisher-king-by-the-numbers-inforgraphic/
34 Koch, Cameron: "Free-to-Play Games Continue to Dominate the MMO Game Marketplace," *Techtimes*, October 24, 2014; http://www.techtimes.com/articles/18666/20141024/free-to-play-games-continue-to-dominate-the-digital-video-game-marketplace.htm
35 N. N.: "Stats," *Kickstarter*, November 28, 2014; https://www.kickstarter.com/help/stats?ref=footer
36 N. N.: "Most Successful Crowdfunding Campaigns," *CrowdfundingBlog*, October 29, 2014; http://www.crowdfundingblog.com/most-successful-crowdfunding-projects/
37 N. N.: *Star Citizen Wiki*, November 2014; http://starcitizen.wikia.com/wiki/Star_Citizen
38 https://robertsspaceindustries.com/funding-goals; as of August 5, 2015.

achieve a certain technical and artistic quality. A decisive structural condition has emerged only over the last decade with the increase of technical options: small groups and even individuals now possess means of production that two decades ago were the exclusive privilege of large companies and corporate groups and, thereby, also only of highly specialized experts. Admittedly, with access to these new technical means comes the challenge to use them artistically in a way that is appropriate and creative. Four developments influenced game design over the last decade:

- A latent stagnation and aesthetic crisis of AAA titles developed through a high degree of division of labor;
- The rise of a so-called indie scene, whose 'small' games are anchored outside of the commercial mainstream and tend towards artistic experimentation and breaking out of traditional schemas;
- A proliferating differentiation into evermore specific subgenres combined with a strong increase in the number of titles being produced;
- The introduction of practices and mechanisms of game development into other production and service areas.[39]

The last of these proves the outstanding position that digital games occupy in the emerging digital media dispositif. Once upon a time the new medium of film influenced the other, older arts: theater and the novel, painting and music developed cinematic qualities. No differently, digital games—namely their aesthetic qualities, such as the mass phenomenon of their interactive reception—are influencing media production and consumption today, especially in the areas of the competing audiovisual media of film and television. Parallel to that the procedures of game design as a production method for audiovisual media are becoming a central practice of digital culture—from the adoption of 'world building'[40], as it is a common practice in game design, by advanced film productions or by the diverse visualization attempts in research and industry to the 'gamifying' applications of game design principles in marketing or knowledge transfer.[41] As a

---

39 See for gamification below p. 224ff.
40 See Freyermuth, Gundolf S.: "Der Big Bang digitaler Bildlichkeit: Zwölf Thesen und zwei Fragen," in: Freyermuth, Gundolf S./Gotto, Lisa (ed.), *Bildwerte: Visualität in der digitalen Medienkultur*, Bielefeld: transcript 2013, pp. 287-333, here p. 293 ff.
41 See for example Zichermann, Gabe/Cunningham, Christopher: *Gamification by Design: Implementing Game Mechanics in Web and Mobile Apps*, Sebastopol, Calif.: O'Reilly Media 2011.

basic tendency one can thereby identify a 'democratization of game design': a steady cheapening and simplification of the financing, conception, production, global distribution and use of digital games.[42]

In *II Game Design* I will first analyze the double origins of game design: on the one hand from practices of analog design, especially its principles of prototyping and iteration that have arisen since the beginning of Industrialization in the context of producing hardware artifacts (*II-1 Analog Design*); on the other hand from practices of digital design that developed since the mid-20th century in the context of software production and visual design (*II-2 Digital Design*). Due to these dual origins during the last half-century in the design of digital games, the development of highly different procedures took place: The non-commercial beginnings in the academic hacker culture of the 1960s and 1970s gave way to the professionalization of the game industry, following in the footsteps of the industrial, highly collaborative role model of film production and especially that of Hollywood. Since the turn of the century an indie scene is also thriving that in its methods of working orients itself more closely toward the rather artistic role models of indie music and indie film (*II-3 A Short History of Game Design*). Next, I analyze the role of the Game Designer and the most important fields in the production of digital games (*II-4 Areas of Game Design*) as well as the standard procedures and processes in game production, including the basic principle of world building. In a special contribution, Nathalie Pozzi and Eric Zimmerman then provide a primer for the all-important method of playtesting (*II-5 Practices of Game Design*). Evidently game design is becoming a central discipline of creative production in digital culture. Its role model effect is changing the design of soft- and hardware, processes and experiences.

THINKING GAMES—GAME STUDIES

In contradistinction to the central and still growing importance of games as well as game design in digital culture, Game Studies continue to play only a minor role both in public perception and in academia. Groundbreaking monographs,

---

42 On the question regarding the most exciting development tendency in the game industry, the game developers Randy Smith and Josh Holmes answered with "the democratization of game development," i.e., "the 'democratization' of game development and the rise of the indie developer." (Cited after Fullerton, Tracy. *Game Design Workshop: A Playcentric Approach to Creating Innovative Games*. Boca Raton: CRC Press/Taylor & Francis (Kindle edition) 2014, loc. 1800 und loc. 5148).

which understood and interpreted games as a new medium and a new form of expression, were first published in the last decade of the 20th century, roughly 40 years after the development of early forms of digital games in research labs. The institutional establishment of Game Studies as an academic field only began in the early 21st century and parallel to the establishment of the first artistic-technical degree paths for game design. Anglo-Saxon and Scandinavian universities were pioneers of this process. In the German speaking world such an establishment is still pending:

"Although individual professors and assistant professors are, by now, beginning to make game studies a focal point, this is still not reflected in the disciplines (e.g. at the Technical University for Visual Arts Braunschweig, the University of Paderborn, and the University of Cologne). Beyond that, both small and large third-party-funded projects as well as (virtual) institutes for computer game research sprung into existence (for instance, at the Center for Art and Mediatechnology in Karlsruhe and at the University for Media in Stuttgart, or the Zurich University of the Arts). Finally, at the beginning of 2014, a novel professorship for game studies was established in the context of the artistic-academic bachelor 'Digital Games' at the Cologne Game Lab at the Cologne University of Applied Sciences. However, despite these advances, it is still impossible to speak of any fundamental establishment of the field in the German language-space."[43]

The formation of new disciplines is nothing special *per se*. Since the sciences and humanities followed the example of the industrial division of labor and became specialized, 'Taylorized,' perpetual processes of differentiation have led to literally hundreds of new disciplines and fields of study. Only very rarely, however, was it possible to found a new discipline whose subject was a culturally defining medium, i.e., a medium which influences and changes the thinking of a majority of people—their view of the world, their understanding of life, and even of their own identity.

The modern process of establishing new disciplines dealing with defining media started during the first half of the 19th century when the analysis of and reflection on language and literature became academic endeavors. Since the En-

---

43 Beil, Benjamin/Freyermuth, Gundolf S./Gotto, Lisa: "Vorwort," in: Beil, Benjamin/ Freyermuth, Gundolf S./Gotto, Lisa (ed.), *New Game Plus: Perspektiven der Game Studies. Genres – Künste – Diskurse*, Bielefeld: transcript 2015, pp. 7-24, here p. 8; the Cologne University of Applied Sciences has since been renamed TH Köln—University of Applied Sciences. (All quotes from German language sources have been translated for this edition.)

lightenment and especially in the German-speaking world, literature was thought to promote what had otherwise proven elusive: cultural identity and political unity. Consequently, literature, which during the 19th and early 20th century influenced public consciousness more than any other medium in most developed regions of the world, separated into nationally defined categories despite cultural exchange. Along similar lines, literary studies grew into national academic disciplines operating in the context of national self-assurance and nationalism.[44]

Next, a good half-century after the advent of motion pictures—a new medium of artistic expression particularly symptomatic of the industrial mentality[45]—, the academic study of film was organized and institutionalized. Just as economic factors of movie production encouraged (or coerced) planning and production beyond national borders,[46] so too did film studies develop—in line with the supra-national influence, distribution and reception of its material—mostly beyond national boundaries and specialization.

Now, since the turn of the century and again several decades after the social and aesthetic emergence of a new medium, digital games, the new discipline of Game Studies is finally forming.[47] As an audiovisual medium of expression, representation and storytelling, video games are produced, distributed and used not just nationally or internationally within larger cultural realms, but globally. In digital culture they influence the perception of the self and of the world beyond all borders, i.e., transnationally. As the youngest of the disciplines that deal with a single medium and art form, Game Studies remains in its early stages and continues to draw sustenance from its respective geographical roots. To date the dis-

---

44 See Lämmert, Eberhard: "Germanistik – eine deutsche Wissenschaft," in: Lämmert, Eberhard, et al. (ed.), *Germanistik – eine deutsche Wissenschaft*, Frankfurt a. M.: Suhrkamp Verlag 1967, pp. 7-41.

45 See Benjamin, Walter: "The Work of Art in the Age of Mechanical Reproducibility" (3rd version), in: Benjamin, Walter, *et al. Selected Writings*. 4 vols, Cambridge, Mass.: Belknap Press 1996, vol. 3, pp. 251-283, here p. 281, note 42: "Film is the art form corresponding to the increased threat to life that faces people today."

46 See, Arnold: *The Social History of Art*, 4 vols., London, New York: Routledge 1999 (*1951), p. 159.

47 See, for example, Egenfeldt-Nielsen, Simon/Smith, Jonas Heide/Tosca, Susana Pajares: *Understanding Video Games: The Essential Introduction*, New York: Routledge 2008; Mäyrä, Frans: *An Introduction to Game Studies*, London: SAGE (Kindle edition) 2008.

cipline, in regard to its subject matter and institutional organization, has yet to follow in the footsteps of its art form, which is inherently global.[48]

Their status quo indicates, however, not only a low degree of institutional presence, but also an extreme diversity of topics and approaches. Practice-oriented game design theories formulated since the early 1980s confront approaches from the social sciences and humanities that date their origins to the 1990s: an eclectic mix of theories taken from older disciplines, such as educational research, media pedagogy, psychology, and design theory, as well as sport and social sciences, literature, art, and media studies. In a positive light, this diversity can be interpreted as a naturally developing interdisciplinarity. In a negative light, it can be seen as a lack of theoretical coherence and, thereby, also as a lack of the disciplinarity required for the creation of a common ground to serve as a necessary precondition for interdisciplinary research.

For example, what Mark Butler stated a few years ago: "The texts about computer games that exist so far suffer mostly from too restricted subject horizons," is true still today: "Computer games fall into the scope of numerous disciplines that either want nothing to do with them, or attempt to coopt them for their own use."[49] Butler's institutional perspective correlates with Franz Mäyrä's view, which is oriented toward content: "scholars [...] bring with them the methodologies typical for their original disciplines."[50] The same conclusion is reached by Simon Egenfeldt-Nielsen, Joan Heide Smith, and Susana Pajares Tosca:

"[G]ame researchers are an eclectic bunch with a multidisciplinary background. Humanist scholars with film or literature backgrounds constitute the largest single group, but game research conferences are also attended by social scientists (mostly sociologists) and, very importantly, game designers. [...] Most researchers, at least at present, choose to adopt

---

48 The Anglo-Saxon and Scandinavian countries' head start continues. In Germany the first university-level educational offerings are starting to arise. For German-language research, three more recent publications are: Beil, Benjamin: *Game Studies: Eine Einführung*, Red guide, Berlin: Lit 2013; Michael Hagner and Games Coop: *Theorien des Computerspiels zur Einführung*, Hamburg: Junius 2012; Freyermuth, Gundolf S./Gotto, Lisa/Wallenfels, Fabian (ed.): *Serious Games, Exergames, Exerlearning: Zur Transmedialisierung und Gamification des Wissenstransfers*, Bild und Bit (Bielefeld: transcript, 2013).
49 Butler, Mark: *Would you like to play a game? Die Kultur des Computerspielens*, Berlin: Kulturverlag Kadmos 2007, p. 8.
50 Mäyrä, Frans: *An Introduction to Game Studies*, loc. 2333.

methods and approaches from their primary fields. Ethnographers tend to observe players. Those trained in film studies tend to analyze the games themselves and communication scholars tend to analyze interactions between players."[51]

This diversity results in, on the one hand, the necessity for creating a common ground for Game Studies: defining the object and the borders of the discipline, as well as specific approaches and methods. On the other hand, this diversity also presents the twofold question: To what degree, in a time of transmedial media technology and also transmedial media production, can individual disciplines of media—especially of the audiovisual media of film, television, web video, and games—still understand the transmedial development and the embedding of different media in this process? Or is, maybe, an all-encompassing comparative media studies required?

Part *III Game Studies* presents the development and central positions of various approaches in the theoretical and—more or less—academic study of digital games. The starting point is formed by philosophical and single-field studies of analog games, from Gottfried Wilhelm Leibniz, to Johan Huizinga, all the way to Marshall McLuhan (*III-1 Theories of Analog Games vs. Theories of Digital Games*). This prehistory of Game Studies closes with an outline of the existing three big avenues for research: approaches from game design theory, the social sciences, and the humanities (*III-2 The Schisms of Game Studies*). The observation and description of them working together and, even more frequently, side by side, reveals the necessity for replacing the existing schisms in Game Studies with an analysis that no longer operates with imported approaches. Instead its focus and methods would arise from the direct confrontation with and the analysis of digital games themselves (*III-3 Desideratum: Overcoming the Schisms*). In conclusion and looking ahead, research perspectives will be developed that could serve the desired evolution of Game Studies (*III-4 Perspectives of Research 1: Digital Games; III-5 Perspectives of Research 2: Serious Games*).

The prevention of a rift between artistic and academic practices—as it exists in older forms of media—is equally important for a successful adaptation of Game Studies to its subject. The epilogue reflects, therefore, how game design and Game Studies are and should be conveyed in academic and artistic education. In a special contribution, André Czauderna analyzes the structures of six undergraduate game design programs from five different countries, while I discuss the objectives and the organization of game design education by the example of one artistic-academic bachelor program. In conclusion, I reflect on the

---

51 Egenfeldt-Nielsen et al.: *Understanding Video Games*, loc. 351 und loc. 360.

consequences of this on-going academization—from changes in aesthetic production to a possible maturation of the medium and an increase of game literacy. (*Epilogue: Academization and Aesthetic Production*).

ACKNOWLEDGMENTS

This book has many co-authors. I would like to mention them in the order of their appearance. First of all my sons, Leon and George Freyermuth, made me play again in the 1990s after a long pause—even if I could never be an equal opponent for them on any console. I would also like to thank my director-colleague Björn Bartholdy for, over a decade ago, giving the first push towards founding a stand-alone games education—even if it became a long, strenuous road that would appear to transform into a dead end before our very eyes more than once, until we could take on the first bachelor students at the Cologne Game Lab in the fall of 2014. Those, without whom we could never have reached this goal and without whom this book would also never have been written, are Rainer Weiland and Joachim Metzner, who helped us during the founding phase of the Cologne Game Lab.

For more than a decade now, I have gained motivation, information, and most importantly inspiration from the students of the BA and MA programs at the ifs international film school Cologne and since 2010 from the students of the further education Master's Degree at the Cologne Game Lab. My thoughts on digital games were continuously influenced by conversations and debates with three colleagues, with whom I've had the privilege of editing two anthologies on games over the last few years: Benjamin Beil, Lisa Gotto, and Fabian Wallenfels, as well as through lectures and encounters with numerous guest lecturers, whom we were able to invite to the Cologne Game Lab, including Espen Aarseth, Georg Backer, Csongor Baranyai, Chris Crawford, Tracy Fullerton, Martin Ganteföhr, Thomas Hensel, Jörg Müller-Lietzkow, and Eric Zimmerman.

Different versions of parts of this text have already appeared in anthologies—in German and English; I must also thank the editors of those versions for their proofreading.[52]

---

52 Freyermuth, Gundolf S.: "Spiel // Film. Prolegomena zu einer Theorie digitaler Audiovisualität," in: Kaminski, Winfred/Lorber, Martin (ed.), *Clash of Realities 2010: Computerspiele: Medien und mehr...*, Munich: kopaed 2010, pp. 27-46; Freyermuth, Gundolf S.: "Movies and Games: Audiovisual Storytelling in the Digital Age," in: Enyedi, Ildiko (ed.), *New Skills for New Jobs / New Skills for Old Jobs: Film and Me-*

Numerous suggestions and corrections from my Game Lab colleagues Björn Bartholdy, André Czauderna, and Katharina Tillmans as well as Carmen Schneidereit helped to improve the German manuscript. Carmen Schneidereit also provided the layout. For this edition, André Czauderna, Nathalie Pozzie and Eric Zimmerman graciously provided valuable contributions for which I am very grateful.

Leon Freyermuth diligently translated most of the German text and helped me edit my own translations. Curtis L. Maughan helped with the copy editing of the English manuscript, thereby significantly improving its linguistic quality and clarity—which of course does not change the fact that all of the remaining mistakes and deficiencies remain my fault alone.

Last but not least, Elke Freyermuth patiently followed along with the protracted process that went into creating this book in its different versions.

To all of you: Thank you!

I dedicate this book to my academic mentor Eberhard Lämmert (1923-2015). I owe him so much.

---

dia Schools in the Digital Revolution, Budapest: University of Theatre and Film Art 2012, pp. 21-39; Freyermuth, Gundolf S.: "Ursprünge der Indie-Praxis. Zur Prähistorie unabhängigen Game Designs," in: Kaminski, Winfred/Lorber, Martin (ed.), *Gamebased Learning. Clash of Realities 2012*, Munich: kopaed Verlag 2012, pp. 313-326; Freyermuth: "Der Big Bang digitaler Bildlichkeit"; Freyermuth, Gundolf S.: "Angewandte Medienwissenschaften. Integration künstlerischer und wissenschaftlicher Perspektiven in Lehre und Forschung," in: Ottersbach, Beatrice/Schadt, Thomas (ed.), *Filmlehren. Ein undogmatischer Leitfaden für Studierende*, Berlin: Bertz + Fischer 2013, pp. 263-278; Freyermuth, Gundolf S.: "Serious Game(s) Studies. Schismen und Desiderate," in: Freyermuth, Gundolf S./Gotto, Lisa/Wallenfels, Fabian (ed.), *Serious Games, Exergames, Exerlearning: Zur Transmedialisierung und Gamification des Wissenstransfers*, Bielefeld: transcript 2013, pp. 421-464; Freyermuth, Gundolf S.: "Vom Drama zum Game. Elemente einer historischen Theorie audiovisuellen Erzählens," in: Kaminski, Winfred/Lorber, Martin (ed.), *Clash of Realities 2014: Computerspiele: Spielwelt-Weltspiel: Narration, Interaktion und Kooperation im Computerspiel*, Munich: kopaed 2014, pp. 29-37; Freyermuth, Gundolf S.: "Der Weg in die Alterität. Skizze einer historischen Theorie digitaler Spiele," in: Beil, Benjamin/Freyermuth, Gundolf S./Gotto, Lisa (ed.), *New Game Plus: Perspektiven der Game Studies. Genres – Künste – Diskurse*, Bielefeld: transcript 2015, pp. 303-355; Freyermuth, Gundolf S.: "Game Studies und Game Design," in: Sachs-Hombach, Klaus/Thon, Jan-Noël: *Game Studies. Aktuelle Anstäze der Computerspielforschung*, Cologne: Herbert von Halem 2015, pp. 67-100.

I Games

Introduction

Game Studies cannot seem to find an adequate definition for its central object of analysis. Of course Game Studies shares this problem with more than a few academic disciplines and fields of study. Both these facts have been observed before, as seen in *Understanding Games*, one of the few existing introductions to Game Studies: Just as sociology cannot quite arrive at a term for society and media studies fail to fully define what a medium is, so Game Studies have been incapable of coming to a consensus on what a game is.[1] There has been no shortage of attempts to arrive at such a definition. On the contrary, this number continues to grow, its proliferation driven mainly by three forces: practical and theoretical media interests, as well as academic policy debates.

Game designer and game design theoretician Jesse Schell, for example, has expressed the ambivalent position taken by media practitioners in face of the unavoidable theoretical challenge of formulating an exact description of "game." On the one hand, those who most vocally complain about the lack of "standardized definitions" are "mostly academics" and "farthest removed from the actual design and development of games."[2] On the other hand, the work of many practitioners would suffer from a lack of insight into their own actions and requirements: "[G]ame designers follow their gut instincts and feelings about what makes a good or a bad game, and sometimes have difficulty articulating what exactly it is about a certain design that is good or bad."[3] Only the attempt to clearly define what games are would force practitioners "to think about them clearly, concisely, and analytically."[4]

---

1 See Egenfeldt-Nielsen et al.: *Understanding Video Games*, loc. 281.
2 Schell, Jesse: *The Art of Game Design: A Book of Lenses*, Amsterdam und Boston: Elsevier/Morgan Kaufmann (Kindle edition) 2008, loc. 849.
3 Ibid., loc. 866.
4 Ibid., loc. 879. See Egenfeldt-Nielsen et al.: *Understanding Video Games*, loc. 1103.

This game design-oriented perspective is similar to those approaches in Game Studies that attempt to systematically conceive of and describe "both the necessary and sufficient features of games and play," as Frans Mäyrä remarks: "Such careful formulations are particularly instrumental to any formalist study of games."[5] These theoretical efforts are also not always free from practical and, in this case, academic and cultural policy interests. For, depending on how the definitions are approached—as games are described as aesthetic artifacts or social phenomena—, they connect themselves either with different existing disciplines or cultural practices:

"Defining anything is a highly political project. Define games as narrative and the research grants are likely to end up with departments devoted to film or literature studies. Define games as a subcultural teenage phenomenon and studies of games are less likely to be funded by ministries of culture, to reach the pages of the 'serious' press, or to be available in public or research libraries."[6]

Overview

The first part of this introduction provides a theoretically grounded history of digital games and at the same time a historically-oriented theory that tries to determine their relation on one hand to analog games and on the other hand to the linear audiovisions of film and television. In the first chapter, an overview of preceding attempts to define games systematically leads to the insight that such a definition can be achieved only within the concrete historical context of digital games *(1 What is a Game? Systematic and Historic Approaches)*. The second chapter demonstrates, in a short media history of games and playing, the different medial characteristics and qualities of analog and digital games *(2 Games in the Modern Era. A Short Media History)*. Chapters 3 to 5 trace the history of digital games from the middle of the last century until the present. These chapters also outline three fundamental and accumulative steps of development that can be identified as having created the medium of digital games as we know it today *(3 Procedural Turn, 4 Hyperepic Turn, 5 Hyperrealistic Turn)*. Chapter 6 comprises these historical findings through a theoretical assertion of the unique otherness of digital games *(6 The Double Alterity of Digital Games)* and chapter 7 focuses on possible trends that seem to characterize the near-term development of digital games *(7 A Look Ahead: Hyperimmersive Turn?)*.

---

5   Mäyrä, Frans: *An Introduction to Game Studies*, loc. 543.
6   Egenfeldt-Nielsen et al.: *Understanding Video Games*, loc. 738.

1 What is a Game?
Systematic and Historical Approaches

Parallel to the cultural advancement of digital games, an almost infinite variety of competing and contradictory suggestions have emerged regarding how games—as the object of game design as well as Game Studies—should be defined.

ATTEMPTS AT SYSTEMATIC DEFINITIONS

Three notable examples from the area of game design are:

- "A game is a form of art in which participants, termed players, make decisions in order to manage resources through game tokens in the pursuit of a goal." (Greg Costikyan)[1]
- "A game is: a closed, formal system, that: Engages players in structured conflict and: Resolves its uncertainty in an unequal outcome." (Tracy Fullerton)[2]
- "All games share four defining traits: a goal, rules, a feedback system, and voluntary participation [...] Everything else is an effort to reinforce and enhance these four core elements." (Jane McGonigal)[3]

---

1 Cited in Salen, Katie/Zimmerman, Eric: *The Game Design Reader: A Rules of Play Anthology*, Cambridge, Mass.: MIT Press 2006, p. 78.
2 Fullerton, Tracy. *Game Design Workshop*, loc. 1638.
3 McGonigal, Jane: *Reality Is Broken: Why Games Make Us Better and How They Can Change the World*, New York: Penguin Press (Kindle edition) 2011, loc. 375-389.

The accumulation of definitions over the past decade has inevitably led to attempts at synthesis, and thereby to meta-definitions as well. Katie Salen and Eric Zimmerman, for example, analyze a row of existing attempts at defining "play" and "game" in their standard reference work *Rules of Play*, including those by Johan Huizinga[4], Roger Caillois[5], and Brian Sutton-Smith[6]. Thereby they isolate common elements, specifically the rule-governed, goal-oriented nature of games, as well as their voluntariness and artistic character, in order to distill their own definition. For one: "Play is free movement within a more rigid structure."[7] And for another: "A game is a system in which players engage in an artificial conflict, defined by rules, that results in a quantifiable outcome."[8]

Comparatively, Jesper Juul approached the problem two years later in *Half-Real* by distilling his "classic game model" from seven definitions:

"A game is a rule-based system with a variable and quantifiable outcome, where different outcomes are assigned different values, the player exerts effort in order to influence the outcome, the player feels emotionally attached to the outcome, and the consequences of the activity are negotiable."[9]

This model, as Juul holds, laid the medial groundwork for "at least a 5,000-year history of games": "It corresponds to the celluloid of movies; it is like the canvas of painting or the words of the novel."[10] Only in the last third of the 20th century would it have been called into question by the new genre of analog role-playing games and their institution of a game master, as well as by aspects of digital games.[11]

Similarly, Jesse Schell examines diverse definitions in *The Art of Game Design* and abstracts ten qualities that are assigned to games:

---

4   Huizinga, Johan: *Homo Ludens: A Study of the Play Element in Culture*, Boston: Beacon Press (Kindle edition) 1955 (*1938).
5   Caillois, Roger: *Man, Play, and Games*, New York: Free Press of Glencoe 1961.
6   Avedon, Elliott M./Sutton-Smith, Brian: *The Study of Games*, New York: J. Wiley 1971; Sutton-Smith, Brian: *The Ambiguity of Play*, Cambridge, Mass.: Harvard University Press 1997.
7   Salen, Katie/Zimmerman, Eric: *Rules of Play: Game Design Fundamentals*, Cambridge, Mass.: MIT Press (Kindle edition) 2003, loc. 934.
8   Ibid., loc. 1281.
9   Ibid., loc. 400.
10 Ibid., loc. 98.
11 Ibid., loc. 311 and loc. 578.

"Q1. Games are entered willfully.
Q2. Games have goals.
Q3. Games have conflict.
Q4. Games have rules.
Q5. Games can be won and lost.
Q6. Games are interactive.
Q7. Games have challenge.
Q8. Games can create their own internal value.
Q9. Games engage players.
Q10. Games are closed, formal systems."[12]

From these characteristics Schell arrives at his own definition: "A game is a problem solving activity, approached with a playful attitude."[13]

FAILURE OF SYSTEMATIC DEFINITIONS

What these diverging efforts to systematically define the object of game design theory and Game Studies have in common is that they all fail equally when confronted with the reality of digital games and the current status of aesthetic theories. Frans Mäyrä and Egenfeldt-Nielsen et al. have pointed out that the majority of circulating definitions disregard newer game types, such as simulations, MMORPGs (Massively Multiplayer Online Role-Playing Games), or open-world and sandbox games, in the name of establishing coherent definitions.[14] In the context of the history of theories, these ontologically-oriented attempts and their utilitarian search for definitions prove themselves bound to the normativity of pre-modern poetics. Thus, from the perspective of aesthetic theory, they seem equally backwards and futile. Insofar as digital games are aesthetic constructions, whose contents are underlain by forms of social and cultural change, all efforts to arrive at an ahistorical, systemically normative definition seem destined to fail from the outset. Advanced artistic production in modern times, after throwing off the chains of religion and tradition, has to approach the evolving lifestyles, topics, and contradictions of its time in new ways, again and again—it knows little of exemplary rules, the relevance of which are timeless. Like works

---

12 Schell, Jesse: *The Art of Game Design*, loc. 1079.
13 Ibid., loc. 1149.
14 Egenfeldt-Nielsen et al.: *Understanding Video Games*, loc. 1095; Mäyrä: *An Introduction to Game Studies*, loc. 580.

of literature or the fine arts, like theatre plays or movies, digital games can be reduced to single concepts solely from a historical perspective.[15]

At present such a view should focus on the understanding of the categorical difference between analog and digital media and, thereby, on the conceptual and historical separation of analog and digital games. Most attempts at systematic definition, however, hardly take such a differentiation into consideration.[16] Jesper Juul admittedly recognizes a historical development—since the 1970s games have arisen that no longer fit into the "classic game model."[17] But in his analyses he purposefully does not differentiate between analog and digital games. Rather, he understands the latter simply as "continuations of a history of games that predate these [video games] by millennia."[18] Salen and Zimmerman target this non-differentiation even more directly:

"The definition of 'game' that we proposed in the previous chapter makes no distinction between digital and non-digital games—the qualities that define a game in one media (sic!) also define it in another."[19]

HISTORICAL DEFINITION: THE ALTERITY OF DIGITAL GAMES

By contrast, I will argue for a twofold alterity of digital games. This otherness aims at more than the drastic technical and aesthetic disparities between, say, a board-game like *Trouble* and a first-person shooter, such as TITANFALL (2014). That these differences alone render an attempt at a common definition questionable is hardly a new insight. Frans Mäyrä writes, for example, of "specific forms into which digital games and their playing have evolved during the last dec-

---

15 The necessity of an historical analysis of ahistorical-systematic attempts at definition is stressed by Mäyrä: *An Introduction to Game Studies*, loc. 550.
16 See Egenfeldt-Nielsen et al.: *Understanding Video Games*, loc. 1112: "... the definitions say nothing about digital computation and thus are definitions of games and not merely video games."
17 See, for example, Juul: *Half-Real*, loc. 103: "[T]he history of video games is partly about breaking with the classic game model."
18 Ibid., loc. 63: Juul also sees digital games as explicitly outside of the tradition of "cinema, print literature, or new media."
19 Salen/Zimmerman: *Rules of Play*, loc. 1358.

ades"[20]: "As games have moved from streets and living room tables into various computer systems, the associated activity has also altered its character, or, at least, gained different dimensions."[21] His argument for the "specificity of digital games" focuses particularly on the moment of their dependence on audiovisual technology: "The absolute majority of digital games is based on screens of various kinds."[22]

To others, however, such a perspective seems bound to surface similarities, since analog and digital contents are of totally different medialities, even if they appear on the same screens. Dieter Mersch, for instance, writes: "At first sight we seem to be dealing with audiovisual phenomena, which, however, have starkly separated themselves from film or video as they are different not just technologically and mathematically, but in fact in every way."[23] Mersch's "media theory of the digital game" defines their specificity as their dependence on decision logic: "It determines the foundations of games and sets the mathematical frame of their programs."[24] Mersch indicates thereby a difference of digital games mainly from older audiovisual media.[25]

Alterity, however, designates more than any arbitrary differences, no matter how peripheral or fundamental they may be. The Latin "alter" describes—for example in the term *alter ego* or in the words alternative and alternating—a particular other: an other, which stands in a specific and describable relation to a first, a related other. Insofar as "alter" implies a binary relationship, it has to do with (1) the philosophical-historical discussion of the term "alterity" regarding the relationship of an individual or subject to another individual or subject, (2)

---

20 Mäyrä, Frans: *An Introduction to Game Studies*, loc. 715.
21 Ibid., loc. 691.
22 Ibid., loc. 812.
23 Mersch, Dieter: "Logik und Medialität des Computerspiels. Eine medientheoretische Analyse", in: Distelmeyer, Jan/Hanke, Christine/Mersch, Dieter (ed.), *Game over!?: Perspektiven des Computerspiels*, Bielefeld: transcript 2008, pp. 19-41, here p. 20.
24 Ibid., p. 35.
25 In regard to analog games, Mersch says: "While it's true that classical forms of play can be as well reduced to operators in decision logic and thereby mathematized as chess computers demonstrate, decision logic is not constitutive for many game situations—I should like to mention children's games, competitions, ritualized forms of play, sports etc." (Ibid., p. 37) Thereby the question remains what sort of relationship should arise between digital and analog games, i.e., between the two "kinds" of analog games: those, which like digital games are bound by "logical decision making operators," and those, which remain independent of them.

the relationship between races (considerably in the context of modern relations of Jews and non-Jews as well as postcolonial relations of whites and non-whites), and (3) the relationship between genders. Thus, in the second half of the 20th century, a thread of philosophizing about alterity ran from Emmanuel Levina's contemplations on the radical alterity of death, which is always experienced as the dying of another,[26] to the reflections of his friend Jacques Derrida on memory and sorrow as a destruction of the alterity of the other through internalization.[27] Next, trains of thought on the postmodern disposition of media, especially Jean Baudrillard's work, focused on the fears that medial and networked audiovisual communication in particular—from television to the World Wide Web—would destroy the experience of otherness of subjects and cultures.[28] These texts in turn influenced modern gender theory. Judith Butler, for example, understands alterity as "the constitutive outside,"[29] against which the respective inside forms itself and finds its identity.

By adapting the term alterity in order to make what it structurally contains fruitful for the historical theory of media, the first half of my assumption claims that *digital games are not something entirely different from analog games, but rather that digital games are the specific other of analog games.* As a medium, digital games form themselves through their indispensable intermedial relation to

---

26 See Bergo, Bettina: "Emmanuel Levinas," *Stanford Encyclopedia of Philosophy*, August 3, 2011; http://plato.stanford.edu/entries/levinas/. See also Lévinas, Emmanuel: "The Philosopher and Death," in: (ed.), *Alterity and Transcendence*, New York: Columbia University Press 1999, pp. 153-168.

27 See Reynolds, Jack: "Jacques Derrida (1930-2004)," *Internet Encyclopedia of Philosophy – A Peer-Reviewed Academic Source*; http://www.iep.utm.edu/derrida/; Derrida, Jacques: *Mémoires: for Paul de Man*, New York: Columbia University Press 1986.

28 See Baudrillard, Jean/Lotringer, Sylváere: *The Ecstasy of Communication*, Brooklyn N.Y.: Autonomedia 1988. For Baudrillard, in the end the object and above all machines remain as the "radical Other": "the inhuman alterity of an intelligent device [...] artificial alterity" (Baudrillard, Jean/Guillaume, Marc: *Radical Alterity*, Los Angeles, CA; Cambridge, Mass.; London: Semiotext(e); Distributed by the MIT Press 2008, p. 110.

29 Butler, Judith: *Bodies that Matter: On the Discursive Limits of "Sex,"* Abingdon, Oxon; New York, NY: Routledge 2011 (*1993). Butler introduced the term "constitutive outside" to the context of the development of the medium: "The exclusionary matrix by which subjects are formed thus requires the simultaneous production of a domain of abject beings, those who are not yet 'subjects,' but who form the constitutive outside to the domain of the subject." (Ibid., p. xiii)

the medium of analog games. Only through this experience of alterity were digital games able to find their identity over the course of several decades. The second half of my assumption claims the same relationship—the dichotomous relationship of identity and alterity—between digital games and the linear audiovisions of cinema and television: *that digital games are neither the same as nor radically different from linear audiovisions, but that digital games are the specific other of linear audiovisions.*

2 Games in the Modern Era. A Short Media History

Games are media, this much seems indisputable. Still, it is seldom attempted to situate analog or digital games in the context of the history and theory of media. Quite clearly, however, digital games are positioned in the continuity of modern audiovisuality.[1] In particular, they are the latest step in the process of the steady

---

1 The German noun 'Spiel' can mean both game and play (which includes both connotations of 'play' as they are found in English usage, i.e., leisure activity and theater); the verb 'spielen' can express both the acts of playing as well as acting or performing. So already the German language itself reveals the shared origins and ongoing aesthetic proximity of 'Spiel' to the most important variations of audiovisual representation in modern times: from the stage play (Bühnen*spiel*) with its subcategories of comedy (Lust*spiel*), tragic drama (Trauer*spiel*), music play/drama (Sing*spiel*) or festival (Fest*spiel*) a clear line connects to the moving picture (Licht*spiel*), which appeared around 1900 in both of its variations—the fiction film (*Spiel*film) and the documentary film, which gave way to the television show (Fernseh*spiel*) and the video and computer game (Video*spiel* and Computer*spiel*). Moritz Lazarus remarked already in 1883, "that the etymology of the German word 'Spiel' indicates a light, aimlessly floating, self-returning movement, a movement that is not caught in a narrowly focused action and is not directed toward an approaching goal, but rather is concerned with the here and there, and the back and forth between polar positions." (Cited from Krämer, Sybille: "Ist Schillers Spielkonzept unzeitgemäß? Zum Zusammenhang von Spiel und Differenz in den Briefen 'Über die ästhetische Erziehung des Menschen'," in: Bürger, Jan (ed.), Friedrich Schiller: Dichter, Denker, Vor- und Gegenbild, Göttingen: Wallstein-Verl. 2007, pp. 158-171.) Until this day, a widespread connotation of the German word 'Spiel,' which has this aimless 'here and there' at its core, has to do with a mostly unintentional freedom of movement within and among machine parts:

rationalization of image and sound production aimed at perspectival realism that began in the Renaissance. As photography, film, and video did before, digital games have made this process faster, simpler, and cheaper: It started with painterly realism, moved to photorealism and now has reached hyperrealism: from Alberti's perspectival window view—"una finestra aperta"[2]—, which had to be manually constructed with great effort, to analog photography, which semi-automated the production of still and moving pictures, to real-time image generation via 3D engines. Just as the industrial media of film and television did not signify a radical break from the preindustrial medium of theater, but rather continued its aesthetic interests in numerous ways on a higher technological level—for instance the optical functionalization of the gaze or the century-long striving for an audiovisual synthesis, a total work of art—, in the same way current digi-

---

'The steering has too much play ("Spiel").' This is just how Katie Salen and Eric Zimmerman define human play: "Play is free movement within a more rigid structure." (Salen/Zimmerman: *Rules of Play*, loc. 4730) The fact that the most important audiovisual modern media have the same German language 'last name' of 'Spiel', which has its roots in free motion, points to what binds these media together irrespective of their great variety: the principle of aesthetic play. According to Friedrich Schlegel, aesthetic play also possesses narratological and mimetic features, within which the "appearance of acts" ("Schein von Handlungen") is generated through artistic means (Athäneums Fragments, in: Schlegel, Friedrich von/Behler, Ernst/Anstett, Jean Jacques/Eichner, Hans: *Kritische Friedrich-Schlegel-Ausgabe: Erste Abteilung: Kritische Neuausgabe*, vol. 2, Munich; Paderborn; Wien: F. Schöningh 1967, p. 180).—This definition has bestowed validity upon many later attempts—from Johan Huizinga up until contemporary game theorists like Jesse Schell—through the advantage of an openness which transcends the boundaries of the arts (and media). While this definition generally covers the similarities of the stage play (Bühnen*spiel*) and the digital game (digitales *Spiel*), it inevitably avoids their differences. For the close relationships among audiovisual media say little about the quality of those actual relationships. Cain slew Abel and everyone would like to find their own familial example of the dialectic of attraction and repulsion, of alternating states of cooperation, coexistence, and constant strife. In particular, the various—aesthetic, artistic, practical, technological, economic—aspects of the cultural relationships between game and film demand a more precise, historical clarification. See *Intermezzo: Game//Film*, p. 107ff.

2   Alberti, Leon Battista: *On Painting. Translated with Introduction and Notes by John R. Spencer*, New Haven: Yale University Press 1970, *1956, Chapter 19; http://www.noteaccess.com/Texts/Alberti/

tal forms of play are more than just distantly related to older forms of media such as theater, film, and television.

GAMES

In fact, historically speaking, games have been around far longer than all other forms of audiovisual representation. They are, as Chris Crawford argues in his "Phylogeny of Play," older than mankind.[3] Many animal species simulate real world movements and actions, such as hunting, in order to practice them in relative safety. To play in such a manner and to go beyond and develop more complex, rule-governed games appears to also be a fundamental tendency of Homo sapiens. Board games such as SENET (Egypt, 3100 BCE) or the ROYAL GAME OF UR (Sumer, 2600 BCE) belong to the earliest evidence of human culture. In 5th century BCE, the Greek historian Herodot described how, supposedly, 700 years earlier the Lydians in Asia Minor, who are also credited with the invention of money, survived long periods of starvation through the use of board, dice, and many other games and then finally, with one last game, found a solution that insured the survival of the entire community.[4] The game design theoretician Jane McGonigal speculates about the future of digital games by appealing to the historical function of analog games:

"When Herodotus looked back, he saw games that were large-scale systems, designed to organize masses of people and make an entire civilization more resilient. I look forward to a future in which massively multiplayer games are once again designed in order to reorganize society in better ways, and to get seemingly miraculous things done."[5]

Such positive use and valuation of games correlates with equally continuous, fundamental criticism and recurring attempts at banning them. Frans Mäyrä speaks of the "continuous history of bans or restrictions on games playing."[6] In the western and Christian-influenced modern era they range from the numerous

---

3   Crawford, Chris: "The Phylogeny of Play," (2010); http://www.erasmatazz.com/library/science/the-phylogeny-of-play.html
4   Herodotus/Macaulay, G. C.: *The History of Herodotus*, 2 vols., London; New York: Macmillan and Co. 1890, here Book 1, Clio, 94; http://www.sacred-texts.com/cla/hh/index.htm
5   McGonigal: *Reality Is Broken*, loc. 242.
6   Mäyrä: *An Introduction to Game Studies*, loc. 621.

attempts by British kings between the 14th and 16th century to ban soccer, to the ban of pinball machines in New York from the 1930s to the 1970s, all the way to the present, constantly flaring up cries to ban violent videogames. From a historical perspective, Jesper Juul writes, "the current preoccupation with the assumed dangers of video games is a clear continuation of a long history of regulation of games as such …"[7] The culture war surrounding play and specific forms of games shapes the social framework for the theoretically-oriented media history of games in the modern era, which I will attempt to outline in this chapter.

The categorical framework I will apply goes back to Harry Pross's study on media research from the 1970s.[8] In it Pross identifies different medialities in accordance with "the apparatus of the messaging system,"[9] i.e., in accordance with the extent to which technology is implemented and used. However, since the availability of technologies and of techniques is subject to constant change in different cultures, Pross's approach has the advantage of operating both systematically *and* historically at the same time. Thereby his theory of mediality allows for the understanding of the history of media as a process of progressive accumulation and differentiation.

PRIMARY, SECONDARY, AND TERTIARY MEDIALITY

Primary media do not require any technology. They "depend on bringing together special skills within a person."[10] In regard to communication media, Pross includes gestures and mimicry as well as pre-language and language-based sounds. Concerning forms of primary media that convey aesthetic experiences, he names rituals and ceremonies, among others. "The one thing they all have in common is the lack of an intermediate apparatus between the sender and receiver and that the human senses are sufficient for the production, transportation, and consumption of the message."[11] According to Pross's criteria—even if he does not name them—pre-technical variants of the theater, such as improvisational theater and street theater, as well as games that function without technology, belong to pri-

---

7   Juul: *Half-Real*, loc. 272.
8   Pross, Harry: *Medienforschung: Film, Funk, Presse, Fernsehen*, Darmstadt: Habel 1972.
9   Pross: *Medienforschung*, p. 119.
10 Ibid., p. 68.
11 Ibid., p. 78.

mary media: for instance, movement games like TAG and HIDE-AND-SEEK or games of skill, such as ROCK, PAPER, SCISSORS.

Addressing secondary media, Pross writes: "The communicator requires an apparatus."[12] This refers to images such as drawings, paintings, caricatures, or photographs, also coins and paper money bills, as well as texts like letters, leaflets, flyers, books, newspapers, and magazines. Secondary media, of course, already existed for millennia before the Renaissance. In modern times, however, they received a three-fold push in their evolution:

1) In the textual realm: through book printing that allowed for standardized reproduction of texts in greater numbers for the first time;
2) In regard to the image: through the mathematically-based perspective technique, which led to a visual realism that was previously unattainable;
3) In terms of audiovisual representation: through the accumulation of numerous mechanical technologies employed in the creation of unprecedented theater structures, including sets painted and arranged in perspective, hoists and lifting platforms, curtains, and the perspectival-oriented seating arrangements for the manipulation of the audience's gaze—the sum of which resulted in a new audiovisual realism.

As a modern complement to the church nave that was the central phantasmatic and public sacred space of the agrarian era, the theater and its proscenium or picture-frame stage advanced to become the central phantasmatic and public secular space of individual reflection, education, and self-understanding by the end of the mechanical era—a time characterized by gradual secularization. The new horizon opened up by the realistic audiovisual imitation of life turned the stage into the leading medium of the age:

"Drama, in a glittering succession of figures ranging from Shakespeare and Calderon to Racine, then dominated the literature of the West. It was the fashion to liken the world to a stage on which every man plays his part."[13]

At the same time games of secondary mediality—especially board and card games like CHESS or BLACKJACK—underwent a continual process of standardization, facilitated by the production of games through print and other mechanical means and the establishment of local, regional, national, and finally international

---

12 Ibid.
13 Huizinga, Johan: *Homo Ludens*, loc. 129.

distribution. The Industrial Age brought about the invention of numerous new games of secondary mediality as well—from the distinctly Prussian WAR GAME (1824) to the distinctly American MONOPOLY (1933) to DUNGEONS AND DRAGONS (1974). Although most of these new creations were identifiable as an expression of specific national (sub-)cultures, they nevertheless found massive, even intercultural, distribution.

Parallel to this, completely new tertiary media, in which "both the sender and receiver require apparatuses,"[14] arose through industrial technology. Harry Pross names the electric telegraph as the first tertiary medium. It was followed by, among others, the telephone, the gramophone, animated and live action film, audio and video recording on magnetic tape. In particular, the industrial broadcast media radio and television changed how and what people played in a lasting way. Live transmission transformed sport and competition games of first and secondary mediality—like SOCCER and FOOTRACES, BLACKJACK and CHESS—from local events, in which participants and audience were physically present, into national and international events, which were passively experienced by millions. Furthermore broadcast media created a variety of new spectator games that were staged purely for radio and television.

Many of these radio and TV shows sought to involve not only studio guests directly, but also—through remedial media—a select few representatives of the 'absent' and passively situated radio and television audience. An especially interesting example was presented by the German game show DER GOLDENE SCHUSS (1964-1970), which was adapted for British TV as THE GOLDEN SHOT (1967-1975). Viewers of this show could call in to control and shoot an apparatus that consisted of a crossbow connected to a camera. This innovative combination of a new visual perspective and interactivity can be seen as an anticipation of experiences that would be delivered a few decades later by online first-person shooters. Through the transmission of sporting events as well as quiz and game shows, whose adaptation to the needs of radio and television transformed them from games of secondary mediality into ones of tertiary mediality, broadcast media created the largest shared experiences of industrial culture over several decades.

The medial difference between games can, thereby, be determined with respect to their mode of representation:

- Games of primary mediality such as CATCH are based on a real simulation of reality;

---

14 Pross: *Medienforschung*, p. 69.

- Games of secondary mediality such as CHESS are based on a symbolic representation of reality;
- Games of tertiary mediality, such as radio and television broadcasts of sporting events or quiz shows are based on a medial representation and adaptation of games of primary and secondary mediality, i.e., they allow for tele-audio-visual participation—mostly passive and remote—in edited simulations of reality as well as edited symbolic representations of reality.

The role of players and that of the audience differ radically across medialities: games of primary and secondary mediality allow players, as well as physically present observers, to engage in interactions that are partly self-determined and partly determined by others, whereas the proportional relation between audience and players remained relatively equal through the early 20th century. Games of tertiary mediality, on the other hand, do not only lead to an audience of millions watching a few players, they also subjugate the tiny minority of players to diverse medial regimes—from the selection of which sporting event to broadcast all the way to the live direction of several cameras and their perspectives through which every "real" game play is audiovisually fragmented and distorted.

CASE STUDY:
SOCCER—A GAME'S JOURNEY THROUGH MEDIALITIES

The historical process, in which individual forms of play accumulate numerous medial forms, can be demonstrated with the example of SOCCER, the "most universal cultural phenomenon in the world"[15] and at the same time a central "sector of the global entertainment industry."[16] Estimates from the international soccer association FIFA say that at the start of the 21st century there were a billion ac-

---

15 Goldblatt, David: *The Ball is Round: A Global History of Football*, New York: Riverhead Books (Kindle edition) 2008, loc. 217. The subsequent outline of the history of soccer follows Goldblatt's narrative.
16 Ibid., loc. 239.—An important exception is displayed by American culture. Within American culture, FOOTBALL established itself as a combination of SOCCER and RUGBY. Characteristic of the sport is the oval shape of the ball as well as the case that, at certain times, players may use both hands and feet to interact with the ball, and, finally, an entirely different game experience for both player and spectator: "Perhaps most fundamentally of all, soccer offers modes of storytelling and narrative structures that the American sporting public finds unsatisfactory." (Ibid., loc. 133)

tive soccer players and 50 million referees, while the total length of white lines painted on soccer fields across the world could cover 25 million kilometers, "enough to circle the earth over a thousand times."[17] The beginnings of the game were less spectacular.

Pre-technical and largely unregulated variants can still be observed today when players kick around rocks or round fruit, such as apples, oranges, and melons. The game advanced from primary to secondary mediality around 4,000 years ago with the handcrafting of the first—still solid—balls from various materials, including leather and rubber, and the development of basic rules.[18] However, the various ball games from Asia to Middle America emerged within the socio-cultural context of religious rites and warlike conflicts:

"Sometimes a substitute for war, the game could also provide its denouement as defeated opponents first played the game before being sacrificed—their heads cut off or their hearts torn out."[19]

The preference to play ball games not with one's hands but rather with one's feet originated in prehistoric times as well as antiquity and continued through modern European times via Celtic cultures, as they maintained some independence from the Christian, game-hostile Middle Ages:

"All appear to have played large-scale and often riotous ball games in large open spaces with innumerable participants divided into two teams trying to get the ball to a particular place with few formalities or restrictions.[20] [...] Often the games were played between two parishes or villages, the ball carried across the open fields between them.[21] [...] It was certainly violent enough for deaths and injuries to be recorded."[22]

The historical process through which SOCCER found its modern form began in the British public schools of the 18th and early 19th centuries, especially at Rugby and Eton. Athletic activities in general and SOCCER in particular played a prominent role in both Rugby and Eton's curriculum as well as in the establishment of their self-image. In order to enable tournaments, a successive codification and

---

17 Ibid., loc. 182.
18 See ibid., loc. 269.
19 Ibid., loc. 422.
20 Ibid., loc. 490.
21 Ibid., loc. 492.
22 Ibid., loc. 516.

standardization of rules had to be set in place, first within schools and then between different schools. In a second step SOCCER burst from the upper-class and upper-middle-class world of these schools into broader population groups: "Almost from the moment of its codification football was colonized by the British working classes as both players and spectators."[23]

In Great Britain, the homeland of industrialization, the popularization of SOCCER followed the examples set by sports like horse racing, rowing, boxing, or cricket, which were already entrenched in the aristocratic and merchant classes: first agreement by different clubs on common rules and procedures, then formation of leagues, and then establishment of regional and national championships. The important standardization of the ball—its size, material, and quality—occurred in 1872.[24] The role of the field referee was introduced in 1881, though he only attained his current function in 1898.[25] In 1882 the goal gained a crossbar, in 1892 a net.[26] Since the mid-1880s amateurs were slowly replaced with paid professionals despite standing bans on the practice. At the start of the First World War around 5,000 professionals earned their living with SOCCER.[27]

In the context of this professionalization of the most popular sport of industrial culture, the medialization of SOCCER took place as well. A first step consisted of—as it did already in the modern medialization of the theater—the construction of specialized buildings that allowed ever-larger numbers of people to follow the game from a variety of perspectives which were at least tolerable. Within a few decades these novel soccer stadiums in Great Britain reached and exceeded the capacity of the previously largest entertainment structure in human history: the Roman Coliseum with its 50,000-80,000 seats. The 1907 completed stadium in Glasgow, for example, then the largest in the world, could house over 120,000 spectators.[28]

Concurrently, various attempts were carried out to make soccer games, or at least their final scores, available to those who could not be there in person. Since the 1880s important results were transmitted via telegraph to faraway cities in order to announce them in post offices, restaurants, and bars.[29] SOCCER newspapers and magazines sprung up and reached ever-higher circulation numbers. For

---

23 Ibid., loc. 1119.
24 Ibid., loc. 818.
25 Ibid., loc. 822-824.
26 Ibid., loc. 809.
27 Ibid., loc. 1394.
28 Ibid., loc. 1436.
29 Ibid., loc. 1344.

example, the weekly newspaper *Scottish Referee*, founded in 1888, circulated 500,000 copies in the first decade of the 20th century, at a time when Scotland had around five million residents.[30] In 1907, the British *Daily Mail* published the first photos of soccer games.[31]

The crucial next step of this medialization resided in the live broadcasting of games. On the radio this took place for the first time in January of 1927, three weeks after the founding of the BBC.[32] And so SOCCER arrived in tertiary mediality. The first transmission via television, again through the BBC in an experimental broadcasting operation, happened only a decade later in September 1937.[33] In the founding years of television, the 1950s and 1960s, SOCCER and television entered into a symbiotic relationship—at least in Great Britain and continental Europe: Next to the transmission of game and entertainment shows as well as the broadcasting of motion pictures, SOCCER decisively contributed to television's status as the new defining medium of the era. Vice versa the integration of sports into tertiary mass media through live-broadcasts, announcements in news programs, and special sport shows ensured that SOCCER went from being a proletarian participation game of British provinces to a global game that excited all classes and was experienced by the majority of humanity as spectators.

With the rise of analog-electronic and then digital games since the 1960s, SOCCER inevitably migrated to this medium as well. The first electro-mechanical soccer game CROWN SOCCER SPECIAL came out in 1967.[34] Many other arcade and PC games followed. The decisive breakthrough of SOCCER into virtuality, however, occurred only with soccer manager and soccer simulator games starting in the 1990s. Of these ANSTOSS—DER FUSSBALLMANAGER (1993-2006), FIFA INTERNATIONAL SOCCER and FIFA (since 1993) as well as PRO EVOLUTION SOCCER (since 2001) were the most successful. Of the diverse incarnations of the FIFA series alone, Electronic Arts sold over 100 million copies, by their own ac-

---

30 Ibid., loc. 1442.
31 Ibid., loc. 1355.
32 Grieves, Kevin: "On This Day in History: First Live Radio Broadcast of a Soccer Match, 1927," *The Modern Historian*, January 23, 2009; http://modernhistorian.blogspot.de/2009/01/on-this-day-in-history-first-live-radio.html
33 N. N.: "Happened on This Day—16 September," *news.BBC*, September 16, 2002; http://news.bbc.co.uk/sport2/hi/funny_old_game/2260280.stm
34 N. N.: "Crown Soccer Special," *The International Arcade Museum at Museum of the Game* o.J.; http://www.arcade-museum.com/game_detail.php?game_id=16047

count.[35] In this way digital soccer games ushered in a new phase of massively active participation, which was no longer played out in reality, but in virtuality. SOCCER seems to be transforming anew from a spectator to a player sport. Whoever enters a living room today and sees people in front of an HD screen cannot—at least from some distance—immediately discern whether a match is 'running' and being 'watched' or if the supposed spectators are playing the game themselves.

QUATERNARY MEDIALITY: FROM SPECTATOR TO PLAYER

When Harry Pross presented his taxonomy of mediality a half-century ago the development of the digital transmedium—especially in the context of European culture—was hardly predictable. In this respect his theories need to be expanded and even partially corrected to account for our current situation. Tertiary media required, as Pross recognized, technology on both sides of the communication process. But with regard to digitalization, the tertiary broadcast and reception technology need to be defined more clearly. The analog mass media radio and television allowed merely the transmission of fixed and standardized works in one direction: from a few producers or broadcasters to many consumers or receivers. Those watching and listening could not 'send back.' They were, therefore, incapable of interacting with those offering the content nor with the offered content itself or with other listeners or viewers. Therefore, Pross's definition of tertiary mediality has to be expanded beyond the current perspective in respect to the fact that the technology used for broadcast media is principally one-way technology. It does not empower the receiver with any sort of responsive or interactive capability and, vice versa, hinders the broadcaster and the content being broadcasted from receiving any responses.[36]

---

35 N. N.: "EA Sports FIFA Soccer Franchise Sales Top 100 Million Units Lifetime," *Business Wire*, November 4, 2010; http://www.businesswire.com/news/home/201011 04006782/en#.VH8zdIs2JVo

36 A good example of the Industrial path from activity to passivity can be seen in the radio, which was originally developed as a medium with two-way channels (radio, after all, means a device that sends and receives radio signals) and only mutated after the First World War in the process of its popularization into a receiver. On the evolution of the broadcast medium radio from the amateur radio movement, see Campbell-

In the course of digitalization yet another mediality came into being that uses technology on both ends of the communication process, yet has back channels at its disposal—whether this potential for interaction is placed at the user's disposal or not. For also under the conditions of digital production and distribution the creators of linear audiovisions follow the tradition of film and its artistic prerogatives. Whether they continue to operate in the context of traditional offline media of film and television or already in online media, they present their audiences a *final cut* version as a closed work. They reserve, therefore, for themselves and their creative manipulation of software files the inherent interactive possibilities of the transmedium. Game designers, on the other hand, integrate the capability of interacting with particular elements of digital audiovisions through the interface of their games, and furthermore, they often give players control over deeper changes in the game via so-called *Mods* or modifications.

From a media historical perspective, therefore, quaternary mediality[37], i.e., the transition to the digital transmedium and its multichannel communication, directly influences the production as well as the reception of audiovisions. For one, it initiates a fusing of the creative authority that characterizes the manual production of imagery with the qualities of industrial reproduction. From the 1970s through the 1980s the technical and aesthetic development of hyperrealistic audiovisuality occurred primarily in the context of the—American—motion picture industry and on the technical basis of pre-rendering. However, since the 1990s, game engines have been realizing the potential of quaternary mediality for the real-time generation of virtual images and sounds—in nearly 'photorealistic', i.e., lifelike quality.[38]

Secondly, the integration and drastic escalation of reception methods associated with primary, secondary, and tertiary mediality were attained on the side of the receivers or users. In virtuality, it is possible for the first time to almost arbitrarily choose and switch between other-determined, self-determined, and interactive use of medial artifacts. Thereby it appears that the digital transmedium is ushering in a historical turnaround, or perhaps a reversal, to a mode of thinking in regard to the culturally dominant behavior towards aesthetic artifacts.

Kelly, Martin/Aspray, William: *Computer: A History of the Information Machine*, New York: Basic Books 1996, p. 234 ff.

37 The digital as a quaternary medium has already been addressed by Fassler, Manfred: *Was ist Kommunikation?*, Munich: Wilhelm Fink Verlag 1997, p. 117.

38 The following game engines have been and continue to be of particular importance for the history of games: the *Unreal Engine* (Epic Games, since 1998), the *CryEngine* (Crytek, since 2004) and the *Unity Engine* (Unity, since 2005).

The sweeping immobilization of the audience—in the theater, the museum, the movie theater, in front of radio and television—was, as is generally known, an achievement of industrial culture. Until late in the 19th century, for example, theater auditoriums were not darkened. Contemporary illustrations and descriptions document to what degree the audience, who could see and hear each other and understood attending the theater as a social event, interacted among each other and even with the actors, whether by praising or heckling them. It was Richard Wagner in Bayreuth who first introduced collective tunnel vision from the darkened auditorium toward the stage. For reasons of aesthetic contemplation, his arrangement constituted a proto-cinematic form of reception that the movies would later require for technical reasons.

The early cinema was then also faced with the difficult task of preventing the audience—now mostly from the middle and lower classes—from general uproar and outbursts of dissatisfaction, especially from throwing objects at the actors, i.e., the projection screen, as theater attendees were accustomed to doing at live performances. The obvious connection between what the new industrial media demanded of their audiences, and what the industrial way of life demanded in general, has often been commented on.[39] A relatively clear line from the training for physical and communicative passivity combined with the necessity to pay exceptional attention to quickly changing situations in art and entertainment, can be traced to a dual phenomenon: first, the experiences enabled by new transportation methods such as railroad and automobiles; secondly, the challenges of industrial work that relied on standardized, passive behavior that seemed to almost be controlled remotely but had to be, of course, self-controlled.

In contrast, digital knowledge work is characterized by acting independently in the creative, also thoroughly exploratory, and thereby playful, manipulation of software programs and files and their virtual symbols.[40] From this perspective it is hardly surprising that at the same rate as empowered knowledge work— especially in the so-called 'creative industries'—is becoming the most important source of economic growth, so, too, are changes in cultural behavior toward aesthetic artifacts taking shape. Playfulness, which was important in pre-industrial times, was forced by industrialization into the private sphere (and from there ex-

---

39 See for example: Friedberg, Anne: *Window Shopping: Cinema and the Postmodern*, Berkeley: University of California Press 1993.
40 See for the term *Knowledge Worker*: Drucker, Peter F.: *Post-Capitalist Society*, New York NY: HarperBusiness 1993. And to the term *Symbolic Analyst*: Reich, Robert B.: *The Work of Nations: Preparing Ourselves for 21st-century Capitalism*, New York: A.A. Knopf 1991.

pelled to the edges of what was considered high culture)—with some good reason, considering the violence and danger arising from industrial machines and processes. In an attempt to belittle games in comparison to books, Harry Pross wrote: "In the [...] sector [...] of free-time and incompetence, the game is at home in numerous forms."[41] From there, however, it is returning—in the course of a "movement from a culture of calculation to a culture of simulation"[42]—into the center of postindustrial civilization. The contradiction between work-ethic and play-ethic that industrial rationality assumed, and that existed in factories as well as in bureaucracies, is gradually dissipating.

With some consequence the phantasmic secular space, in which digital knowledge workers collect their aesthetic experiences, is no longer to be found in material reality but rather in virtuality. There, the process of dematerializing dislocation that began with the movies comes to completion: where on stage human beings of flesh and blood stand, the cinema projects images of light. Online, spectators and actors alike are now also shedding their corporeality in favor of mediated presences by turning into virtual co-players. In this way games profit from the changing nature of work in digital culture. The readiness to be passively entertained over long periods of time is on the decline, while inversely, the readiness for interactive participation is on the rise. Players see the need for making your own decisions that analog and digital games require not as a burden but rather as a pleasure.

Today we must, therefore, differentiate between games of primary, secondary, tertiary, and quaternary mediality. Games of primary mediality are based on real simulations of reality, those of secondary mediality on symbolic representations of reality, and those of tertiary mediality on tele-auditive or tele-audiovisual participation at real simulations of reality as well as symbolic representations of reality. In contrast, digital games now enable interactive participation not only at virtual, real-time simulations of symbolic representations of reality, but also, most importantly, at virtual, real-time, and hyperrealistic simulations of the imaginary.

Because of these singular medial characteristics, digital games seem to correspond to the experiences of cultural digitalization more fully than other forms of representation and storytelling: digital games relate to the changing ways of perceiving time and space and to new conceptions of how, under the requirements of digital production and communication, humans have to be and act.

---

41 Pross: *Medienforschung*, p. 104.
42 Turkle, Sherry: *Life on the Screen: Identity in the Age of the Internet*, New York: Simon & Schuster 1995, p. 22.

The three successive developmental pushes in which the new digital medium gained its current characteristics, between the mid-20th and the start of the 21st century, will be presented in the next three chapters.

3 Procedural Turn (since the 1950s)

> "In the historical blink of an eye, video games have colonized our minds and invaded our screens."
> SIMON EGENFELDT-NIELSEN ET AL.[1]

QUADRUPLICATE ORIGIN OF DIGITAL GAMES

An affinity between games and digital computers had been noted many times before Eric Zimmerman's landmark ludic manifesto of 2013.[2] Jesper Juul, for example, argued that both share several qualities, in particular transmediality and regularity: "[G]ames are not tied to a specific set of material devices, but to the processing of rules."[3] The use of computers for the execution of those rules, however, enables the creation of games that follow "rules more complex than humans can handle."[4] The very same observation—at first, merely a hope—was made at the dawn of digital games. Their origin in the mid-20th century is marked by the convergence of four different interests:

1) the scientific pursuit of artificial intelligence;

---

1 Egenfeldt-Nielsen et al.: *Understanding Video Games*, loc. 213.—My portrayal of the history of digital games is based on Donovan, Tristan: *Replay*; Egenfeldt-Nielsen et al.: *Understanding Video Games*; Kent, Steve L.: *The Ultimate History of Video Games: From Pong to Pokémon and Beyond: The Story Behind the Craze That Touched Our Lives and Changed the World*, Roseville, Calif.: Prima Pub. 2001; Mäyrä: *An Introduction to Game Studies*; Wolf, Mark J. P.: *The Medium of the Video Game*, Austin: University of Texas Press 2002.
2 See above, p. 7.
3 Juul: *Half-Real*, loc. 575.
4 Ibid., loc. 580.

2) the military-economic desire for the simulation of real events in order to develop risk-free, affordable training, particularly in air and space travel;
3) the player's wish for acceleration and facilitation of the complicated and lengthy processes associated with analog games, specifically so-called *War Games* and other strategy games;
4) the wish to use the new universal machine, the computer, in a playful manner, i.e., to create new forms of play impossible in older analog media.

The common thread among all four of these efforts was the virtualization and algorithmic automation of processes, which previously had to be managed in the real world through material processes.

The theoretical foundation of such virtualization as the basic innovation of digital technology was laid in three steps. First in 1936, Alan Touring conceived the theoretical model of a digital computer as the universal machine.[5] Then in 1945, John von Neumann invented the technical model for such a universal machine, which is still valid today.[6] Its novel characteristic was the categorical separation of material equipment from the control system. This separation provided the basis for what we now refer to as hardware and software, or more precisely, the software which we refer to as programs.[7] The third fundamental innovation occurred in 1948, when Claude Elwood Shannon proposed a method to digitize all communicative processes and artifacts of civilization: the adequate transfer of analog qualities and functions into mathematical values.[8] Thereby he provided

---

5 Turing, Alan: "On Computable Numbers, with an Application to the Entscheidungsproblem," *Proceedings of the London Mathematical Society*, ser. 2. vol. 42 (1936-7). http://www.abelard.org/turpap2/tp2-ie.asp
6 Neumann, John von: "First Draft of a Report on the EDVAC," (1945). http://www.virtualtravelog.net/wp/wp-content/media/2003-08-TheFirstDraft.pdf
7 The term 'software' itself was coined 13 years later. See Leonhardt, David: "John Tukey, 85, Statistician; Coined the Word 'Software'," *The New York Times*, July 28, 2000; http://www.nytimes.com/2000/07/28/us/john-tukey-85-statistician-coined-the-word-software.html
8 Shannon, Claude Elwood: "A Mathematical Theory of Communication," *The Bell System Technical Journal* Vol. 27, July / October (1948), republished with corrections from *The Bell System Technical Journal*; http://cm.bell-labs.com/cm/ms/what/shannonday/paper.html.—Even the basic technical invention of digitalization, Bill Shockley's transistor, dates to 1948. With it began the steady process of performance optimization, miniaturization, and reduction in price, which transformed the computer from large-scale technology—still part of Industrialization—to a private machine for

the universal machine with its universal bit-material: texts, sounds, pictures, etc.; the software which we call files.

DIGITAL TECHNOLOGY

The technical realization of these concepts proceeded in two phases early in the digitalization process. By the middle of the 1950s, ca. 500 digital mainframe-computers had been built worldwide. They used cathode rays, required large teams for their maintenance and operation, and, with the exception of a few experimental situations, they lacked any sort of interactive in- and output capabilities, such as keyboards or screens. With the advent of microcomputers at the end of the 1950s—the result of transistors and, by the 1960s, of semiconductors as well—, the second phase began, during which procedures for digital sound and image production developed in the fields of telephony, television, and air and space travel. At the same time the first theoretical as well as practical resistance against the industrial-collaborative use of computing power arose. In 1960, J.C.R. Licklider proposed the concept of interactive use of digital computers under the buzzword "man-computer-symbiosis."[9]

One year later, at a time when approximately 9,000 computers were running worldwide, about 1,000 of which were mid-sized computers used by individuals,[10] MIT students set the standard for 'rebel computing' when they programmed the game SPACEWAR! With their deliberate 'waste' of expensive processing power, these students replaced work-ethic with play-ethic.[11] Thus, the economic efficiency principal of collective organization was displaced by the luxurious pleasure principle of the individual.

---

the first time. In this way, the computer developed into a means for individual empowerment.

9   Licklider, J. C. R.: "Man-Computer Symbiosis," *IRE Transactions on Human Factors in Electronics* HFE-1 (1960); http://www.memex.org/licklider.pdf

10 See Friedewald, Michael: *Der Computer als Werkzeug und Medium: Die geistigen und technischen Wurzeln des Personal Computers*, Berlin: GNT-Verlag 1999, p. 16. Also Carlson, David E., "David Carlson's Online Timeline [Carlson's New Media Timeline] (1960 to present). Interactive Media Lab., University of Florida," (since 1998).

11 See Stone, Allucquere Rosanne.: *The War of Desire and Technology at the Close of the Mechanical Age*, Cambridge, Mass.: MIT Press 1995, p. 13f.

Artificial Intelligence

SPACEWAR! was, however, by no means the first digital game. Already in the 1940s the thought had circulated in leading-edge research, originating from Alan Turing's and Claude Elwood Shannon's deliberations that computer games in general, but specifically digital versions of CHESS, could eventually demonstrate an attempt at artificial intelligence through competition with human players. Shannon wrote in 1950:

"Although perhaps of no practical importance, the question [of computer Chess] is of theoretical interest, and it is hoped that a satisfactory solution of this problem will act as a wedge in attacking other problems of a similar nature and of greater significance."[12]

However, with its high potential of possible moves, CHESS proved to be too complicated at first for algorithmic representation, which requires decontextualizing abstraction. The matchstick game NIM was easier to algorithmatize; this process was made possible through a specially constructed computer, Nimrod.[13] Its programmer, John Bennett, like Shannon, connected his digital game with greater hopes:

"It may appear that, in trying to make machines play games, we are wasting our time. This is not true as the theory of games is extremely complex and a machine that can play a complex game can also be programmed to carry out very complex practical problems."[14]

Then in 1952, A.S. Douglas programmed NOUGHTS AND CROSSES, a digital version of TIC TAC TOE, as part of his doctoral thesis. In the same year IBM presented the first digital game of CHESS. By 1955 the program was so advanced that it learned from its own mistakes. In the 1960s chess programs started to win against amateurs. However, it would take another two decades until finally, in 1997, IBM's Big Blue beat reigning world champion Garry Kasparow.

---

12 Cited from Donovan: *Replay*, loc. 112.
13 The 1951 presented Nimrod-Computer defeated headline-grabbing German Secretary of Commerce, and later Federal Chancellor, Ludwig Erhard.
14 Cited from Donovan: *Replay*, loc. 136.

FLIGHT SIMULATION

The second area of research that led to digital games concerned military and civilian flight simulators, which were developed at great cost for training purposes. Analog simulators with limited capabilities existed since the First World War. Their digitalization began in the last months of World War II, when the *Servomechanisms Laboratory* at MIT received the contract to develop a "universal flight trainer," a real-time flight simulator that, unlike previous ones, could simulate more than just a single, predetermined airplane model.[15] *Project Whirlwind* was planned as a two-year endeavor. However, this first attempt at the construction of a—first analog, then digitally conceived—computer designated for real-time control of simulations ultimately failed. Only in the 1960s did regular mainframe and microcomputers become powerful enough for such an undertaking.

The National Aeronautics and Space Administration (NASA) was the driving force behind this development. Flight training through simulation promised to provide long-term savings in exchange for large short-term investments. However, in the case of the planned moon mission, the only possibility for training was through realistic simulation.[16] Already in 1967, General Electric delivered the first electronic real-time 3D simulator to *Johnson Space Center* in Houston, Texas. David Evans, together with computer graphics pioneer Ivan Sutherland, constructed another digital prototype in 1968. Their combination of optimized hard- and innovative software calculated new images from digital recordings of real scenes, which could change their perspectives to match the actions of the pilot or astronaut. With the virtual perspectival modeling of 3D images, the basic defining innovation of digital games had been realized.

The first commercial flight simulator, which generated markedly abstract virtual images in real-time, became available in 1971. During this time, after Intel had introduced the microprocessor in 1970, the social and technical construction of the personal computer began in the West Coast hacker-scene in the US. Two types of programs proved to be the most successful because they satisfied needs that were suppressed in the regulated-usage of the expensive mainframes found at universities, in management, and at large companies: the need for personal productivity and creativity as well as for entertainment. Among commercial software products, computer games earned the highest number of sales at the end

---

15 See Campbell-Kelly et al.: *Computer*, p. 157ff.
16 See Rolfe, J. M./Staples, K. J.: *Flight Simulation*, Cambridge [Cambridgeshire]; New York: Cambridge University Press 1986, p. 234.: "The Mercury, Gemini and Apollo missions were supported by a wide variety of training simulators."

of the 1970s. They were played both on hobbyist PCs and on consoles equipped with microprocessors. Thus digital games (and among them notably flight simulators) served as a 'gateway drug' for a new generation of computer enthusiasts.[17]

The first flight simulators for personal computers like the Apple II and the Tandy TRS-80 were released at the end of the 1970s. In 1981 one of the most popular Apple programs was FLIGHT SIMULATION by a company called SubLogic, which was later acquired by Microsoft. In 2001, MS FLIGHT SIMULATOR secured a place in the Guinness Book of Records for earning 21 million sales.[18] During this time other successful digital simulations were created—most notably Will Wright's SIM CITY (1989) and Peter Molyneux's POPULOUS (1989), both of which generated complex situations and behavior patterns from relatively simple rules and thereby offered experiences of open play.

VIRTUALIZATION OF ANALOG GAMES

Playable simulations, both old and new, function through the virtualization and algorithmic automation of real-world processes and procedures. The digitalization of analog games occurred in the same way. In the beginning it affected board and sports games equally. Unlike the virtualizations programmed in the area of AI-research and under the auspices of academic insight, the motivation behind this third group of early digital games was focused on improving playability and the fun factor. Trailblazers of this movement were war games of the classical Prussian tradition and other types of strategy games. While the analog versions of these games demanded time-consuming calculations, sometimes requiring the aid of a sliding rule, desk or hand calculator, the digital versions drastically accelerated gameplay through the use of computers; in principle, they enabled real time play.

In the fifties and sixties such digitalization was largely restricted to military training due to the high cost of digital technology. With the rise of the affordable personal computer, however, digital adaptations of analog games became one of the most successful areas of game production. A deciding factor of their success can be attributed to the performance enhancement enabled by virtualization and algorithmization. This boost motivated, for example, Chris Crawford already in

---

17 See Campbell-Kelly/Aspray: *Computer*, p. 249.
18 *Guinness Buch der Rekorde*, Hamburg: Guinness Verlag GmbH 2001, p. 113. Sales figures from the year 1999 were used.

1977 to realize TANKTICS, a digital war game programmed on his university's IBM mainframe: "I was playing board war games and I was acutely aware of the absence of the fog of war, which I consider to be crucial to simulation of warfare [...] I considered that computers could solve the problem. I don't think people fully appreciated just how big a leap this was."[19] The first commercial war games for PCs came out in the eighties, mostly as adaptations of board war games.[20]

Similarly around 1960 academic research began to strive for the algorithmization of sports games. Already in 1958 TENNIS FOR TWO, played on the screen of an oscilloscope, was created through the use of an analog computer at the Brookhaven National Laboratory. Over a decade later, when the first digital game console became available for purchase, it included a table tennis game. Atari-founder Nolan Bushnell played a prototype of this console and then had a similar game programmed. With PONG in 1972, Bushnell brought the first digital game to the arcades and, three years later with the Atari console, into the living room as well. And thus began a long tradition of digital sports games as home entertainment. Today there is hardly a sport in existence, which does not have its virtual equivalent. In particular, licensed league games such as FIFA or MADDEN NFL comprise one of the most popular and lucrative game genres.

So it is true for the majority of digital games then, as Frans Mäyrä writes, that they are "in fact remediated, or 'disguised' versions of non-digital ones,"[21] i.e., they remediate "activities or forms of representation that have originally appeared elsewhere."[22]

PLAYFUL USE OF DIGITAL TECHNOLOGY

A rare exception from the 1960s is SPACEWAR! Instead of looking to board games or sports, SPACEWAR! designer and programmer Steve Russell was inspired by science fiction novels and movies, but especially by Edward Elmer

---

19 Cited from Donovan: *Replay*, loc. 1372.—With EASTERN FRONT 1941 (1981) Chris Crawford later wrote Atari's first War Game, whose conflicts played out in real time.
20 See Egenfeldt-Nielsen et al.: *Understanding Video Games*, loc. 1812. This has to do with Ralph Baer's conceptualization of the Magnovox Odyssee.
21 Mäyrä: *An Introduction to Game Studies*, loc. 811.
22 Ibid., loc. 539.

Smith's "Lensman" series.[23] In its rudimentarily narrative orientation, SPACE-WAR! thereby pointed to the hyper-epic future of the new medium, and in its graphical form it indicated a hyperrealistic future: The advanced vector-graphic monitor showed, on top of the mostly astronomically accurate night sky, two spaceships that shot torpedoes at each other and evaded each other per hyperspace jump, while taking care not to fall into deadly gravitational fields.

The game, programmed by MIT students in the sixties, spread throughout the computer labs of American universities. Computer manufacturer DEC finally included it with all $120,000 PDP-1 systems because it served to effectively demonstrate the machine's capabilities. The future founder of Atari, Nolan Bushnell, was among the thousands of Computer Science students who were deeply influenced by SPACEWAR! In 1971, he produced COMPUTER SPACE, an arcade adaptation of SPACEWAR! and thereby initiated the transition from mechanical-electrical to digital arcade games. A further adaptation for the digital home console Atari 2600 followed in 1978 under the title SPACE WAR.

PROCEDURALITY

In the early stages of the digitalization of games, a categorical turn toward procedurality manifested itself among the virtual adaptations of board and sports games as well as simulations and other ludic creations. At the end of the 1990s, Janet H. Murray recognized procedurality as a special quality of digital narrations, which she called "cyberdrama": "The most important element the new medium adds to our repertoire of representational powers is its procedural nature, its ability to capture experience as systems of interrelated actions."[24] Ian Bogost later introduced procedurality into Game Studies as a term describing the medial affordance for the construction of dynamic models of real-world processes: "This ability to execute a series of rules fundamentally separates computers from other media."[25] Digital games use procedurality as their "core representa-

---

23 Smith, E. E.: *First Lensman*, Reading, Pa.: Fantasy Press 1950; *Gray Lensman*, Reading, Pa.,: Fantasy Press 1951; *Second Stage Lensmen*, Reading, Pa.,: Fantasy Press 1953; *Children of the Lens*, Reading, Pa.,: Fantasy Press 1954.—These novels were originally published in installments between 1934 and 1948.

24 Murray, Janet Horowitz: *Hamlet on the Holodeck: The Future of Narrative in Cyberspace*, New York: Free Press 1997, p. 274.

25 Bogost, Ian: *Persuasive Games: The Expressive Power of Videogames*, Cambridge, MA: MIT (Kindle edition) Press 2007, loc. 125.—Bogost himself points out that Janet

tional model."[26] They possess then, in contradistinction to both their analog predecessors and to linear audiovisual media, a new systemic modus of representation. Because of their medial characteristics they do not simply—as is the case with literature—describe systems, or merely—as is the case with visual arts and photography, theater, film, television—represent them visually or audiovisually. Rather digital games are able to simulate how systems function and thereby they enable players to experience these systems.

Until now, the procedurality of digital games has primarily resulted from individual design and human programming. It is, so to speak, produced by heads and hands, through knowledge-work and manual labor. Only recently have attempts been made to automate these processes, i.e., to procedurally generate procedurality; for example, in the production of central elements of game worlds like the galaxies of ELITE: DANGEROUS (2014), the planets of NO MAN'S SKY (2015, in development) and STAR CITIZEN (2015, in development) or even procedurally-generated quests like in the MMO EVERQUEST NEXT (2015, in development).[27]

Such automation seems to be the telos of procedural narration. From simple rules, algorithms allow for the creation and manipulation of complex game situations in real time; a feat which could never be matched by human calculation and deduction. This could lead to emergent and truly surprising storylines, both unplanned and unanticipated in nature; an imminent narratological phenomenon far beyond what is possible in analog games, and of course linear audiovisions as well.[28]

When one looks at early digital games—even the truly innovative SPACEWAR!—it seems hardly imaginable that, only a few decades later, their descendants would challenge cinema and television. This competition arose from two more qualitative developmental advancements that would radically change the digital medium once again.

H. Murray, already in 1996, recognized procedurality as a central characteristic of the digital transmedium, from which its special storytelling capabilities result. See ibid., loc. 119.

26 Ibid., loc. 36.
27 See Lauro, Christina: "MMO Mechanics: Procedural Generation is the Future," in: *Massively by joystiq*, February 26, 2014; http://massively.joystiq.com/2014/02/26/mmo-mechanics-procedural-generation-is-the-future/
28 See "Emergent gameplay is usually taken to be situations where a game is played in a way that the game designer did not predict." (Juul: *Half-Real*, loc. 837)

4 Hyperepic Turn (Since the 1970s)

> "[A] video game is a set of rules as well as a fictional world."
>
> JESPER JUUL[1]

GAME ECONOMICS

During the seventies digital games left the confines of American universities and research institutions, which they had occupied since the fifties. First manufactural methods of organization developed in both production and distribution, following the example set by the producers of arcade machines. Industrial methods of organization following Hollywood's studio model were introduced in the early eighties. The rise of Atari, the most influential game studio of its time, illustrates this process. Founded in 1972, the company already made $3 million in revenue in 1973; in 1975 $40 million. In 1976, Warner Brothers bought Atari and in 1979, following a long line of successful digital games made for both arcades and home entertainment—incl. ASTEROIDS, BATTLEZONE, and BREAKOUT—, Atari reached $200 million in revenue.[2] Finally, in 1982, shortly before the big video game crash, Atari games accounted for 70 percent of Warner Brothers' profits and thereby far exceeded the revenue the studio attained from its movie and music businesses.[3] In the second half of the eighties, Electronic Arts (founded in 1982), among other developers, carried forward game produc-

---

1   Ibid., loc. 43.
2   See Egenfeldt-Nielsen et al.: *Understanding Video Games*, loc. 1530 ff.
3   See Donovan: *Replay*, loc. 2198.

tion using the Hollywood model with the explicit goal to set aside "the traditional distinctions between art and entertainment and education and fantasy."[4]

Hollywood-orientated game production intensified around 1990 when it became possible to integrate filmed sequences into digital games. Writing about the influential game studio Cinemaware, Donovan maintains that its "movie influences ran deeper than just surface presentation and storytelling however. Hollywood's movie development processes would also inform its approach to game development."[5]

FROM MAINFRAME AND ARCADE GAMES TO CONSOLE AND PC GAMES

The economic success of digital games was accompanied by their social and cultural pervasiveness, especially in the US.[6] The *conditio sine qua non* for this new preeminence was the transition of games from the arcade to the living room. This move became possible through a development which took place in the television industry independent of digitalization: the attempt to make use of millions of television sets for more than usual programming. The TV engineer Ralph Baer, who in 1966 first imagined interactive entertainment, knew nothing of computer games like SPACEWAR![7] After many long years of work in develop-

---

4   Ibid., loc. 3259. EA also followed the Hollywood model in that it presented its game designers in public "as if they were movie directors—artistic visionaries of the new era of interactive entertainment."

5   Ibid., loc. 4260.

6   For the situation outside of the US See "While the Americans were enjoying a steady stream of variously innovative or derivative games [...], there were many parts of the world which were still waiting for their first electronic game to appear." (Mäyrä: *An Introduction to Game Studies*, loc. 941.) Also: "At the time the whole of Europe was lagging behind the US in the rise of home computers and video games. While the US and Japan forged ahead building a new entertainment industry on the back of the digital revolution, Europeans had largely settled into the role of consumers rather than producers of video games." (Donovan: *Replay:* loc. 2638.)

7   See Baer's recollection: "I knew nothing about Steve Russell's or Nolan Bushnell's work. I was just a guy with a TV engineering degree who wanted to do something with all those 60 million TV sets out there besides tuning in Channel 2, 4, or 7. And I did." (Baer, Ralph H.: "Foreword," in: Wolf, Mark J. P. (ed.), *The Medium of the Video Game*, Austin: University of Texas Press 2002, pp. ix-xvi, p. xv.).

ment, he managed to create a television console that was released by Magnavox under the name *Odyssey* at the same time Nolan Bushnell brought PONG to the arcades: "It was the only way to approximate the *PONG* experience at home," Baer writes. "Nearly 100,000 *Odyssey* units wound up in people's homes [...] The home video game industry was launched."[8] *Odyssey* and other early consoles enabled an active engagement with audiovisions on home TV screens for the first time. Playing, Nolan Bushnell states, "gives you a sense of control, whereas before all you could do was sit and watch channels."[9]

In the seventies, however, the most important digital games continued to originate in university mainframes and in the game-machines of arcades. But for the second half of the decade, most digital games were quickly ported to consoles and PCs. Thereby they not only became ubiquitous in homes, but also in the general media landscape, on the front-page of newspapers and magazines, in movies and television series.[10] By the mid-eighties every fourth American household was home to a game console and every eighth to a PC. At the same time, popular digital games released in the first decade of consoles and home computers—incl. COLOSSAL CAVE ADVENTURE (1972), ZORK (1977), SPACE INVADERS (1978), FLIGHT SIMULATOR (1978), MYSTERY HOUSE (1979), BATTLEZONE (1980), PAC-MAN (1980), DONKEY KONG (1981), MARIO BROS. (1983), SUPER MARIO (1985)—established many of the game genres which still exist today; among them platformer, simulation, action, and finally adventure, which at the time was the most influential.

THE INNOVATIVE GENRE OF TEXT-ADVENTURES

The prototypical COLOSSAL CAVE ADVENTURE came into being during the early seventies as a purely text-based game on a timesharing computer. After several revisions—which added, among other things, fantasy elements in the Tolkien

---

8   Ibid., p. xv.
9   Cited from Donovan: *Replay*, loc. 801.
10 Time Magazine, for example, featured the 1982 leading headline: N. N.: "Gronk! Flash! Zap! Video Games Are Blitzing The World," *Time*, January 18, 1982; http://content.time.com/time/covers/0,16641,19820118,00.html.—Video games were prominently featured in and substantially influenced numerous Hollywood films of the early 80s, especially: TRON (1982) and THE LAST STARFIGHTER (1984). Both films operated extensively with digitally-generated images, as did the sorts of games these films depicted.

tradition and the original cave adventure—it attained a great deal of popularity through the ARPAnet starting in 1976; at least in the circles of the few who already had access to a networked computer. The commercial distribution of PC versions of this game and other adventure games influenced by it began towards the end of the seventies—among them, ZORK and ADVENTURELAND (both 1978). Quickly text games, often billed as *interactive fiction*, rose to become the most popular contemporary genre.[11] Their charm lay in the player's ability to navigate branching plots by answering text prompts or, later, by clicking on hyperlinks. With the text adventure, digital games started to form their very own modus of narration. In the beginning, it was shaped by literary world creation. Using the specific abilities of digital writing for multi-linearity, however, text-based adventures enhanced literary storytelling far beyond the possibilities of analog literature. Temporal linearity was replaced by a spatiality whose temporal dimension realized itself anew with every play-through.

Whoever read, wrote, and clicked their way through these 'webbed' text passages, was introduced to unknown experiences of decision-making and independence, of immersion and calculation. Particularly the company Infocom, founded in 1979 near MIT, wished to differentiate its productions through literary quality from the mass of contemporary games:

"Expect the unexpected the first time you experience Infocom's interactive fiction. Because you won't be booting up a computer game. You'll be stepping into a story. [...] For the first time, you can be more than a passive reader—you can become the story's main character and driving force."[12]

One of the most advanced text-adventures was the 1984 Infocom adaptation of Douglas Adams' novel THE HITCHHIKERS GUIDE TO THE GALAXY. When the game came out, however, text-based adventures had already passed the zenith of their success. By the end of the seventies, the endeavor to tell demanding and touching stories in ever increasing immersive and interactive ways began to outgrow the limitations of purely text-based representations. The move to audiovisual storytelling unfolded in three ways.

---

11 See Mäyrä: *An Introduction to Game Studies*, loc. 1194.
12 Cited from Furtwängler, Frank: "Im Spiel unbegrenzter Möglichkeiten. Zu den Ambiguitäten der Videospielforschung und -industrie," in: Distelmeyer, Jan/Hanke, Christine/Mersch, Dieter (ed.), *Game over!?: Perspektiven des Computerspiels*, Bielefeld: transcript 2008, pp. 59-72, here p. 70.—The ad is located here: http://archeogaming.blogspot.com/2012/11/infocom-advertising-real-trick-is.html

THE EVOLUTION OF AUDIOVISUAL STORYTELLING

First, the increasingly capable home computer—enabled especially by better graphics cards and data storage for distribution (diskette, CD-ROM)—made it possible for the narrative text of adventure games to be accompanied by illustrations and animations. This development began around 1980 with MYSTERY HOUSE[13], which Roberta and Ken Williams published for the Apple II with still relatively simple graphics. It culminated at the beginning of the nineties in Robyn and Rand Miller's narratively as well as graphically complex masterwork MYST.[14] This CD-ROM game offered its players interactive exploration of a multimedia-created island world from a subjective perspective. MYST—with its fascinating combination of independent action and puzzle solving, textual and nonverbal storytelling, music, and interactive graphics, altogether which constitute a first-person slideshow dependent upon the player's location—sold around six million copies to become the most successful game in the history of the young medium.[15]

The second effort to overcome the limitations of text-adventures was aimed not at the medial restriction to text, but rather against the fact that these texts, in which the stories and narrative experiences unfolded, were predetermined—an essential characteristic of these games which made truly organic interaction impossible.[16] However, a higher level of interaction could be produced when hu-

---

13 The game designers were inspired by the board game CLUEDO and Agatha Christie's novel *And Then There Were None* (New York: St. Martin's Griffin 2004, *1939). See Donovan: *Replay*, loc. 1314.
14 The title is an allusion to Jules Verne's novel *L'Île mystérieuse* (1874/75).
15 MYST sold 4.2 million copies by 1999, followed by MS FLIGHT SIMULATOR with 2.8 million and DOOM II with 1.5 million copies. See Dunnigan, James F.: *The Complete Wargames Handbook: How to Play, Design, and Find Them*, New York, N.Y.: Morrow 1992, Online: http://www.strategypage.com/wargames-handbook/chapter/content s.aspx. The numbers can be found in the introduction: http://www.strategypage.com/ wargames-handbook/chapter/Introduc.aspx.—MYST was only surpassed in 2002 by THE SIMS, when MYST had already been sold around 6 million times. See Walker, Trey: "The Sims Overtakes Myst," *Gamespot* 2002; http://www.gamespot.com/arti cles/the-sims-overtakes-myst/1100-2857556/
16 See Schell, Jesse: "Die Zukunft des Erzählens: Wie das Medium die Geschichten formt," in: Beil, Benjamin/Freyermuth, Gundolf S./Gotto, Lisa (ed.), *New Game Plus: Perspektiven der Game Studies. Genres – Künste – Diskurse*, Bielefeld: transcript 2014, pp. 357-374, here p. 365.—This essay is based on Jesse Schell's talk: "The Fu-

man actors no longer played against a preprogrammed game but rather against each other within the confines of a game. The first so-called MUDs—Multi-User Dungeons—, in which a multitude of (role)players could communicate textually in real-time, emerged in local networks and special dial-up networks during the second half of the seventies. Historically they have two roots: first, the text-based online games, which students and teachers programmed for university mainframes since the early seventies—for example, STAR TREK (1971), MAZE WAR (1974) or AVATAR (1977); and second, the analog roleplaying game *Dungeons and Dragons*—a combination of elements from war games, amateur theater and fantasy tales—that also had a significant influence on text-adventures.

Published in 1973, *Dungeons and Dragons* started the modern role-playing game movement. At the same time, its complicated statistical rules and processes lent themselves to virtual automation. The first—unlicensed—attempt at a virtual adaptation for a mainframe computer was made by then-student Don Daglow (DUNGEON, 1975/76).[17] At the end of the decade, British students Roy Trubshaw and Richard Bartle programmed MUD. With a connection from their university mainframe computer—which hosted the game—to the ARPAnet, MUD went from being a locally networked online game to being the first internationally networked online game in 1981—and thereby became the predecessor of all later multiplayer online games on the Internet and the World Wide Web.[18] Contemporary digital games continue to adopt the mechanics of this role-play classic.[19]

A third key area for the development of the narratological aspect of digital games was the creation of strong and relatable characters—something missing in most text-adventure games despite their crucial importance (alongside plot and setting) for effective storytelling. Developed characters in digital games also had their origins in the eighties. Surprisingly they appeared more often in platformers and action games than in adventure games. A predecessor to this (alternate) route

---

ture of Storytelling: How Medium Shapes Story," held on March 03, 2013 at the Game Developers in San Francisco. A recording of the talk can be found here: https://soundcloud.com/schell-gamesmarketing/gdc-13-future-of-story-telling

17 See Daglow's comments: "It was so well-suited to simulate on a computer." Cited from Donovan: *Replay*, loc. 1195.

18 With HABITAT (1985) MUDs also made the transition from purely text-based games to graphically designed worlds.

19 "The systems for digital role-playing games such as DIABLO III, BALDUR'S GATE, EVERQUEST, ASHERON'S CALL, and WORLD OF WARCRAFT are derived from the paper-based system of DUNGEONS & DRAGONS." (Fullerton: *Game Design Workshop*, loc. 5274.)

to narration was Pac-Man, the hero of the 1980 arcade game of the same name.[20] Through uncounted adaptations—including games for consoles and PCs, an animated TV series, a hit single, and action figures—Pac-Man became the first iconic video game figure in contemporary mass-culture and thereby the "precursor for later gaming icons like Mario, Sonic the Hedgehog and Lara Croft."[21] Their audiovisual representation and characterization developed parallel to the first attempts at imparting games with technically as well as aesthetically photorealistic qualities; from short animated sequences in image spaces organized in a rather static theatrical manner (which became possible in the early eighties, e.g. MARIO BROS., 1983), to cinematically produced and designed scenes (which became possible around 1990, e.g. IT CAME FROM THE DESERT, 1989).

Thereby a decisive change was initiated: film began to replace literature as a model for non-linear storytelling. As a consequence, digital games started to develop a new hyperepic as well as hyperrealistic aesthetic.

THE HYPEREPIC

The formation of evermore interwoven multi-linear stories occurred during the time of and following the procedural turn—that is, during the second phase of digital games between the early seventies and early nineties. This led to the development of open spaces of action as they could already be more or less freely explored in predecessors of contemporary sandbox games like MYST. "The guiding principle," Frans Mäyrä writes, "was to incorporate the storyline into the playable structures of interactive game levels, thereby creating a unified, highly playable story-world."[22] The establishment of complex story structures in the medium of digital games—starting with text-adventures, and subsequently other genres as well[23]—can be described as a hyperepic turn. The prefix "hyper" refers to Ted Nelson's compound noun from the mid-1960s, "hyperlink": a direct, in-

---

20 "Unlike all previous game hits, this one had an identifiable main character." (Egenfeldt-Nielsen et al.: *Understanding Video Games*, loc. 1729.) Today PAC-MAN is still the arcade game with the highest one-player gross sales, see Wikipedia: "search term 'Arcade game'," (2014); http://en.wikipedia.org/wiki/List_of_highest-grossing_arcade_games#List_of_highest-grossing_arcade_video_games
21 Mäyrä: *An Introduction to Game Studies*, loc. 1103.
22 Ibid., loc. 1138.
23 Already in 1983, ULTIMA III: EXODUS tried to bring roleplaying games and storytelling together. See Donovan: *Replay*, loc. 3430.

teractively realizable reference, which allows for navigation between data complexes, whether they are texts, images, or 3D-worlds.

With the development of hyperepic structures and qualities, digital games eliminated several barriers hindering audiovisual storytelling in older mechanical and industrial media. This is demonstrated with the various means of representing time and space in different media. While literary storytelling is free to manipulate both time and space, audiovisions of stage, film, and television are faced with strong restrictions which constitute the unique qualities of each respective medium:[24]

- Mechanization and its corresponding culture produced the proscenium—or picture frame—stage with its perspectival space of illusion, with the curtain, and numerous other tools better suited to manipulate time and space than those available in reality or street theatre.
- Within Industrialization and its corresponding culture, film and television came into being. These new audiovisual media replaced the curtain with the cut and montage. By interconnecting changes of time and space in greater scope and nearly without a trace, film and television allowed for radically new relationships between time and space in audiovisual storytelling.
- With the transmedium of digital software, new possibilities are once again being developed to manage time and space. These new methods are predicated on replacing hardware manipulation—the wooden stage, sets, and curtain or celluloid—with the interactive, real-time manipulation of software. By making local and networked virtuality into a narratological playground, a dual aesthetic effect takes place: time and space relations become virtualized and, simultaneously, the virtual realm of data is made temporal and spatial.

Therefore, hyperepic narratives differ categorically from older, analog variants of literary and audiovisual storytelling in regards to both media and technology—and they are also their 'other.' Namely, the hyperepic narrative continues to depend on its predecessors, especially novels and films, which serve as role models whose aesthetic qualities can be modified through adaptation to fit the virtual transmedium. In contrast to these forms of linear media, however, games

---

24 Compare the following with the exhaustive discussion in Freyermuth, Gundolf S.: "Der Big Bang digitaler Bildlichkeit: Zwölf Thesen und zwei Fragen," in: Freyermuth, Gundolf S./Gotto, Lisa (ed.), *Bildwerte: Visualität in der digitalen Medienkultur*, Bielefeld: transcript 2013, pp. 287-333.

offer—as Hans-Georg Gadamer had already analyzed in light of the analog, i.e., non-hyperepic games—fictitious rule-governed worlds for potential action.[25]

In continuing these observations, Lev Manovich in "Database as Symbolic Form"[26] addressed the relationship between (analog) narration and (digital) databases, which can elucidate the alterity of the stories experienced in digital games. He describes databases and storytelling as "natural enemies," because both constitute meaning that contradicts one another. Arbitrary real-time access, which algorithms make possible for the majority of digital data collection—from e-commerce websites like Amazon or Ebay all the way to social networking platforms, like Flickr or Facebook—is fundamentally anti-narrative, since it knows neither a necessary beginning nor a necessary end, no logical sequence, no development whatsoever. In opposition to, for example, the reading of a novel or the viewing of a movie, the world never forms an aesthetic or meaningful whole when we are researching databases.

Digital games, however, behave differently. At their core they also are made up of databases. Their thoroughly diverse algorithms allow stored data to be experienced as narration for two reasons. For one, algorithms steer player experience by posing specific tasks—quests, puzzles, etc.: "Everything which happens to her [the player] in a game, all the characters and objects she encounters either take her closer to achieving the goal or further away from it."[27] Second and more importantly, the worlds of digital games formed from databases are themselves constructed through algorithms and thus allow for their reconstruction:

"As the player proceeds through the game, she gradually discovers the rules which operate in the universe constructed by this game. She learns its hidden logic, in short its algorithm. Therefore, in games where the game play departs from following an algorithm, the player is still engaged with an algorithm, albeit in another way: she is discovering the algorithm of the game itself."[28]

---

25 Gadamer, Hans-Georg: "The Relevance of the Beautiful. Art as Play, Symbol and Festival", in: *The Relevance of the Beautiful and Other Essays*, Cambridge University Press 1986, pp. 3-53.
26 Manovich, Lev: "Database as Symbolic Form," *Millenium Film Journal*, Fall 1999; http://www.mfj-online.org/journalPages/MFJ34/Manovich_Database_FrameSet.html
27 Ibid.
28 Ibid.—In the meantime, even database websites design their algorithms proto-narratively: 'Your friends have also searched for…,' 'this photo is similar to these,' 'your friend recommends this article …,' etc.

On the one hand hyperepic storytelling is database-oriented, and on the other hand it is structured through (proto-)narratological algorithms. It is a unique characteristic of its storylines, which were in the beginning textual and later visual and audiovisual, that the sequence from which they result is not exactly predetermined. Rather it is realized as players make their way through the game and encounter interactive structural possibilities—the combinatorics of data and algorithms—in a virtual, as well as algorithmically-constructed narrative space. With regard to the structure and function of narration, Jesper Juuls differentiates between two archetypal poles, which supposedly marked the beginning of digital games:

"[T]here is a general scale from the highly replayable multiplayer game (the emergence game) where the player can gradually begin to ignore the fiction to, at the other extreme, the 'complete-once' adventure game (the progression game), where the player only faces each setting once and is therefore more likely to take the fictional world at face value."[29] [...] The history of video games can be seen as the product of two basic game structures, the emergence structure of Pong and the progression structure of adventure games."[30]

Over the last decade, however, the rise of Open World and Sandbox games has all but eliminated the opposition of emergence and progression with a synthesis of the two. Within this synthesis, narration is organized spatially, rather than temporally, as Henry Jenkins writes, "spatial exploration over plot development."[31] In the multi- or nonlinear narrative spaces where hyperepics open up as "environmental storytelling,"[32] players become semi-autonomous actors. The resulting aesthetic experience is not set—as it is in classic adventure tales, but rather it emerges out of the inherent tension between hyperepic construction and each potential interaction. More specifically: Only in the fusion of the—programmed and designed—narrative potential with the numerous individual preferences and decisions, user reactions and interactions within the new time-

---

29 Juul: *Half-Real*, loc. 87.
30 Ibid., loc. 799. See also: "The progression structure yields strong control to the game designer: Since the designer controls the sequence of events, this is also where we find the games with cinematic or storytelling ambitions." (Ibid., loc. 822)
31 Jenkins, Henry: "Game Design as Narrative Architecture," in: Wardrip-Fruin, Noah/ Harrigan, Pat (ed.), *First Person: New Media as Story, Performance, and Game*, Cambridge, Mass.: MIT Press 2004, pp. 119-129. Cited from: http://web.mit.edu/21 fms/People/henry3/games&narrative.html
32 Ibid.

space 'inbetween'—medium—of the game form the singular experiences of hyperepic narrative form.

The hyperepic's aesthetic charm, like its enduring popularity, however, results primarily from the fact that it has ceased to be text-based for some time.

5 Hyperrealistic Turn (since the 1990s)

At the start of the third phase of digital games, the most influential changes no longer originated from arcade games and only seldom from console games. Rather games (originally) designed for multimedia PC were the technical as well as aesthetic trendsetters of this period.

DIGITAL TECHNOLOGY

Around 1980 altogether 2 million PCs existed worldwide. By 1990 that number had climbed to 50 million and included computers of considerably greater computational power. Another ten years later, shortly after the turn of the 21st century, there were already a billion PCs in use.[1] This exponential growth correlated with a qualitative transformation: Statistically, the personal computer went from being an un-networked office and work machine, which was typically used for text editing, data management, and bookkeeping, to a multimedial and—with the introduction of the first browsers for the World Wide Web after 1993— networked communications and culture machine. This new breed of computer was outfitted with video and audio subsystems whose capabilities also grew exponentially throughout the nineties. Its use shifted increasingly to multimedia communication and production as well as the reception of art and entertainment,

---

[1] See N. N.: "Milliardster PC verkauft," *Heise Newsticker*, July 1, 2002.; Jusko, Jill: "Milestone Reached," *Industry Week*, August 2002; http://www.industryweek.com/; Rupley, Sebastian: "One Billion PCs Shipped," *PC Magazine*, July 3, 2002; http://www.pcmag.com/article2/0,4149,340368,00.asphttp://www.pcmag.com/article2/0,4149,340368,00.asp

of games, music, photographs, videos, and—after the DVD was introduced to the market in 1996—films and television series.[2]

The first push towards the multimedial outfitting of PCs with faster processors, more powerful graphics cards, and larger data storage came from digital games. This was driven by the desire of many game designers and players alike for an ever increasing photographic realism. In the seventies, arcade games possessed simple black-and-white graphics.[3] The same held true for early console and PC games. At the start of the eighties, arcade games with color screens finally became available. Console and PC games hurried to follow this example. However, at first PC games were doubly handicapped: on the one hand, through the lack of color monitors (the result of high prices), and on the other hand, through the file size restrictions imposed by diskettes. Even if the "nasty arms race over graphics" (Chris Crawford)[4] already started in the mid-eighties, then the arms race in the field of computer games still faced strong restrictions thanks to the lack of storage and distribution media. At the end of the eighties, numerous PC games were published on half-a-dozen or more diskettes that had to be installed painstakingly.

Starting in 1991, the implementation of the CD-ROM in conjunction with multimedia standards led to more complex graphics and realistic sound design as well as the integration of animation and video clips. By the mid-nineties, PCs portrayed 3D audio and image worlds which had previously only been seen in far more expensive arcade installations. The privatization of access supported the potential for aesthetic personalization, as was impossible with public offerings like arcades due to their collective and temporally limited use. After 1995, digital games became the dominating software branch once again.[5]

---

2   Digital technology thereby came into unavoidable competition with analog electronic home entertainment, which had been dominant up until that point. See Freyermuth, Gundolf S.: "Freizeitpark im Fernsehsessel," *c't - magazin für computertechnik*, September 13, 1999; http://www.heise.de/kiosk/
3   Color effects were generated for arcade and console games by creating transparent color foil over the black and white displays for specific games—for instance BREAKOUT and SPACE INVADERS.
4   Cited from Parkin, Simon: "30 Years Later, One Man Is Still Trying To Fix Video Games," *kotaku.com*, December 27, 2013; http://kotaku.com/30-years-later-one-mans-still-trying-to-fix-video-gam-1490377821
5   See for example: "For the third consecutive year, PCs are being used more to run entertainment software than for any other function, including word processing, online

From the Model of the Novel to the Model of the Film

The media-aesthetic realization of increasingly technically-complicated image and sound worlds now strove toward a new ideal: If the premiere role model for the most successful games of the seventies and early eighties was still the novel, then in the mid-eighties, film—in particular, Hollywood—took over this role. By transforming a text- and graphic-based medium into a genuinely audiovisual one, the first phase of mutual influence began in production practices as well as in the aesthetic realm. It showed itself first in the increasing number of film companies and filmmakers reaching into the games market and, in turn, in the rising number of game studios adopting techniques and methods of film production.

George Lucas, for example, founded Lucasfilm Games in 1982—later renamed to LucasArts—and began to produce a number of influential games, as well as adaptations of the STAR WARS and INDIANA JONES movie series and graphical adventure games including LABYRINTH (1986), MANIC MANSION (1987), INDIANA JONES AND THE LAST CRUSADE: THE GRAPHIC ADVENTURE (1989), THE SECRET OF MONKEY ISLAND (1990). The cinematic roots of the game studio clearly revealed themselves in the steady ongoing development of the adventure genre. "Lucasfilm [sic!] became more and more interested in applying the techniques of cinematography, moving from the largely static scenes of MANIAC MANSION to the panning cameras and close ups of THE SECRET OF MONKEY ISLAND."[6] The fusion of game and movie aesthetics reached its first highpoint in 1993 with STAR WARS: REBEL ASSAULT. This successful game, which significantly contributed to the pervasiveness of the CD-ROM, integrated digitized actual scenes from the STAR WARS movies, self-staged real-movie images, pre-rendered 3D-CGI-scenes of the highest quality, and film music.

The same path toward a combination of game-experience and cinematic aesthetic was explored—only in the opposite direction: originating from the game industry—by game studios like Cinemaware and Sierra Online. Cinemaware published, for example, THE KING OF CHICAGO (1986), inspired by American mobster movies of the 1930s, and IT CAME FROM THE DESERT (1989), inspired by B-movies of the 1950s. Sierra Online even built a complete movie studio for its game productions: "It was a true studio with all that goes with it: sound rooms; blue-screen stage; editing bays," company founder Ken Williams re-

---

activities and business applications." (Tucker, Greg: "Interactive Entertainment Industry Matures," *Patriot News-Harrisburg PA*, June 7, 1998, www.nexis.com)
6   Donovan: *Replay*, loc. 4319.

members.[7] While the adoption of film-aesthetic elements—for example Mise en Scène, camera direction, dialog direction, sound design, etc.—improved the audiovisual form of digital games and, thereby, also the game-experience, the integration of real-movie sequences proved to be a temporary mistake. This was due to the disruptive nature of these sequences, which were filmed with real actors in the form of non-interactive cinematic cut scenes. They disrupted the playful immersion doubly: for one, they halted the flow of the game; for another and more importantly, the striking difference between their photorealistic quality and the comparatively low visual quality of the animated game scenes endangered the aesthetic unity of the game. Prominent game designers like Chris Crawford accused the game industry around 1990—in allusion to the Freudian penis envy—of suffering from an unfortunate "movie envy."[8]

The impetus for Crawford's complaint was Chris Roberts's PC spaceflight-simulator WING COMMANDER (1990). In the context of its time, this game had a strong cinematic aesthetic. However, unlike other contemporary CD-games—and also unlike later episodes of the Wing Commander franchise[9]—its cinematic look was not achieved through real-movie material, but rather through its graphics engine. Next to pre-rendered animation scenes, where the characters even spoke in lip sync, the engine gave the impression of perspectively correct 3D worlds, even in the game itself. Its advanced aesthetics, as well as its success, made WING COMMANDER one of the milestones of the early nineties that showed the new medium the way to a cutting-edge cinematic-photorealistic audiovisuality. The speed and sustainability of this innovation is most noticeable, for example, when one compares the crude graphics (by today's standards) of WING COMMANDER or DOOM (1993) with the enhanced realism of games like MAX PAYNE (2001) which appeared around the turn of the century, and finally with the nearly lifelike appearance of current games like CRYSIS 3 (2013).

Digital visuality and particularly the hyperrealistic images of digital games striving for the impression of photorealism indicate the return to a tradition thousands of years old, which analog film pushed to the margins of industrial culture

---

7   Cited from ibid., loc. 5623.
8   See Mäyrä: *An Introduction to Game Studies*, loc. 1402.
9   WING COMMANDER II: VENGEANCE OF THE KILRATHI (1991), WING COMMANDER: ACADEMY (1993), WING COMMANDER: PRIVATEER (1993), SUPER WING COMMANDER (1994), WING COMMANDER: ARMADA (1994), WING COMMANDER III: HEART OF THE TIGER (1994), WING COMMANDER IV: THE PRICE OF FREEDOM (1996), PRIVATEER 2: THE DARKENING (1996), WING COMMANDER V: PROPHECY (1997), WING COMMANDER: SECRET OPS (1998)

and now moves into the center of digital culture: the production of moving images not through the imprint of reality—stored light or sound waves—but through animation.[10]

HYPERREALISM

Of course the photorealistic animation of today represents a completely new variant of realistic image production: After the proliferation of perspectival 2D realism following the Renaissance and of 2D and 3D photorealism in the 19th and 20th century, the digitalization of still and moving pictures combined the characteristics of painterly realism—that its images do not need an index—with those of the camera-produced photorealism—that its images indeed give the impression of indexical quality. Such imagery was anticipated in painting since the 1960s and was described by art criticism as hyperrealism since the early 1970s.[11] The imitation of works of art and the complete reproduction of actual structures, as became the norm in US theme parks and entertainment architecture after Disney, was described by Umberto Eco[12] and Jean Baudrillard[13] as too much reality; an uber-reality. This hyperreality, they feared, would dethrone more modest 'original' reality, producing de-realization.

The analog arts of painting and architecture thus anticipated an imagery that at once appears photographic, but whose images do not refer to any reality or ac-

---

10 See Manovich, Lev: *The Language of New Media*, Cambridge Mass.: MIT Press 2000.
11 In hindsight the picturesque hyperrealism of the sixties and seventies proved to be, like large parts of analog special effects technology, an aesthetic anticipation of digital media technology and its effects. For picturesque hyperrealism see Chase, Linda: *Hyperrealism*, London: Academy Editions 1975.—For cinematic hyperrealism see Brinkemper, Peter V.: "Paradoxien der Enträumlichung Zur Philosophie des 3-D-Films," *Glanz und Elend. Literatur und Zeitkritik* (2012); http://www.glanzundelen d.de/Artikel/abc/s/starwars.htm.—For the historical and aesthetic differentiation of realism, photorealism, and hyperrealism see Freyermuth, Gundolf S.: "Cinema Revisited. Vor und nach dem Kino—Audiovisualität in der Neuzeit," in: Kloock, Daniela (ed.), *Zukunft Kino*, Marburg: Schüren 2007, pp. 15-40.
12 See Eco, Umberto, "Travels in Hyper Reality, in: (ed.), *Travels in Hyper Reality: Essays*, San Diego: Harcourt Brace Jovanovich 1986, pp. 1-58.
13 Baudrillard, Jean: *Simulacra and Simulation*, Ann Arbor: University of Michigan Press 1994 (*1981).

cessible 3D world. However, in their "virtuality" they often appear more real than reality. This hyperrealism found its media-technological realization in the mathematically based transmedium of software and especially in the context of American film production.[14] Already in the early 1980s, analog special effects could be replaced with digitally edited and even completely generated images. More and more, motion pictures and television series distinguished themselves through a hybrid of photorealistically produced and virtually edited or generated imagery, until finally George Lucas brought the first completely digitally-rendered movie to theaters with STAR WARS: EPISODE I: THE PHANTOM MENACE (1999).[15]

In game production this development took longer, since digital games cannot, in contrast to movies, pre-render their hyperrealistic worlds but rather—outside of cutscenes—have to generate them in real-time. In the course of the 2000s, however, even these pre-produced linear sequences gave way to real-time images of evermore photorealistic quality. In present audiovisual production—film, television, games, visualizations, and simulations—three variants for the production of hyperrealistic imagery coexist:

1) *Virtual generation* in the tradition of analog animation, i.e., a digital production *ex nihilo*, for example through key-frame animation, motion and performance capturing combined with pre-rendering;
2) *Hybrid generation* in the tradition of the analog production of movies and television series, i.e., the hyperrealistic modification of previously taken photorealistic image materials or the mixture of such shots with completely digitally generated ones, in both cases combined with pre-rendering;
3) *Procedural generation* in the tradition of digital games, i.e., the algorithmically automated generation of images *ex nihilo* through real-time rendering game engines dependent on the (inter-)actions of the players.[16]

---

14 See Freyermuth, Gundolf S.: "Die Zukunft des Kinos: Synthetische Realitäten / The Future of Cinema: Synthetic Realities," in: Wolfgang Jacobsen, Hans Helmut Prinzler, Werner Sudendorf (ed.), *Filmmuseum Berlin*, Berlin: Nicolaische Verlagsbuchhandlung 2000, pp. 315-382 (English / German).

15 Freyermuth, Gundolf S.: "Der Tod des Tonfilms—Revisited," in: Polzer, Joachim (ed.), *Weltwunder der Kinematographie—Beiträge zu einer Kulturgeschichte der Filmtechnik. Aufstieg und Untergang des Tonfilms / Die Zukunft des Kinos: 24p?*, Potsdam: Polzer 2002, pp. 17-33.

16 This variant comes into use not only in digital games but also in the production of movies, where it serves the creation and fixation of linear audiovisions. See for exam-

All three variants of digital hyperrealism have a design freedom nearing that found in literature and the visual arts: While analog photography and analog movies inevitably run into limitations because they can only show what actually existed or took place before a camera—no matter what trickery was used—, hyperrealistic images and audiovisions can represent whatever their creators are capable of imagining and technical-artistically rendering.

AUTHENTICITY AND OPERATIVITY

The realization of universal manipulability results in the loss of the medially-generated authenticity that comes from photorealism through the basic process of taking an audial and visual imprint of reality. Hyperrealistic images do not document reality even when they show something real. In this way the imprint paradigm of industrial media can be recognized as a historical intermezzo. In the digital transmedium the question of an object's authenticity arises just as it did in pre-industrial times: as something that does not bind itself to medial guarantees, but rather to authorship and its authority.[17]

Beyond that loss of authenticity, the third procedural variant of hyperrealistic image production characterizes a special feature that has a genuine relationship to authenticity and authorship: operativity.[18] The engagement that these hyperrealistic image worlds afford is no longer passive—as is the case with painting and photography, movie, and TV—, but rather active:

"Kevin Kelly was probably one of the first to realize that screens and their content, the images, are turning into 'portals.' Thomas Elsaesser put this change in the perception and use of perspectival imagery into more concrete terms: 'We are moving from Alberti's window, through which we passively look onto the world out there—behind the pane—to portals that allow us to enter the world of the images or at least to interactively influence

---

ple Freyermuth, Gundolf S.: "Prinzip Weltenbau. Digitale Spiele & Film: Konkurrenz, Kooperation, Komplementarität," *Film-Dienst*, May 7, 2009, pp. 6-10.

17 This circumstance applies especially to those games referred to as Serious Games, which in the tradition of nonfiction books and documentaries seek to do more than simply entertain.

18 For a discussion of the term 'operative image' see Krämer, Sybille: "Operative Bildlichkeit. Von der 'Grammatologie' zu einer 'Diagrammatologie'? Reflexionen über erkennendes 'Sehen.'" in: Hessler, Martina/Mersch, Dieter (ed.), *Logik des Bildlichen: zur Kritik der ikonischen Vernunft*, Bielefeld: transcript 2009, pp. 94-123.

the more or less hyperrealistic virtualities: 'pictures on a computer screen are not something to look at, but to *click* at ...'"[19]

This quality of operativity influences the specific imagery of digital games deeply, particularly in comparison with film and television. Next to more or less photorealistic game scenes, a multitude of direct and indirect instructions, which overlay the "actual" scenes, determine their effect and use. Benjamin Beil writes about the "computer game image":

"Often it is covered with interface controls, usually in form of pictograms or text inserts that inform display information concerning health, ammunition or objectives; in addition there are maps that help determine positions and in multiplayer games a chat window for communication with other players. Some of these elements are animated, others are interactive."[20]

THE INNOVATIVE GENRE OF THE FIRST-PERSON SHOOTER

The specific visual ability of procedurally generated hyperrealistic images to lend themselves to operativity comes to the fore in the first-person perspective, as it is orchestrated in the medium of digital games but especially by first-person shooters.[21] A rudimentary, perspectivally-immersive view could already be

---

19 Freyermuth: "Der Big Bang digitaler Bildlichkeit," p. 298. Reference to Kelly: Kevin Kelly, "Window on the World," in: N. N., "13 of the Brightest Tech Minds Sound Off on the Rise of the Tablet," *Wired*, April 2010; http://www.wired.com/magazine/2010/03/ff_tablet_essays/all/1; Quote from Elsaesser: Elsaesser, Thomas: "Die 'Rückkehr' der 3D-Bilder. Zur Logik und Genealogie des Bildes im 21. Jahrhundert," in: ibid., pp. 25-67, here p. 54, quoted from the English manuscript.—A similar though not identical passage can be found in: Elsaesser, Thomas, "The 'Return' of 3-D: On Some of the Logics and Genealogies of the Image in the Twenty-First Century," in: *Critical Inquiry* 39 (Winter 2013), pp. 240-241.

20 Beil, Benjamin: *Game Studies: Eine Einführung*, Red guide, Berlin: Lit 2013, pp. 55-56.

21 Dieter Mersch reaches a similar conclusion, though he grounds it in a mix of content concern (simulation of objectivity) and reception-logical argumentation (constitution of playing self-confidence) rather than media-aesthetics: "It must be considered among the hereby proposed theses, that with the 'First Person Perspective,' the partic-

found in the online and arcade games of the 1970s, for example SPASIM (1974), MAZE WAR (1974), NIGHT DRIVER (1976) and BATTLEZONE (1980). Its aesthetic beginnings, however, date to the start of the 20th century, the early movies and the first flight simulators that used point-of-view silent films. While the narrative film, with a few exceptions, avoided the first-person perspective—the most famous of these exceptions is the noir film LADY IN THE LAKE from 1947—, it found its further technological development first in the analog flight simulators of the 1950s and 1960s and then in the digital simulators of the seventies and eighties. The first of these two types operated with TV cameras and model landscapes. The second worked with real-time generated 2D and later 3D-polygon graphics in the areas of professional use and digital games. The first-person perspective became especially effective in numerous virtual-reality experiments, which in the eighties advanced from 3D simulators with a specific function to universal simulators like the CAVE (Cave Automatic Virtual Environment), which was demonstrated for the first time in 1991.

Around the same time—with ULTIMA UNDERWORLD: THE STYGIAN ABYSS (1992), WOLFENSTEIN 3D (1992), DOOM (1993), QUAKE (1996), HALF-LIFE (1998)—the aesthetic and commercial breakthrough of the 3D first-person shooter (FPS) took place. In particular, DOOM "would prove to be a landmark release that would shake up the entire video game industry."[22] Apart from all content elements that are connected with first-person shooters—as a rule violent ones—, their special formal attraction lies in the combination of three elements:

1) The elimination of distance. Frans Mäyrä, for example, writes: "When playing an FPS like Doom, the player gets a strong sense of 'being there' herself, as no mediating character is brought to the centre of attention."[23]
2) The radicalization of our worldview. Schooled on the linear perspective, our views are always "I"-focused. From the beginning, however, the first-person perspective was related as violence—Andrea Mantegna's painting "Archers Shooting at Saint Christopher (1451-55) stages this, when the arrow of the linear perspective strikes a watching human eye.[24] With the FPS, this implicit

---

ular mediality of digital games comes into its own, because FPP simulates subjectivity and possesses an incomparable status within the constitution of the 'playful' state of mind." Mersch: "Logik und Medialität des Computerspiels," p. 11.
22 Donovan: *Replay*, loc. 6045.
23 Mäyrä: *An Introduction to Game Studies*, loc. 1584.
24 See also: "Already in 1646 the Jesuit Athanasius Kircher pointed, in his text about light and shadows, the Ars Magna Lucis et Umbrae, to the connection between aiming

relationship with violence becomes explicit: The player's view of the world runs along the barrel of a gun, the blade of a sword or a knife, and of course along the shaft of an arrow, which Mantegna's painting chose as the symbol of the harmful effect of the central perspective.

3) The operativity of the game space. The world, which we see through the eyes of someone who must continually act—through the eyes of an actor then—is presented as a space that is fundamentally operative, i.e., something that can be 'handled' and conquered in a way that is dangerous and harmless at the same time. On the other hand, everybody else can perceive me, the acting 'ego-shooter,' solely down the barrel of gun as well. The result is the thrill of not only aggressively gazing at the world, but also surveying and colonizing it violently.

Since digital games gained the capability for procedural hyperrealism, they have possessed an entirely *new mode of image production*: the possibility for non-indexical real-time generation of seemingly photorealistic images and cinematically staged 3D action-spaces that users can "enter" and navigate by selecting from myriad procedural courses; a level of interactivity and immersion that was merely imagined in the storytelling-spaces of text-based adventures.[25] However, precisely in its otherness, the operative hyperrealism remains connected aesthetically to the imagery and soundscapes of older visual, auditive, and audiovisual media.

---

and drawing and, thereby, also that between seeing and shooting, which made the first-person shooter the most consequential implementation of the central perspective." (Günzel, Stefan: "Von der Zeit zum Raum. Geschichte und Ästhetik des Computerspielmediums," *Rabbiteye—Zeitschrift für Filmforschung* 2010, pp. 90-108; http://www.rabbiteye.de/2010/2/guenzel_computerspielmedium.pdf)

25 Benjamin Beil correctly notices that with the establishment of the techno-aesthetic possibilities for procedural hyperrealism, older image forms do not vanish. "However noteworthy this transformation may be, of greater significance is the fact that despite advanced technology and the victory march of 3D graphics since the 1990s all forms of visual representation remain in use in contemporary games. [...] Computer game images are not becoming primarily more realistic but rather more diverse. The technological development is not aiming solely for a 'simulation of reality imprints,' it is also expanding consistently the computer games' repertoire of forms of representation." (Beil: *Game Studies*, p. 57)

6 The Double Alterity of Digital Games

To date, digital games have evolved in three significant phases:

- *First phase*: Starting in the 1950s, hardware-based artifacts and processes were replaced with software-based ones. With this *procedural turn* parlor games like chess, sports games like table tennis, and analog (flight) simulations were virtualized and algorithmatized. SPACEWAR! with its design influences in SciFi literature and film signaled the start of a far-reaching interest in narration and audiovisual representation that began in the 1960s.
- *Second phase*: Starting in the 1970s, digital games gained the ability to deliver the interactive experience of multi-linear and increasingly complex stories. This *hyperepic turn* originated in the genre of text-based adventure games. Through the combination of databases and algorithms, an interactive mode of storytelling was realized that exceeded the medial possibilities of its model, analog literature. Around 1980 the growing dissatisfaction with the limitations of preprogrammed textual storytelling resulted in two outcomes: first, the transition from off- to online narrations, in which players no longer competed by themselves against the game but also against each other; and second, a steadily increasing 'arms race' of visual and audial capabilities. This process reflected the desire of both game designers and game players to advance the design of digital games from the standard of the novel to that of the movie.
- *Third phase*: Starting in the 1990s, digital games participated in the development of a new digital form of (audio-)visual representation: virtually produced hyperrealism. Technologically as well as aesthetically, hyperrealism integrates central elements of manually and mechanically produced realism with central elements of the semi-automated industrial reproduction of photorealism. With their *hyperrealistic turn* digital games gained the technical as well as aesthetic potential to generate operative 3D image worlds that in-

creasingly gave the impression of photorealism but were produced nonindexically. The subjective visual construction in real-time that then became possible radicalized the experience of the linear perspective, which since the Renaissance had formed and informed the modern individual. Now virtual realities are subjugated to an ever more powerful perspectival gaze, which has connected worlds through violent acts of optical appropriation since the dawn of modern time. Under the conditions of procedural hyperrealism, this perspectival gaze found its most successful media-aesthetic realization in the new visual regime of the first-person-shooter genre.

THE EVOLUTION OF GAMES INTO AN AUDIOVISUAL MEDIUM

The cumulative completion of the new medium of nonlinear audiovisuality, which took place between the 1950s and 2000s, can be compared to the half-century long formation of the medium of linear audiovisuality, which took place between the 1870s and 1930s in the transition from chronophotography to silent, sound, and color film. In the history of film this evolution manifested itself as continual improvement—for instance from black and white to color film—as well as a radical technological-aesthetic break, especially the turn from silent movies to talkies. The same is true for the path from analog to digital games.

This process is discussed in *Understanding Video Games*: "But it should be clear that video games are a result of the evolution and reconstitution of various elements of games going back several thousand years."[1] And Jesse Schell writes: "Videogames are just a natural growth of traditional games into a new medium."[2] Tom Chatfield, on the other hand, understands digital games as a radically different medium because they enable completely new experiences and forms of expression. Thereby his perception focuses less on the comparison with analog games than on the relation to traditional forms of fiction. Games, he writes, offer "a portal to a new destination in human experience, a space where people could interact in real time within an entirely simulated environment—as if a work of fiction had suddenly become real."[3]

---

1 Egenfeldt-Nielsen et al.: *Understanding Video Games*, loc. 1438.
2 Schell: *The Art of Game Design*, loc. 317.
3 Chatfield, Tom: *Fun Inc.: Why Games are the Twenty-First Century's Most Serious Business*, London: Virgin (Kindle edition) 2010, loc. 321-323.

Chatfield clearly speaks of digital games as they have come into being since the hyperrealistic turn. This last evolutionary jump—the transition to a realism, which appears photographic but does not correspond to any index—led games from the edges of industrial culture to the center of digital culture. It drove their transformation from a medium in the tradition of analog games, or even sports, to the third audiovisual and culturally defining medium of representation in modern times—after the live theater of illusion, which came into being pre-industrially, and the industrial media of film and television, which feature linear audiovisions produced through stored indexical imprints of reality.

DIGITAL GAMES VS.
ANALOG GAMES AND LINEAR AUDIOVISIONS

As a consequence of this transformation, the history of games consists of two distinct parts, the analog and the digital. Two earlier developments can serve as historical models for this categorical division: the industrial transition of visual representation from painting to photography, and the transition of audiovisual representation from theater to film. Subsequently, scholarly analysis of these various media has also divided itself—into the theory of art and of photography, into theater and film studies. Since digital games do categorically differ from analog games, the theories of analog games should have as little or as much validity for digital games as theories of the theater have for film.[4] The same holds true for the relationship between movies and games.

Thus digital games are characterized by a double alterity, i.e., a relative otherness in relation to the two central media from which they grew and in relation to which they form their own specific identity. Despite what they have in common, digital games distinguish themselves from analog games through what they gained over the course of three evolutionary jumps as well as through what established their aesthetic competition with older, and initially, analog media of theater, film, and television: *first*, procedural simulation including virtualized feedback, *second*, hyperepic multi- or nonlinear narration, and *third*, hyperrealistic representation able to generate perspectival images in real-time.

---

4   Despite all the historical differences between theater and film, theoretical concerns of the theater hold validity for the cinema; especially in terms of theories of the practitioners—from the traces of Aristotelian poetry in the theories of script writing to the teachings of staging and directing.

Vice versa, the difference between digital games and older audiovisual media is demonstrated in the way qualities which originate from analog games undergo qualitative and quantitative enhancement through the process of their virtualization: their potential for arbitrary interactions realized through game mechanics. Thus the unique media-technological affordances of digital games produce their alterity in relation to older audiovisual media:

- The stage, as a non-storing medium, allows for specific actors to deliver performances that are original and vary from show to show, i.e., in regard to the representation and manipulation of space and time, the stage presents its audience almost exclusively with continual live-action performances which are experienced as diegetically linear and in real-time.
- As storing media, film and television allow chosen actors to be copied and selected and, thereby, it produces performances which do not vary from iteration to iteration, i.e., in regard to the display and manipulation of space and time, these media present their audiences with dis-continually cut and edited storylines, which are experienced linearly and in a time that is both someone else's time and removed from the present time of the audience.
- Digital games, on the other hand, enable general and equal participation in potential performances which vary from iteration to iteration, i.e., in principle, they no longer 'know' a passive audience and involve the user in rule-determined and, in regard to space and time, continual as well as iterative actions which are experienced multi- or nonlinearly and in real-time (and only rarely in a time removed from that of the user). Thereby one must differentiate between games that enable interaction between players and software and those which organize software-assisted interactions between players.[5]

---

5 This theoretical separation was of course not followed in practice. With tennis or chess, for example, one can usually play against 'the computer' as well as against other human players, all in the same program; where the advantage of the virtual multiplayer game via digital networking rests mainly with the delocalization of the player's opponents. In multiplayer games, the virtual environment also directly impacts gameplay; through simulated weather or, for example, through NPCs, which mix themselves in among the players.

THE DEFINING MEDIUM OF DIGITAL CULTURE

A theoretical perspective of the history of digital games reveals the tight connection between their evolution in three phases and the unfolding and implementation of digital culture. Essentially games worked as a trailblazing force. In the 1960s they allowed several generations of students an independent and playful use of university mainframe computers. In the 1970s digital arcade games and home consoles empowered average citizens to experience digital hard- and software. In this way, games conveyed, asserts J.P. Wolf, "a positive, fun, and user-friendly image of the computer, which helped to usher in the era of the home computer only a few years later."[6] Both the popularization of the PC as well as its evolution from a machine for the processing of numbers and texts into a transmedial entertainment machine during the 1980s and 1990s was then driven by the desire for, and the requirements of, digital games.

Throughout the process of digitalization, digital games took and continue to take on the role that film possessed during the second phase of the industrialization according to Walter Benjamin: familiarization with a new world that has largely been shaped by virtualization. "The games gave us mass training in how to 'live' inside the pure, weightless, scientific space of the Computer," asserts Rochelle Slovin.[7] As an audiovisual medium—whose products are no longer reproduced and edited to a final cut in the fashion of Taylorization but rather unfold virtually, that is in the medium of software, interactively and in real-time— the digital game, more so than older forms of expression, seems to correspond more closely to the experiences of digital culture, to the requirements of digital knowledge work, to the changing methods of perceiving time and space, to the new concepts of how people should exist and act under the conditions of digital production and communication.

So a conclusive question regarding the double alterity of digital games, i.e., the formation of their medial identity, must be asked: Is this process in its completion stage or will it continue, and if so, in what direction will it develop?

---

6   Wolf, Mark J. P.: "The Video Game as a Medium," in: Wolf, Mark J. P. (ed.), *The Medium of the Video Game*, Austin: University of Texas Press 2002, pp. 13-33, p. 5. Also ibid.: "Many people at the time wondered if they really needed a Computer, or what they would use it for, since typewriters, board games, calculators, ledgers, and other technology already served their needs. Games made the Computer a recreational device instead of merely a utilitarian one."

7   Slovin, Rochelle: "Hot Circuits: Reflections on the 1989 Video Game Exhibition of the American Museum of the Moving Image," in: ibid., pp. 137-154, here p. 146.

7 A Look Ahead: Hyperimmersive Turn?

Both the future and the present are most confidently discussed once they have become the past. But some of us are living in the future already, as William Gibson once stated: "[T]he future is already here—it's just not very evenly distributed."[1] From this perspective of cultural nonsynchronism, i.e., that "Not all people exist in the same Now" (Ernst Bloch)[2], three trends stand out.

THE EVOLUTION OF DIGITAL GAMES

First, the past decade has brought a far-reaching *differentiation*. Around the early 2010s, digital games were not far behind older audiovisual media as far as what they could offer in content and artistic diversity.

"Analogously to, for instance, the opposition of feature and documentary films, so-called Serious Games, which specialize in knowledge-transfer and clarification, are flourishing. At the same time, just as with the opposition of million-dollar blockbusters and cheaply produced Independent and Art-House movies, there are AAA and indie games. The diversity also includes art games, which find their place in galleries and museums, mobile

---

1 Gibson, William "Talk of the Nation, The Science in Science Fiction (Interview with William Gibson, [quote at min. 11:50])," *National Public Radio*, November 30, 1999; http://www.npr.org/templates/story/story.php?storyId=1067220. William Gibson had expressed this opinion since the beginning of the 1990s in numerous interviews. For details compare N. N.: "The Future Has Arrived—It's Just Not Evenly Distributed Yet. William Gibson? Anonymous? Apocryphal?," *Quote Investigator*, January 24 2012; http://quoteinvestigator.com/2012/01/24/future-has-arrived/

2 Compare Bloch, Ernst. "Nonsynchronism and the Obligation to its Dialectics," *New German Critique* 11, 1977 (*1932).

games, and hybrid game forms, such as combinations of board and computer games or alternate reality games (ARG) that connect play in reality and virtuality with one another."[3]

A second trend is the proliferation of a new, "easier" to play category of games, so-called social or casual games. Designed to be played in a browser or on mobile devices, they demand less commitment from potential consumers in terms of time and money and, thereby, they lower the entrance threshold. This *democratization* of gaming—in the sense of financial enabling and practical facilitation—has promoted its spread into social classes and age groups that had previously escaped the new medium: "In the short history of video games, casual games are something of a revolution—a cultural reinvention of what a video game can be, a reimagining of who can be a video game player."[4]

Thirdly, the general mobilization of communication and medial consumption has been important for the popularization of video games. Until recently, gaming—like making phone calls and watching TV—was largely technically bound to specific locations: board gamers, for instance, usually sat in the living room, PC gamers at a desk, etc. Only two recent innovations introduced a potential *delocalization* of digital playing: first, the proliferation of smaller high-performance devices, such as PDAs and cell phones, mobile consoles like the PlayStation Portable (2004) and the Nintendo DS (2004), smartphones and tablets like the iPhone (2007) and the iPad (2010); second, the proliferation of wireless broadband connections over local networks (WLAN), cellular radio and GPS. Special attention should be given to the escalating delocalization of playing in so far as it has impacted how we play in and outside of our homes as well as how it influences where other players hang out and can be found.

Differentiation, democratization, delocalization: Despite this rapid economic, media-technological and media-aesthetic evolution, game designers have recently voiced the supposition that digital games are still at the beginning of their medial and aesthetic evolution. In a talk at the 2013 Game Developers Conference in San Francisco, for instance, Jesse Schell said—calling on his colleague Chris Swain—games had only reached a medial state at this point which can be compared to that of the movies in the mid-1920s: impressive media-aesthetic achievements exist in opposition to a lack of media-technological development

---

3   Metzger, Nils: "Können Pixel Kunst sein?, *Neue Zürcher Zeitung*," April 19, 2013; http://www.nzz.ch/aktuell/feuilleton/literatur-und-kunst/koennen-pixel-kunst-sein-1.1 8067546

4   Juul, Jesper: *A Casual Revolution: Reinventing Video Games and Their Players*, Cambridge, MA: MIT Press 2009, pp. 5-7.

that hinders sustained artistic evolution. Therefore, Schell saw digital games as standing shortly before an evolutionary push, which he compared to the transition from silent film to the talkies.[5] As an equivalent to speech, which film once lacked, he identified 'listening' in its broadest form: the still nascent ability of games to recognize the player's words, gestures, and facial expressions within the given narrative and situational frame. Just as film gained psychological depth and artistic merit through their characters' learning to speak, games could now experience a comparable evolutionary push through their AI-characters'—NPCs'—learning to listen, watch, and understand via processes of speech, gesture, and facial recognition.

Whether we share Schell's particular hopes or not, we can hardly overlook the larger changes taking place in the realm of digital media technology. What over the years has evolved as a procedural, potentially hyperepic, and potentially hyperrealistic gaming experience, has been developing over the last few years anew in a manner that targets both the aesthetic form as well as the interactive use of digital games. A complementary dual trend seems to have emerged: on the one hand, the striving for every-day, i.e. 'natural' activity in games, and on the other hand, the pursuit of gamelike, i.e., 'gamish' activity in every-day life.[6]

LIFELIKE AGENCY IN GAMES

Hard- and software interfaces are the media technological basis of all human interaction with digital technology. In their use they allow for the manipulation and control of virtual programs and data through various feedback channels. Since the 1940s, highly varied interfaces determined interaction: from punch cards (which hindered interactivity rather than enabling it) to challenging command line interfaces to GUIs (graphical user interfaces) used in combination with keyboard, mouse, and similar controllers, which have been produced since the late 1960s, but first became popular only in the late 1980s.

This long-time trend towards more intuitive interaction found its continuation with technological-artistic experiments especially in the field of digital games and digital (installation) art. The search for input devices beyond the abstractions that have characterized all interfaces between man and the data-world so far—particularly the effort to overcome the so-called "tyranny of the key-

---

5   Schell: "Die Zukunft des Erzählens."
6   This dual tendency corresponds in part with Schell's observations, even exceeding them.

board"[7]—began in the arcades of the 1970s.[8] Until the present, it led to the integration of real-world objects into the interface design—pistols, rifles, and other weapons, steering wheels and stick shifts, gloves, dance mats, etc.; it also led to the development of 'more physical' interface apparatuses, such as joysticks, gamepads, balance boards or head mounted displays. In the arts, mixed-reality-experiments attempted further anticipations in the direction of less abstract and more corporeal ways of dealing with data-worlds.[9] Since the 1970s, artists have also tried to capture visual, acoustic, tactile, gestural, and geographical data (sight, speech, touch, and balance, bodily movement, position in space) in order to transfer physical actions and synesthetic interactions into medial spaces.

It was on the basis of these experiments that *natural user interfaces* became an industry-standard in the first decade of the 21st century, for instance in Nintendo's Wii (2006), Apple's iOS (2007), Google's Android (2008), Sony's Move (2009) or Microsoft's Kinect (2010).[10] Control through direct touch was of particularly far-reaching importance for digital gaming and beyond. Starting in the late 1980s, the introduction of the mouse and GUI effected a dramatic simplification of computer use and thereby brought desktop and laptop PCs into the majority of households of the developed world. In connection with a natural, gesture-controlled user interface, touch screens—the most recent challenge to the dominance of the mouse and GUI—have now triggered another push for simplification and with that a further escalation of the increasingly symbiotic relationship between humanity and its digital machines.[11]

Alongside the biological naturalness of the user interface, the cultural familiarity with the tablet's physical form contributed to its popularization. For thousands of years, easy-to-handle text and image tablets—from the stone and clay tablets of antiquity to the modern book or notebook—have furthered the transfer of knowledge and everyday written communication. Furthermore the tablet was

---

7   Kelly: "Window on the World."
8   Compare to, for example, Mäyrä, Frans: *An Introduction to Game Studies*, loc. 2116.
9   Fleischmann, Monika: "Die Spur des Betrachters im Bild," in: Weibel, Peter, Zentrum für Kunst und Medientechnologie (Karlsruhe) (ed.), *Vom Tafelbild zum globalen Datenraum: neue Möglichkeiten der Bildproduktion und bildgebenden Verfahren*, Ostfildern-Ruit: Hatje Cantz Edition ZKM 2001, pp. 138-149.
10 Systematically, these can be distinguished as follows: motion control (for example Nintendo's Wii, Sony's Move, Microsoft's Kinect), touch control (for example Apple's iOs, Google's Android) and voice control (for example Apple's Siri as part of the iOS, or Microsoft's Cortana).
11 Compare Licklider: "Man-Computer Symbiosis."

not just a space for text and images, but also a playing field.[12] In the touchpad, all these familiar forms of use found their "natural" digital form. For the past few years, touch-tablet digital media have been penetrating areas of use that were previously reserved for analog media—such as the distribution and reception of texts—or were too technical for a large portion of the population (as seen in digital games), i.e., they appeared too complicated.[13]

In a relatively short time period, touch-control has changed the way audiovisual products and especially games are perceived and consumed. This change is flanked by the proliferation of other NUIs. Monitors are incorporating not only touch-screens, so that they may feel their users, but they are also incorporating cameras and microphones so that they can see gestures and faces, and hear noises and speech. Goggles that allow navigation through 3D image and game worlds by simply turning one's head enhance this 'natural'—multi-sensory—appropriation of digital data.[14]

The consequences for digital gaming brought on by the proliferation of NUIs reach far beyond the facilitation and deepening of existing ways of playing and game experiences. The evolution is working unmistakably towards one of the oldest desires by which media and the arts are driven: immersion.

UTOPIA HOLODECK

The desire to experience fictional worlds as intensely as possible was already a companion to the development of networked gaming, from text-based MUDs of the 1970s and early 1980s to the first-person shooter 'death matches,' which ar-

---

12 The game Tavli—the Greek variation of Backgammon—retains roughly the origin of the tabula (board) also in name.
13 Not least to the surprise of the game industry. See Metzger: "Können Pixel Kunst sein?": "When the iPhone was introduced to the market in 2007, no one from the established Game companies recognized the potential of the new platform. They continued to concentrate on the console market, while students, amateur developers and startups began to program for the entertainment possibilities of Apple's bestseller."
14 The strength of the demand for immersion revealed itself above all in the spectacular 2012 Oculus-Rift Kickstarter Campaign, which raised 2.4 million dollars. Two years later Facebook carried out the acquisition of the company, which could only exhibit prototypes at the time, for over 2 billion dollars. See Rubin, Peter: "The Inside Story of Oculus Rift and How Virtual Reality Became Reality," *Wired* 2014; http://www.wired.com/2014/05/oculus-rift-4/

rived in the 1990s with DOOM, to the extensive virtual 3D worlds of Massively Multiplayer Online Roleplaying Games (MMORPGs) like ULTIMA ONLINE (ELECTRONIC ARTS 1997), EVERQUEST (SONYONLINE, 1999), OR WORLD OF WARCRAFT (BLIZZARD, 2004), whose players numbered in the hundreds of thousands in the nineties and in the millions since the 2000s. Parallel to the rise of networked gaming, the ideal of truly immersive fiction became popular, diverging from the anti-immersive stance of postmodern art and literature as well as poststructuralist theory.[15]

Its aesthetic utopia, however, no longer emerged in the context of high culture, as was the case with the analog ideal of the "Gesamtkunstwerk"—the "total work of art"—, but rather in the context of popular culture: the "holodeck," which ENCOUNTER AT FARPOINT,[16] the pilot episode of the science-fiction TV-series STAR TREK: THE NEXT GENERATION[17], introduced as part of its fictional world. Roddenberry's holodeck was an immersive holographic and interactive entertainment environment, the users of which physically stepped into interactive fiction and influenced their progression by playing. Within a short time, the concept of a holodeck became the model for the digital future of art and entertainment—not only for millions of Star Trek fans but also for academics, scientists, and artists, and especially for filmmakers and game designers.

Three examples from the recent past may demonstrate the lasting influence of this popular utopia on digital practice:

- In 2011 Stevie Bathiche, research director at Microsoft's Edison Lab, announced that he would strive "to create a holodeck-like experience"[18];
- Since 2012 the "Project Holodeck" at the School of Cinematic Arts of the University of Southern California in Los Angeles has been experimenting with interactive-immersive audiovisual experiences, for example through the use of the Oculus-Rift data glasses;[19]

---

15 Ryan, Marie-Laure: *Narrative as Virtual Reality: Immersion and Interactivity in Literature and Electronic Media* (Baltimore: Johns Hopkins University Press, 2001), p. 2.
16 ENCOUNTER AT FARPOINT (USA 1987, D: Corey Allen)
17 STAR TREK: THE NEXT GENERATION (USA 1987-1994, P: Gene Roddenberry)
18 Sottek, T. C.: "To Build a Holodeck: An Exclusive Look at Microsoft's Edison Lab," *The Verge*, December 29, 2011; http://www.theverge.com/2011/12/28/2665794/microsoft-edison-lab-holodeck-tour
19 Stevens, Tim: "Project Holodeck and Oculus Rift Hope to Kickstart Every Gamers' VR dream for $500," *Engadget*, July 23, 2012; http://www.engadget.com/2012/07/23/project-holodeck-and-oculus-rift/

- In 2013 Jeff Norris from the Jet Propulsion Laboratory at NASA announced—fittingly during the Game Developer Conference in San Francisco—the space agency's plan to deliver the experience of space travel to millions of earthbound users: "Everyone exploring the universe through robotic avatars, not just peering at numbers or pictures on a screen, but stepping inside a holodeck and standing on those distant worlds."[20]

GAMELIKE AGENCY IN REAL LIFE

The desire for immersion and interaction in and with fictional worlds correlates with the opposite effort to virtualize reality after the model of digital games, i.e., to overlay it with virtual structures so that play-like acting becomes possible. If the origins of immersive virtual acting lie in stationary-networked games, so do those of immersive everyday acting in mobile-networked games. New mobile hardware has allowed, however, not only existing games to be used in public areas; it has also generated new game forms, especially since the release of GPS for civilian purposes: pervasive- and augmented-reality games, from THE BEAST (2001) and MAJESTIC (2001) to INGRESS (2012) and ENDGAME (2014).

In the last decade, a superposition of reality by digital media—texts, sounds, images—facilitated not only the geographical but also the social, cultural, and playful navigation of the urban environment.[21] What under analog conditions had to remain merely metaphorical speech—that the media, such as images of mov-

---

20 Claiborn, Samuel: "NASA Wants to Design a Holodeck. At GDC 2013, NASA presentation claims 'We are the Space Invaders'," *IGN* (2013); http://www.ign.com/articles/2013/03/28/nasa-wants-to-design-a-holodeck

21 This development can be compared to the labeling, or signposting, of the urban landscape in the early stages of industrialization, as seen in street names, house numbers, guide posts, traffic signs, and advertisements. At that time a new analog mediality laid itself over the natural world, just as a new digital mediality is doing so today. The material transformation of reality into a medium, which began with mechanization and industrialization, and was realized through the collective standardization of symbols, has now been completed through the virtual transformation of reality into a medium, which has been realized through individual customization of symbols. Compare to Freyermuth, Gundolf S.: "Der große Kommunikator. Soziale Konsequenzen von 'media merging' und Transmedialisierung," in: Siever, Torsten/Schlobinski, Peter/Runkehl, Jens (ed.), *Websprache.net. Sprache und Kommunikation im Internet*, Berlin; New York: Walter de Gruyter 2005, pp. 15-45, here p. 33ff.

ies and TV-shows, shape our perception of reality—has become a virtual or hybrid reality. Mobile 'Von Neumann machines,' which since their inception were thought of as talent and intelligence enhancers, advanced to become machines that improve reality. "The real world is too boring for many people," said Daniel Sánchez-Crespo, the Spanish augmented-reality game developer: "By making the real world a playground for the virtual world, we can make the real world much more interesting."[22]

Step by step a historically new connection of imagery and operativity has been achieved. If, in the course of their digitalization, images became operative in the way reality once was—roughly turning *windows*, which allowed one to passively observe worlds, into *portals*, through which one can actively step—then it appears reality is now slowly becoming operative in a way that only virtual image worlds once were. The best example and simultaneously a symbol for this fusion of reality and virtuality are civilian and military drones, which are generally outfitted with systems for real-time transmission of images as well as with remote-controlled weapons systems. Obviously the cultural practices of software-based navigation through virtual worlds and reality differ less and less.

Even such real-world immersion was anticipated in both an utopian and dystopian manner. Already in 1946, during the pioneer years of technological digitalization, Jorge Luis Borges sketched a fictional realm in which cartographers were concerned with the creation of a perfect map in order to improve the navigability of their world. In his short short-story "On Rigor in Science" Borges stated—in the form of a fictitious 'quotation', i.e., in the form of a literary forgery: "In time, [...] the Colleges of Cartographers set up a Map of the Empire which had the size of the Empire itself and coincided with it point by point."[23]

Borges short story, however, was itself an adaptation of another story published by Lewis Carroll in 1893 called *Sylvia and Bruno Concluded*. In it Carroll includes dialogue between the first-person narrator and another person known as "Mein Herr":

"What do you consider the largest map that would be really useful?" [Mein Herr]
"About six inches to the mile." [Narrator]

---

22 Cited from, Berlin, Leslie: "Kicking Reality of a Notch," *The New York Times*, July 12, 2009; http://www.nytimes.com/2009/07/12/business/12proto.html?_r=1&partner=rss&emc=rss

23 Borges, Jorge Luis: "On Exactitude in Science," in: Borges, Jorge Luis/Hurley, Andrew (ed.), *Collected Fictions*, London; New York: Allen Lane The Penguin Press 1999, p. 325.

"Only six inches!" exclaimed Mein Herr. "We very soon got to six yards to the mile. Then we tried a hundred yards to the mile. And then came the grandest idea of all! We actually made a map of the country, on the scale of a mile to the mile!"
"Have you used it much?" I enquired.
"It has never been spread out, yet," said Mein Herr: "the farmers objected: they said it would cover the whole country, and shut out the sunlight! *So we now use the country itself, as its own map, and I assure you it does nearly as well.*"[24]

We are starting to live under similar circumstances. For in the course of its digital augmentation and in connection with mobile hardware as well as natural user interfaces, reality itself is successively evolving. Once only a real space of action, it is now also a virtual, or rather hybrid, playing field, just as Lewis Carroll and Jorge Luis Borges imagined: Reality is replaced with or rather augmented to an operative likeness of itself, the elements of which provide us with information in real-time and allow us to act, interact, and engage with it playfully as well as seriously.

POTENTIAL FOR HYPERIMMERSIVE TURN

Since the development of procedurality, hyperepicness, and hyperrealism, digital games seem to be aiming now for a higher and different degree of immersion than can be created in other media. The title of Janet H. Murray's groundbreaking study *Hamlet on the Holodeck* (1997) indicated its focus on the "enchantment of immersion" as a singular aesthetic quality of the digital transmedium.[25] Two years later, Murray along with Henry Jenkins described immersion as one of two most important "aesthetic pleasures that emerge most immediately from the intrinsic properties of the computer medium."[26] Since then the question of immersion has attained prominence in film theory and Game Studies as well as

---

24 Compare Carroll, Lewis: *Sylvia and Bruno Concluded*, 2 vols., London, New York: Macmillan 1893; http://archive.org/stream/sylviebrunoconcl00carriala/sylviebrunoncl00carriala_djvu.txt. (My emphasis)
25 Murray, *Hamlet on the Holodeck*, p. 125.
26 The second most important pleasure is interactivity. See Murray, Janet/Jenkins, Henry: "Before the Holodeck: Translating *Star Trek* into Digital Media," in: Greg M. Smith (ed.): *On a Silver Platter: CD-ROMs and the Promises of a New Technology*, New York: New York University Press, 1999, pp. 35-57; http://web.mit.edu/cms/People/henry3/holodeck.html

popular debates on the qualities of digital media and culture. For example, Frank Rose—after interviewing filmmakers and game designers—concludes that immersion in fictional worlds is the desire of this age, which is also driving the development of new digital storytelling methods: "We can see the outlines of a new art form, but its grammar is as tenuous and elusive as the grammar of cinema a century ago. We know this much: people want to be immersed. They want to get involved in a story, to carve out a role for themselves, to make it their own."[27]

The term 'immersion,' however, is hardly better defined in academic discourse than the term 'game.' It's not surprising then that there is quite a bit of disagreement over what medium-defining circumstances trigger and promote immersion respectively, and what forms of immersion actually exist. In 2004 Ernest Adams differentiated tactical immersion (achieved through skilled tactile interactions) from strategic immersion (achieved through mental involvement) and narrative immersion (achieved by losing oneself in a story).[28] A year later Laura Ermi and Frans Mäyrä categorized immersion into sensory, challenge-based and imaginative variants.[29] Quite similarly, Staffan Björk and Jussi Holopainen discerned sensory-motoric, cognitive, and emotional immersion, but added spatial immersion to the mix, the feeling of being "really there."[30] Henry Jen-

---

27 Rose, Frank: *The Art of Immersion: How the Digital Generation is Remaking Hollywood, Madison Avenue, and the Way We Tell Stories*, New York: W.W. Norton & Co., Kindle edition, 2011, loc. 166.—It's no coincidence that the ability to achieve exceptional immersion awoke a sensation of Angstlust in traditional media, for example in literature and above all film. The pervasively positive Holodeck-Utopia as seen in STAR TREK contrasts with dozens of dystopian Hollywood films, in which the slave-inducing danger of immersion is portrayed: TRON (USA 1982, D: Steven Lisberger), ARCADE (USA 1993, D: Albert Pyun), STRANGE DAYS (USA 1995, D: Kathryn Bigelow), THE THIRTEENTH FLOOR (USA 1999, D: Josef Rusnak), EXISTENZ (USA 1999, D: David Cronenberg), THE MATRIX (USA 1999, D: Andy and Lana Wachowski), GAMER (USA 2009, D: Mark Neveldine, Brian Taylor), INCEPTION (USA 2010, D: Christopher Nolan).

28 Adams, Ernest: "Postmodernism and the Three Types of Immersion," *Gamasutra*, July 9, 2004; http://www.designersnotebook.com/Columns/063_Postmodernism/063_postmodernism.htm

29 Ermi, Laura/ Mäyrä, Frans: "Fundamental Components of the Gameplay Experience. Analysing Immersion" (paper presented at the DiGRA Conference, Vancouver 2005).

30 Björk, Staffan/Holopainen, Jussi: *Patterns in Game Design*, Hingham, Mass.: Charles River Media, 2005.

kins and Janet Murray have asserted, "immersion and interactive agency reinforce each other."[31] Marie-Laure Ryan, on the other hand, has argued that interactivity conflicts with immersion, in so far as immersion is replaced "by an aesthetics of play and self-reflexivity that eventually produce[s] the ideal of an active participation of the appreciator—reader, spectator, user—in the production of the text."[32]

As with the question of what a game is, defining aesthetic immersion systematically and ontologically appears more promising from a historical perspective as well as from a perspective of medium specificity. A historical sense of the term immersion in audiovisual media can be developed in parallel with the four medialities presented above:[33]

- Primary audiovisuality relates to immersion in the real: losing oneself in real time, actual events which unfold organically or are staged. Participants are transported to times and locations in which they do not live (though they might want to) and allow them to behave as beings which they might be (and might want to be more often).
- Secondary audiovisuality relates to immersion in the realistic: losing oneself in proper time in artifacts—paintings, plays, etc.—that transport spectators to times and places where they are not (but perhaps would like to be) and where they can identify with people who they are not (but perhaps would like to be).
- Tertiary mediality relates to immersion in the photorealistic: losing oneself in a time other than one's own and in artifacts—movies, television shows, etc.—that transport viewers to times and places where they are not (but perhaps would like to be) and where they can identify with people who they are not (but perhaps would like to be).
- Quaternary mediality, finally, relates to immersion in the hyperrealistic: losing oneself in real time, proper time, or a time other than one's own and in artifacts or programmed processes—games and other nonlinear audiovisions—that enable users to explore and experience times and places where

---

31 Murray and Jenkins: "Before the Holodeck: Translating *Star Trek* into Digital Media." Also: "The more we feel we are surrounded by another enticing environment, the more we want to manipulate it. The more the environment responds to our manipulations, the stronger our involvement with it, and the more persuasive the illusion of being there."
32 Ryan: *Narrative as Virtual Reality*, p. 2.
33 See Chapter I, part *2 Games in the Modern Era. A Short Media History*, p. 39ff.

they are not (but perhaps would like to be) and where they can act like people who they might want to be (but are not).

Insofar as quaternary audiovisuality virtualizes the specific qualities of primary, secondary, and tertiary audiovisuality (and in doing so, integrates and enhances these qualities), it empowers immersion—in virtual worlds—in a way that was not allowed in older audiovisual media. Analogous to the terms "hyperepic" and "hyperrealism," this new experience of immersion, as it results to a large extent from the interactive navigation of hyperlinked, hyperepic, and hyperrealistic procedures, can be defined as hyper-immersion. Its rise heralds another turn in the history of digital games. Once again, this should enhance their alterity in relation to analog games as well as to analog audiovisions.

Intermezzo: Game // Film

Introduction

Media have always referenced other media; they have both inspired and rejected one another, and so they have always mutually influenced each other in some way. Within historically changing media environments, however, not all intermedial relationships carry the same weight. The exchange among defining media, i.e., the arts based on them, always stood in a privileged position. In *Laocoon. An Essay upon the Limits of Painting and Poetry* (1766) Gotthold Ephraim Lessing analyzed, for the first time in modernity, such a tension of proximity and distance between the central mimetic and storytelling modes of an era. He maintained that this tension—e.g., the difference between pictorial narration in space, which is merely able to represent relationships in their juxtaposition or, in the best case, represent key scenes of events, and literary storytelling in time, which is capable of unfolding complex plots simultaneously or successively—was not just something that had to be endured, but something that provided opportunities for creative approaches to storytelling.[1]

Today, a quarter of a millennium later, the two primary media of representation and storytelling are audiovisual: film and games. Particularly through their tense relationship, they are defining the epochal change from industrial to digital culture. Feature films, TV movies, TV series—meaning audiovisual narratives that are no longer played out live and in real-time (like the theater), but are rather Tayloristically produced and edited in a final cut—corresponded to the industrial way of life, its perception of time and space, its worldview, the industrial view of how people were supposed to be and act.

Now, however, right before our eyes a new audiovisual culture is emerging. New media, Marshall McLuhan once wrote, "institute new ratios, not only

---

1 Lessing, Gotthold Ephraim/Ellen Frothingham. *Laocoon. An Essay upon the Limits of Painting and Poetry*. Boston: Roberts brothers 1874 (*1766); https://archive.org/detai ls/laocoonessayupon00lessrich

among our private senses, but among themselves, when they interact among themselves."² Thus, the familiar industrial media dispositif is dissolving in two respects.

First there is the digital reinvention of cinema as well as television. Wheeler Winston Dixon calls this process with respect to cinema, "every bit as revolutionary as the dawn of cinema itself"³: "the dawn of a new grammar, a new technological delivery and production system, with a new set of plots, tropes, iconic conventions, and stars."⁴ More or less, the same applies to television. Consequently, the traditional boundaries that used to separate analog cinema and analog television are steadily vanishing. It already makes little sense to categorize feature films according to whether they have been or will be released in movie theaters or on television, on DVD or on the web. In the context of digital culture they are all just movies.

The second fundamental change is the rise of non-linear audiovisuality and multi-linear audiovisual storytelling. The variations of what we have so far categorized under the (mildly inadequate) term 'digital games'—meaning audiovisual narrations that are no longer reproduced and assembled in a Tayloristic manner, like film, but instead unfold in real-time and interactively in the medium of software—seem to correspond to the experiences of digital culture more appropriately than other narrative forms. Digital games best represent the changing perceptions of time and space and how human beings are supposed to be and act under the conditions of digital production and communication.

However, games as a narrative medium are rather underdeveloped, particularly in comparison to film. After directing several game adaptations (MORTAL KOMBAT, 1995; RESIDENT EVIL, 2002, 2004, 2007), Paul W. S. Anderson stated in 2007: "Games are now at the stage that movies were when Talkies were introduced."⁵ Nonetheless, multi-linear interactive narratives are so wildly popular

---

2   McLuhan, Marshall: *Understanding Media: The Extensions of Man*, Berkeley: Gingko Press (Kindle edition) 2013 (*1964), p. 64.
3   Dixon, Wheeler Winston: "Vanishing Point: The Last Days of Film," *Senses of Cinema* 2007; http://www.sensesofcinema.com/2007/feature-articles/last-days-film
4   Dixon, Wheeler Winston: "Twenty-Five Reasons Why It's All Over," in: Lewis, Jon (ed.), *The End of Cinema as We Know It : American Film in the Nineties*, New York: New York University Press. 2001, pp. 356-366, here p. 366.
5   Crecente, Brian: "Convergence, Smergence... Hollywood Director Paul W.S. Anderson Believes Games and Movies Should Remain Separate," *Kotaku*, November 29, 2007; http://kotaku.com/327820/convergence-smergencehollywood-director-paul-ws-anderson-believes-games-and-movies-should-remain-separate

and successful, that they are posing a competitive threat to traditional modes of audiovisual narration, both commercially and artistically, as Tracy Fullerton asserts: "The cultural impact of digital games has grown to rival television and films as the industry has matured over the past three decades."[6] Today, cinema and television's status as culturally defining media is being increasingly called into question: their linear products are coming under pressure to innovate aesthetically their visuals as well as their narratives.

Overview

In this intermezzo chapter I will, therefore, try to analyze the present and emerging relationship between these two defining media of our time, linear movies and non- or multi-linear games. In doing so, my main objective is to reflect on impending changes in audiovisual storytelling. Due to this interest, I will limit myself to addressing today's dominant fictional forms; the live-action feature film and the fictional digital game. That is, regarding linear audiovisuality, I will not consider animated films, documentaries, or video blogs, and regarding nonlinear audiovisuality, I will also not consider so-called serious games, pervasive games, augmented reality games, purely ludic games of skill or sports games. I will proceed in three steps:

1) I will concern myself with the status quo, the present relationship between games and film (*1 Game and Film*).
2) In order to better understand present developments, I will reexamine two earlier audiovisual rivalries: the rise of film and its interchange with theater, the rise of television and its interchange with film (*2 Audiovisual Rivalries*).
3) I will look to the future and apply the results of my historical analysis in order to explore the emerging relationship between digital games and digital movies (*3 Modes of Audiovisual Storytelling*).

---

6   Fullerton: *Game Design Workshop*, loc. 471.

1 Game and Film

> "In the last two decades, with accelerating speed, the media-specific distinctions between cinematic, televisual and computer media have been eroded beyond recognition..."
> ANNE FRIEDBERG[1]

COMPETITION

At first sight movies and games seem primarily to compete head to head with each other, for attention and money, users and talent. The older media industries of cinema and television are under pressure to defend their once dominant position. While they are stagnating or even losing in audience, on- and offline games are experiencing extraordinary growth. The share of games in the average media budget of most developed countries has been rising steadily over the last decade while, relatively speaking, the expenditures for movie theater attendance keep falling, at least relatively.[2] The growing popularity of digital games is detrimental to the primacy of linear audiovisuality: US gamers who spent more time playing in 2013 than in the previous three years, cut back on watching movies at home (47% of those questioned), going to the movies (40%) and watching TV (39%).[3] As a consequence, any number of AAA games often achieve higher box-

---

1 Friedberg, Anne: *The Virtual Window: From Alberti to Microsoft*, Cambridge, Mass.: MIT Press 2006, p. 3.
2 According to Electronic Arts, in Germany the percentage of the media budget spent on games rose between 1999 and 2008 from 9 to 16 percent. In contrast, the expenditures on cinema visits fell from 9 to 8 percent. (Electronic Arts, "Unternehmenspräsentation 12.9," http://www.presse.electronic-arts.de/publish/page204218419835234.phhp3?1=1&aid=41&spieleid=)
3 See ESA: "Essential Facts about the Computer and Video Game Industry 2015."

office results than blockbuster movies. For example, CALL OF DUTY: MODERN WARFARE 2 (2009) grossed 401 million dollars on its first day, thereby—according to the *Guinness World Book of Records*—out-earning every other mass-entertainment product that preceded it.[4] That was exceptional, but not unique. A year later CALL OF DUTY: BLACK OPS grossed 360 million dollars on its first day.[5] Movie box office results pale in comparison, the best first day ever being HARRY POTTER AND THE DEATHLY HALLOWS PART 2 (2010) with almost 92 million dollars, followed by MARVEL'S THE AVENGERS (2012) with 84 million and JURASSIC WORLD (2015) with 82 million.[6] In 2014, the global box office revenue was 38.2 billion dollars, the global video revenue 32.3 billion.[7] In comparison to the combined revenue of 70.5 billion dollars for linear audiovisual entertainment,[8] the revenue from games was 83.4 billion dollars.[9]

The rise of nonlinear mediality and the concurrent marginalization of linear media are reflected in social and cultural change as well. Demographics couldn't

---

4   N. N.: "Modern Warfare 2 Biggest Entertainment Launch Ever," *Guiness World Records* 2010; as of August 10, 2011; not online anymore: http://community.guinness worldrecords.com/_Call-of-Duty-Modern-Warfare-2-Most-Successful-Entertainment-Launch-of-All-Time/BLOG/2308082/7691.html

5   Hayden, Erik. "'Call of Duty' Tears Down Records on Opening Day," in: *The Atlantic Wire*, November 11, 2010; http://www.theatlanticwire.com/entertainment/2010/11/cal l-of-duty-tears-down-records-on-opening-day/22309/

6   As of August 2015: Mojo, Box Office, "Top Single Day Grosses," http://boxoffice mojo.com/alltime/days/?page=open&p=.htm

7   N. N.: "MarketLine Industry Profile: Global Movies & Entertainment," April 2015, p. 9, www.marketline.com. "The movie box office segment is valued as the revenues received by box offices from total annual admissions. The home video segment covers sales of Blu-Ray, DVDs and VHS at end-user (retail) prices including paid downloadable videos."—See Motion Picture Association of America: "Theatrical Market Statistics 2014"; http://www.mpaa.org/wp-content/uploads/2015/03/MPAA-Theatric al-Market-Statistics-2014.pdf. According to this source, global box office revenues were only 36.4 billion dollars. (Ibid., p. 2)

8   Not counting revenues from television and streaming services.

9   N. N.: "Top 100 Countries by Game Revenues."—"Total revenues are based on consumer revenues generated by companies in the global games industry and excludes hardware sales, tax, business-to-business services and online gambling and betting revenues." (Ibid.)—See N. N.: "Global Revenues of the Video Game Industry from 2003 to 2014". According to this source, global game revenue was as high as 86 billion dollars in 2014.

indicate this change more clearly: Film and television audiences are growing older than the average population whereas gamers, once primarily male teenagers, have now expanded into the center of the population. For example, in the US, where more adults are playing games than kids and teens, the average game player is now 35 years old.[10] Several surveys also show that in most developed countries, the percentage of male and female gamers is nearly equal to their proportion in the population.[11]

The growing competition for consumers' time and money correlates with that for creative talent. For every prominent member of the film community who starts to make games at least part time—directors like Steven Spielberg, Peter Jackson, or John Woo, producers like Jerry Bruckheimer, authors such as Jordan Mechner—, there are hundreds of hopeful, young artists (many of them film school graduates) who are enticed by the high-paying game industry and might, therefore, be lost to the film industry for good. "Now, instead of looking to Hollywood and dreaming of writing the next blockbuster," Tracy Fullerton states, "many creative people are turning to games as a new form of expression."[12] At the same time successful game designers have also been pursuing film, for example Chris Roberts (WING COMMANDER, games since 1990, films since 1999) or Hironobu Sakaguchi (FINAL FANTASY, games since 1987, film 2001). This exchange of talent in both directions clearly suggests that movies and games are not just competing but also influencing each other artistically.

COLLABORATION

The most obvious area of collaboration is the adaptation of content. Since the 1980s, an increasing number of movies have been turned into games and, similarly, more and more games have been turned into movies. There are game franchises like SUPER MARIO BROS (games since 1985, movie 1993) and FINAL FANTASY (games since 1987, movie 2001) to TOMB RAIDER (games since 1996, movies since 2001) and RESIDENT EVIL (games since 1996, movies since 2002) to

---

10 ESA, Entertainment Software Association: "Essential Facts about the Computer and Video Game Industry," August 10, 2011; http://www.theesa.com/facts/pdfs/ESA_EF_2011.pdf

11 For the US see ibid. For Germany see BIU, Bundesverband Interaktive Unterhaltungssoftware: "Games Report 2011"; http://www.biu-online.de/fileadmin/user_upload/pdf/games_report_2011.pdf

12 Fullerton: *Game Design Workshop*, loc. 550.

MAX PAYNE (games since 2001, movie 2008). And there are literature and movie franchises like JAMES BOND (novels since 1953, movies since 1962, games since 1983) and LORD OF THE RINGS (novels since 1954, movies since 1978, games since 1982) to STAR WARS (novels since 1976, movies since 1977, games since 1978/79) to HARRY POTTER (novels since 1997, movies and games since 2001) and THE MATRIX (movies since 1999, games since 2003).

However, intermedial adaptation has so far resulted in mostly mediocre movies and games. The difficulties in converting content—stories and characters—from one medium into the other indicate the fundamental aesthetic differences between linear and nonlinear forms of audiovisual expression. Through many difficulties and some failures, the film and game industries have gradually been learning to optimize the important economic exploitation of so-called properties in several media, i.e., the practice of remedialization and adaptation. For example, the traditional separation and sequence of original production and adaptation has been increasingly replaced by parallel development, i.e., the exchange of assets as well as close collaboration between filmmakers and game designers.

Of greater importance and lasting significance—at least from an artistic and academic perspective—is the extensive adaptation of aesthetics between movies and games. Visually both are becoming more and more similar. Advanced nonlinear audiovisions strive for the impression of photorealism,[13] for example BIOSHOCK (2007), ASSASSIN'S CREED (2008), GTA4 (2008), HEAVY RAIN (2010), ALAN WAKE (2010), CRYSIS 2 (2011), UNCHARTED 3: DRAKE'S DECEPTION (2011), CRYSIS 3 (2013) or BEYOND: TWO SOULS (2013). Conversely, since the turn of the century, popular movies are experimenting with hyperrealism, an alienating mixture of photography and graphics following the model of the computer-generated imagery of digital games. Notable examples of this are films like Richard Linklater's WAKING LIFE (2001), Robert Zemeckis' THE POLAR EXPRESS (2004), Robert Rodriguez and Frank Miller's SIN CITY (2005), Linklater's A SCANNER DARKLY (2006), Christian Volckman's RENAISSANCE (2006), Tatsuo Yoshida's SPEED RACER (2008), Zemeckis' BEOWULF (2008)—"looks like a 120-minute video game cut scene"[14]—and, of course, James Cameron's AVATAR (2009).

Clearly the aesthetic influence on film exerted by computer-generated imagery—popularized by hyperrealistic games—undermines the cultural dominance of photorealism. This process of aesthetic evolution calls to mind the proliferation

---

13 Compare above chapter I, part *4 Hyperepic Turn (since the 1970s)*, p. 69ff.
14 Kohler, Chris: "What Beowulf Means For The Convergence Of Movies And Games," *Wired*, November 19, 2007; http://www.wired.com/gamelife/2007/11/what-beowulf-me/

of photorealism itself. One-and-a-half centuries ago, when camera images—semi-automated imprints of reality, no longer produced by the human hand as paintings had been—began to invade everyday life, painting initially reacted to this aesthetic competition with a combination of mimicry and a stressing of its own strengths. A comparable combination of, on one hand, adaptation to digital hyperrealism with, on the other hand, attempts to aesthetically outperform early CGI imagery, resulted in the post-photorealism of movies like A SCANNER DARKLY (2006), which was produced through the synthesis of live-action sequences with computer-assisted interpolated rotoscoping, or BEOWULF (2007), which was animated through the digital 3D-capture of movement.

This mutual aesthetic influence, however, is not limited to the visual alone. Both movies and games have also been adopting key elements of mise-en-scène, choreography, and storytelling from each other. Since their audiovisual beginnings in the early 1980s, digital games have oriented themselves to the narrative conventions of film, the complexity of which they have always struggled to match, albeit with increasing success. Today the "cinematographicity" of games is evident on many levels: for example, in the use of edited cut scenes and split screens or in the appropriation of "classical" camera angles and well-established techniques of flashback and flash forward that transport the eye through space and time. Furthermore, basic structures of cinematic storytelling, such as the hero's journey and genre conventions, have been absorbed by digital games. At the same time, the technological-aesthetic influence of television on games can be seen in the recording practices that allow for instant replay of key scenes, commonly used in sports broadcasting.[15]

But the influence—the adaptation of aesthetics—does not merely run in one direction, from old to new media. Despite all of their aesthetic shortcomings, digital games, along with their cultural influence and their nonlinear storytelling, proved powerful enough to significantly affect the older, more established art of the motion picture. As demonstrated by Tony Scott's ENEMY OF THE STATE (1998), Andy and Lana Wachowski's MATRIX (1999), and Steven Spielberg's MINORITY REPORT (2002), films have employed radically simulative first person views or "god perspectives" that deconstruct cinematic space in a manner reminiscent of games. Writing on THE MATRIX (1999), Bo Kampmann Walther

---

15 The first digital game with "action viewed from TV-inspired angles" was WORLD SERIES BASEBALL (1983), published by Intellivision: "The following year Cinemaware took the union of TV coverage with sports games to its logical conclusion with TV SPORTS FOOTBALL, a title that offered all the razzmatazz associated with broadcasts of American football matches." (Donovan: *Replay*, loc. 5051 and loc. 5120)

claimed, "the spatial gestalt of a potential game is reconfigured into a cinematographic level design."[16]

A similar process of adoption and adaptation can be witnessed in storytelling, particularly in the 'counterintuitive' quest for cinematic nonlinearity. In the last quarter century nonlinear-oriented experiments established themselves in successful entertainment movies such as Harold Ramis' GROUNDHOG DAY (1993), Quentin Tarrantino's PULP FICTION (1994), Peter Howitt's SLIDING DOORS (1998), Tom Tykwer's LOLA RENNT (1998), David Cronenberg's EXISTENZ (1999), Christopher Nolan's MEMENTO (2000), Mike Figgis' TIMECODE (2000), David Lynch's MULHOLLAND DR. (2001), Gaspar Noé's IRRÉVERSIBLE (2002), Alejandro González Iñárritus' BABEL (2006), Nolan's INCEPTION (2010) and Doug Liman's EDGE OF TOMORROW (2014). In the meantime experiments with parallelism and asynchronicities—as simulations of nonlinearity in a linear medium—have also reached television; from 24 and LOST to individual episodes of more traditionally told series such as HOW I MET YOUR MOTHER.[17]

On the one hand, these attempts to hyperrealistically deconstruct Hollywood's well-established three-act-structure of chronological and naturalistic storytelling have a long prehistory in cinema itself. Many avant-garde filmmakers—Luis Buñuel, Akira Kurosawa, Jean-Luc Godard, to name just three—have experimented with non-chronological narrative time and non-naturalistic story spaces, as well as with repetitive and permutational plotlines. On the other hand, the cinematic experiments of the last two decades differ radically from these modernist classics, in their aesthetics as well as in their popular orientation. Their mainstream success is, if nothing else, very suggestive of "gamish-ness." Specifically the intensive play with asynchronicities and loops, real-time and repeat-time, seems to be deeply inspired by games.

CONVERGENCE

This growing economic and aesthetic interdependence of movies and games has encouraged theories of media convergence. John Gaeta, special supervisor of the MATRIX, has predicted the development of a kind of "movie that preserves the singular vision of the creator that also allows the viewer-player to observe it, to play it and to go into hybrid explanatory mode. You can't call it filmmaking, you

---

16 Walther, Bo Kampmann: "Cinematography and Ludology: In Search of a Lucidography," 2004; http://www.brown.edu/Research/dichtung-digital/2004/1/Walther/index.htm

17 For example HOW I MET YOUR MOTHER (2009, S04E13: *Three Days of Snow*).

can't call it games."[18] Reflections of director Guillermo del Toro (PAN'S LABYRINTH, 2004; HELLBOY, 2008) point in the same direction: "I believe, that the future of storytelling is on an interactive level and that it will more or less arise out of a marriage of films, videogames and television. All platforms will mix with each other [...]"[19] And Chris Kohler, after watching BEOWULF (2007), resigned to the fact: "Game industry watchers who have long predicted that the revolution in video games would be about games evolving and becoming movies, as it turns out, had it all backwards. It'll be because movies are becoming video games."[20]

Indeed, there are strong signs of convergence of linear and nonlinear audio-visuality, at least in production, distribution, and reception. George Lucas, for example, re-organized his media empire in 2006 to encourage collaboration between Industrial Light & Magic's film making and LucasArt's game design. Both branches, initially separated organizationally as well as geographically, moved into the same premises and began work on the same internal software platform called Zeno. The movie branch was to profit from real-time (pre-) visualization techniques that the game designers were employing, while the designers could make instant use of high definition movie assets when building game environments.[21] A year later game producer Guillaume de Fondaumiere of Quantic Dreams (FAHRENHEIT, 2005; HEAVY RAIN, 2010, BEYOND: TWO SOULS, 2013) proposed a similar cooperation at the Berlin International Film Festival between European filmmakers and game designers—the exchange of content and actors, technical and artistic talent and, most important, knowhow: "There is a number of technologies that we're using in the games industry that when I show [them] to film people [they say]: Well, I want this, I want this."[22]

Wherever such collaboration is already taking place, not only the multimedia exploitation of content is optimized. Rather, the basic practices of production in both the film and game industries are changing, therefore allowing for conver-

---

18 Crabtree, Sheigh: "Video Games Grow Up," *The Hollywood Reporter,* April 7, 2006; http://www.allbusiness.com/services/motion-pictures/4899000-1.html
19 Brown, Scott: "Q&A: Hobbit Director Guillermo del Toro on the Future of Film," *Wired Magazine,* June 2009; http://www.wired.com/entertainment/hollywood/magazine/17-06/mf_deltoro?currentPage=all
20 Kohler: "What Beowulf Means For The Convergence Of Movies And Games."
21 See Sullivan, Steve/Williams, Chris: "The New Force at Lucasfilm," *BusinessWeek,* March 27, 2006, http://www.businessweek.com/print/innovate/content/mar2006/id20060327_719255.htm
22 Fondaumière, Guillaume de: "Berlinale Keynotes: Rethinking Content," March 1, 2007; http://www.youtube.com/watch?v=zEQrQb7cSrc&hd=1

gence. The digital movie, Lev Manovich wrote in 2001, could "serve as an interface, to play out events in 3D."[23] In recent years, top tier filmmakers have moved from the mental and literary construction of separated aspects of reality—from the mental conception and written description of scenes and specific actions that are eventually to be recorded in built sets or found locations—to the virtual construction of complete audiovisual worlds, in which actions and camera movements can be played through arbitrarily. Thereby digital movie productions such as Zack Snyder's WATCHMEN (2009) or James Cameron's AVATAR (2009) are following the world-building example of games.

"Constructing worlds is the main idea," said WATCHMEN production designer Alex McDowell. "By creating a 3-D virtual production space, you can work with your fellow filmmakers in a very descriptive, data-rich, virtual representation of the film before you even start making it."[24] And James Cameron commented on his—almost 300 million dollar—production that, instead of having sets, a "movie-scape" was created, a virtual movie landscape in which the participants and cameras could be moved about freely: "It's like a big, powerful game engine. If I want to fly through space, or change my perspective, I can. I can turn the whole scene into a living miniature."[25]

As production methods in filmmaking and game design converge—using more or less the same tools and the same pool of technical talent—, something similar has been happening on the side of reception. Since the turn of the century, the line between the consumption of linear and nonlinear audiovisual content in everyday life has blurred, especially for adolescents. Not in the least because both forms of entertainment can be played on the same desktop or laptop computer, the same console and TV set, the same handheld, tablet or smartphone, and. Therefore, rapid switching comparable to channel surfing is made possible. The innovation of commercial offerings that exploit these new habits seems to be inevitable. John Koller, head of Sony's marketing division for the PlayStation 3, said in 2009, "[t]he way that we see the future is that the movie and the game are placed on the same disc."[26]

---

23 Manovich: *The Language of New Media*, pp. 326-327.
24 Hart, Hugh: "Virtual Sets Move Hollywood Closer to Holodeck," *Wired*, March 27, 2009; http://www.wired.com/underwire/2009/03/filmmakers-use/
25 Chatfield: *Fun Inc.*, loc. 623-625.
26 See Ault, Susanne: "Blu-ray/videogame discs to be released for PS3," *Video Business*, March 3, 2009; http://www.videobusiness.com/article/CA6636623.html?desc=topstory.—An early example of such integration featured John Woo's adapted Playstation 3 game *Stranglehold* (2007) along with the 1992 movie of the same title.

The technical combination of film and game in one storage medium opens up new aesthetic potential as well: smooth and continuous transitions between the action of a film and the interactions of a game. A few aesthetic attempts anticipating such transitions have already been made. In some episodes of STAR WARS, for example, sequences were clearly designed as starting points for game productions. The interactive DVD TOMB RAIDER: THE ACTION ADVENTURE, took this concept a step further by basing itself on THE ANGEL OF DARKNESS (2006), the sixth installment of the TOMB RAIDER game series. The interactive DVD not only included a variety of cinematographic effects, like split screens and choices of perspectives and camera angles, but also the option to switch to automated play, thereby converting the interactive game experience into a passive film experience.[27]

These different trends towards convergence—in production, distribution, and reception—are also complemented by economic convergence. More and more, the same media conglomerates tend to finance, produce, and distribute linear and nonlinear audiovisual entertainment. Recent developments clearly indicate that movies and games will probably cooperate organizationally, technically, and artistically even more in the near future.

However, many artists and academics have objected to ideas of total convergence, as well as aesthetic fusion. Director Paul W. S. Anderson noticed: "I love movies and I love video games, but I don't think there is some kind of a hybrid art form between the two [...] the process of playing and interacting with a game make it necessarily different from the movies. I wouldn't know why you would want to combine the two."[28] And media theorist Bo Kamp Walther stated that movies and games are aesthetically incompatible: "The film [...] is a realized action (or string of actions); whereas gaming means to 'frame' actions. [...] The film may thematize the potential of interactivity [...], but it can never materialize this potential."[29]

So far, the relationship between movies and games seems contradictory when one considers the following trends: firstly, economic competition and poaching of talent; secondly, artistic collaboration and strong aesthetic influence; thirdly, technological and economic convergence in production, distribution, and reception. However, the question of where the limits of this rapprochement might be,

---

27 See Höltgen, Stefan: "Phallische Heldin in Paris. Das sieht nach seltsamen Experimenten aus 'Tomb Raider' als Hybrid zwischen Spiel und Film," *Telepolis*, December 2, 2006; http://www.heise.de/tp/r4/artikel/24/24090/1.html
28 Crecente: "Convergence, Smergence..."
29 Walther: "Cinematography and Ludology."

are still open: Will digital film be able to maintain its aesthetic autonomy in the face of its escalating proximity to games? And vice versa: Will games be able to maintain their aesthetic autonomy in the face of their escalating proximity to film?

2 Audiovisual Rivalries

A short historical investigation might help to better understand the give-and-take relationship of film and game, as there have been two earlier and comparable instances of such audiovisual rivalry between defining media: the tense relationship between theater and cinema at the beginning of the 20th century and the tense relationship between cinema and television fifty years later.

MEDIA HISTORY

After 1900, when cinema started its triumphal ascent, it came into direct competition with the theater, "the world's wide stage", i.e., the stage that signifies the world.[1] However, the dominant audiovisual medium of the preindustrial age was ill-equipped to counter the assault, as its new opponent was a genuine industrial medium which produced a visual narrative that progressed at twenty-four frames per second in a temporal and spatial segmentation, following the logic of industrial work and technically anticipating the rhythm of the assembly line. In comparison to the silver screen, the theater stage suddenly seemed outdated, theatric. Soon the powerful new medium dominated economically. As the majority of theaters that existed in the years before film went out of business within two decades, the film industry poached massive amounts of stage talent—from D. W. Griffith to Ernst Lubitsch.

At the same time both audiovisual art forms began to collaborate and influence each other. Many artists—authors and actors, directors and set designers,

---

1 Schiller, Friedrich: "To My Friends" (1802): "Yet we see the great of every age / Pass before us on the world's wide stage". See online http://www.readbookonline.net/readOnLine/20462/

make-up artists, lighting technicians, and musicians—switched back and forth between theater and film. Searching for content but also striving for reputation, the film industry initially took to recording stage performances and then to adapting dramas and other forms of theater. Likewise, dramatic stage action in the age of the screen became increasingly "cinematic"—from the famous Berlin productions of Max Reinhardt and Erwin Piscator to the plays of Bertolt Brecht and Arthur Miller. The longtime-genre of the theater-film, however, stayed a niche-product and never gained any lasting influence. Additionally, no institutionalized collaboration between theater and film ever materialized.

That might not come as a surprise as over the decades this distant relationship has been the de facto norm. However, it still needs a theoretical explanation, not least for the reason that the audiovisual rivalry that came next in media history, the competition between cinema and television, was to turn out quite differently.

During the 1950s, cutthroat competition once again characterized the relationship between an old and a new audiovisual medium. But now cinema was at the receiving end and found it hard to keep up with its new competitor. The rapid implementation of the so-called 'tube' or home cinema followed a long-term trend in modernity towards home entertainment, i.e., the private use of or access to works of art and entertainment as well as means of communication. In a short time, television became the new rich kid on the block, the defining medium of the age, and started to poach cinema's audience. In the US, for example, average weekly cinema attendance fell from around 50% of the population in the mid-1940s to around 10% in the mid-1960s.[2] In Germany almost half of all movie theaters had to close within the first two decades after TV was introduced.[3] Attendance fell from 800 million moviegoers per year in the mid-1950s to 140 million in the mid-1970s.[4]

Consequently, talent migrated from film to television and again collaboration followed suit. Adaptation of content in both directions became rampant, accompanied by the adaptation of aesthetics. Hampered by contemporary small

---

2   See Pautz, Michelle: "The Decline in Average Weekly Cinema Attendance: 1930-2000," *Issues in Political Economy*, 2002, Vol. 11, appendix; http://org.elon.edu/ipe/pautz2.pdf

3   Deutsches Filminstitut: "50 Jahre Kino in Deutschland," 2000; http://www.deutsches-filminstitut.de/hdf/cont_k_12.html. In the Federal Republic of Germany, there were 7085 movie theaters in 1959, ten years later just 3739.

4   Spitzenorganisation der Filmwirtschaft: "Filmbesuch 1925-2009," 2010; http://www.spio.de/index.asp?SeitID=381

screens, TV-series, for example, resorted to cutting back and forth between close-ups. Soon enough, film adopted these and other elements of TV aesthetics. "There's so much cutting and so many close-ups being shot today I think directly as an influence from television," Steven Spielberg complained in 1990: "That has carried over indelibly into motion pictures of the late twentieth century."[5] And in 2001, Wim Wenders lamented that "television has eliminated the long-shot, which so beautifully conforms to the human eye, and replaced it with the tedium of close-ups."[6] On the other hand, television strived for cinematic qualities. As most Hollywood studios withheld new product from their TV competitors, the networks resorted to licensing old feature films, thereby turning TV into the first movie museum: Tens of thousands of movies from the first half of the century of cinema, which after a few weeks of run-time had been stowed away in archives, were given a new mass-audience again (and again). In the early 1960s, at the height of the rerun era, when black-and-white movies were a perfect match for black-and-white television, Marshall McLuhan wrote, "that the 'content' of any medium is always another medium."[7]

At the same time, television started to finance and produce new feature films and made-for-TV movies. Competition slowly gave way to institutionalized cooperation. The American model of commercial television led to a partial vertical integration of movie studios and TV networks within the same national and multinational media companies. The Western European model of public service television brought forth public partnerships forced and controlled by regulators. New German Cinema, for example, was mainly financed by public television already in the late 1960s. Since then hardly any German films have been made without co-funding—directly or through film boards—by public and private TV stations. In the process, even a new aesthetic form emerged: the so-called amphibious movie, partly cinema, partly television. Its first specimen was Wolfgang Petersen's DAS BOOT (THE BOAT, 1981), edited in radically different versions for theatrical release and broadcasting.[8]

Clearly, the audiovisual rivalry between cinema and television came to quite a different solution than the older rivalry of theater and cinema. While Broadway

---

5 Ebert, Roger/Siskel, Gene/Scorsese, Martin/Spielberg, Steven/Lucas, George: *The Future of the Movies*, Kansas City Mo.: Andrews and McMeel 1991, p. 73.
6 Cited after Ostrowska, Dorota/Roberts, Graham: *European Cinemas in the Television Age*: Edinburgh University Press 2007, p. 75.
7 McLuhan: *Understanding Media*, p. 10.
8 Freyermuth, Gundolf S.: "Das Boot. Ein Meilenstein der Film- und Fernsehgeschichte," *Schnitt. Das Filmmagazin*, July 2011; http://www.schnitt.de/211,0063,01

theaters never bought a Hollywood studio and Hollywood never really tried to buy into Broadway, cinema and television were able to develop economic and practical partnerships that led, more or less voluntarily, beyond competition and sporadic collaboration to their organized cooperation and partial economic and institutional integration.

The still open question, of course, is how to explain these very different outcomes and what they might tell us about the future of film and games, i.e., linear and not-so-linear audiovisuality. Will their relationship follow either one of these two historical models?

MEDIA THEORY

An answer to this question might be found with recourse to the systematic-historical model of medialities originally introduced by Harry Pross. In its context the rivalries between theater and cinema and between cinema and television present themselves quite differently. Since its conception and construction as a media system in the sixteenth century, the theater, with its perspectival picture-frame stage, has employed mechanical, as well as industrial, technology for its production of imagery and perspectives. In contrast to earlier audiovisual spectacles like most religious rites, street theater, or carnival, which do not use special media technology, modern theater is a secondary medium. Cinema, however, required advanced industrial technology not only for the production but also for the storage, editing, distribution, and reception of its audiovisual works. As a tertiary medium, film was technologically incompatible with the older medium, theater. Both media operate on different levels of development; they are, so to speak, separated generationally. Cinema could not even become a museum for the theater though it tried early on to appropriate the content of the stage. But when filmed, that is, when transferred from secondary (live) to tertiary (stored) audiovisuality, theater plays lose their media-specific qualities, i.e., their main attraction.

By comparison, television was very similar to cinema as both belonged to the same third generation of media technology. During the second half of the 20th century they distinguished themselves primarily through details of their techno-logical-social organization: their analog storage media (celluloid vs. magnetic tape), their distribution channels (physical lending vs. airing), the social control over production and distribution (un- or self-regulated movie studios vs. state-licensed commercial or public networks), the social control over the apparatus necessary for consumption (service by projectionist vs. self-service by home viewer). Accordingly, television stations did not have to re-shoot or adapt movies; they could reuse—air—them without any essential change.

Of course, in the early days of television it made quite a difference whether one watched a film on the "silver screen" or on a TV monitor. But this loss in quality lamented by early TV audiences was only caused by nascent technological development—the relatively small size of TV screens, their low definition, the lack of color, the different aspect ratios, the bad sound quality. At least from today's perspective these differences were incidental, not essential. The only difference that could not be done away with, at least under the constraints of analog technology, came with the change of venue, from semi-public cinema to private living room: Watching a movie on TV was no longer an anonymous-communal experience.

In conclusion, the different outcome of both audiovisual rivalries can be sufficiently explained by Harry Pross' taxonomy: The technological gap between secondary and tertiary audiovisuality is responsible for the distance that theater and cinema have maintained while the technological similarity between two variants of tertiary audiovisuality allowed for the relatively close collaboration and partial integration that cinema and television eventually developed.

But do these two historic models also shed light on the present and future relationship of film and games? Simply asked: In terms of media technology, are the two defining audiovisual media of our time, film and games, incompatible like theater and cinema, or are they compatible like cinema and television?

At first glance the theater-cinema model seems to apply as digital games are not just using technology in production and reception—like film and television—, but also require permanent communication between both poles: the so-called feedback channel. It removes the categorical separation between production and reception and enables interactive play. Thus digital games are of quaternary mediality and seem as incompatible with a tertiary medium like film, as film once was with a secondary medium like theater.

At second glance, however, this analysis proves to be shortsighted, as it does not take into account the fact that film transforms from a tertiary into a quaternary medium upon entering the digital realm. Parallel to the rise of digital games, which were always created as software, film developed from a hardware medium into a software medium. In fact, it was the film industry with its financial power that expedited the digitalization of audiovisual production in the 1980s and early 1990s, at a time when narrative games were still text-based or relied on simple non-photorealistic graphics. However, from the moment software replaced celluloid, cinematic narration—digital linear audiovisuality—could utilize the capabilities and qualities of quaternary mediality. If created as software, whether through digital recording, computer animation, or scanning during postproduction, films stay open for arbitrary interactive manipulation by their producers and, in principle, also their viewers, or perhaps, users.[9] As linear audiovisual narratives, digital films put the same digital technology to use in a different way than nonlinear audiovisual narratives.

Digital film and digital games are of the same quaternary generation of audiovisuality, just as analog cinema and analog television once belonged to the same tertiary generation. Consequently, there seems to be a trend in the production and distribution of both forms of media, from competition and occasional collaboration to a further reaching medial integration. Around the middle of the past century, television appropriated not only film, but almost all existing media: literature, painting, music, and particularly radio with its various forms of content including radio features, game shows, news, and live transmissions directly from theaters, sport stadiums, and political events. In the context of the emerging digital media dispositif, nonlinear audiovisuality could have a similar integrative function, as Jesse Schell writes:

"As technology advances, more and more aspects of human life and expression will be integrated into games. There is nothing that cannot be part of a game. You can put a painting, a radio broadcast, or a movie into a game, but you cannot put a game into these other things. ... At their technological limit, games will subsume all other media."[10]

Whether we want to believe in Schell's vision or not, there seems indeed to be little doubt that the future of making and consuming movies and games will be more integrated—organizationally, technically, and also artistically. The obvious potential for convergence notwithstanding, there is still one unresolved question, perhaps the most important question thus far: Will games, as John Gaeta and Guillermo del Toro have envisioned, become films and films games? Will there be aesthetic convergence as well?

---

9   Fan cuts demonstrate the possibility of a participatory use of movies; compare: Rojas, Peter: "Hollywood: the People's Cut. The Fans are Now Editing Hollywood Blockbusters," *The Guardian*, July 24, 2002; http://www.theguardian.com/film/2002/jul/25/internet.technology
10 Schell: *The Art of Game Design*, loc. 1326-29.

3 Modes of Audiovisual Storytelling

Since the digitalization of games and their transition into a medium of narrative, the discussion over the compatibility of playing and storytelling has not ceased. At first this discussion was confined to the field of game design; since the late nineties it has spread to Game Studies.[1] Content-wise, the discussion has centered on the relationship between games and literature—especially the novel—since the seventies and early eighties and on games and film since the mid-eighties. As the same questions have repeated throughout this discourse, it is clear that none of the hitherto given answers have been satisfactory. A possible reason for this insufficiency could be the constant focus on defining the relationship between play and storytelling from a systematic perspective.[2]

Therefore, this chapter will examine the specific aesthetic effects of three audiovisual media—theater, film, game—and their central modes of representation and storytelling from a historical perspective. I will sketch the development of audiovisual storytelling in (Western) modernity, which constitutes the prehistory and genesis of narrative digital games. Finally, I will suggest the emergence of a new audiovisual narrative form that is a combination of gameplay and storytelling, and serves as a compliment to film through its shared aesthetic qualities.

STORYTELLING IN SPACE AND TIME

All forms of audiovisual storytelling differ from literature in a similar way: while literature conveys whatever can be written, analog audiovisions—on the stage or in the cinema—can only represent that which can be staged. Audiovisual storytelling, therefore, must always cope with the constraints of space and

---

1 For the ludology-narratology debate, see below p. 203ff.
2 See chapter I, part *1 What is a Game? Systematic vs. Historic Approaches*, p. 31ff.

time. The aesthetic effect of the audiovisual narrative as well as the aesthetic experience of the viewer/user is largely shaped by these constraints. Thus, every audiovisual medium—in contrast to literature—is innately limited by its foundational technology, which defines and restricts its artistic potential to construct and manipulate of space and time.

If a certain incompatibility exists among storytelling methods across various analog media, whether game, novel, or film, then it seems that, with new methods of digital image and sound production, a new medium is emerging which overcomes significant restrictions underlying mechanical and industrial technologies used in audiovisual media, and also, thereby, opens up nonlinear storytelling.

Storytelling in this new audiovisual medium must fulfill those fundamental needs in human culture that storytelling in theater, film, and television has done for millennia, as Janet H. Murray writes: "Games, like stories, are ancient forms of human communication, connected to the earliest human experiences of culture-making and part of our basic cognitive apparatus for making sense of the world."[3] That which is conveyed narratively we grasp and memorize more quickly and easily. Storytelling thereby serves the management and transfer of knowledge, norms, and values; how we behave and act. Narrative helps us understand the world by endowing it with rational and emotional meaning. Thereby it appears to follow certain fundamental patterns, at least in Western culture: the custom of beginning, middle, and end—though not necessarily in that order, as Jean-Luc Godard once remarked;[4] the stages of the hero's journey, which begins with a challenge, forces its hero to make a choice, and ends with a resolution to

---

3   Murray, Janet/Bogost, Ian/Mateas, Michael/Nitsche, Michael: "Asking What Is Possible: The Georgia Tech Approach To Game Research and Education." in: *International Digital Media Media and Arts Association Journal* 2, no. 1 (Spring 2005), pp. 59-68, here p. 64.

4   The origin of this remark is hard to determine. However, the quote is widely attributed to Godard. See for example: N. N., "Godard only knows... For decades he was regarded as a genius and a revolutionary, but Jean-Luc Godard—70 years old next week—has spent the last 20 years alienating everyone. Has he finally succeeded in biting off the hand that feeds him?," *The Observer*, November 25, 2000.—In his biography of Primo Levi, Berel Lang quotes the following dialogue: "Interlocutor: But surely, M. Godard, you would agree that every film should have a beginning, a middle and an end. / M. Godard: Yes, of course—but not necessarily in that order." (Lang, Berel. *Primo Levi : The matter of a Life*. New Haven: Yale University Press 2013, motto, before content page).

the conflict. This fulfills the central wish that stories have consequences, that the world will be different at the story's end than it was at its beginning.

PRE-INDUSTRIAL AUDIOVISIONS: THEATER

Before the rise of film, three genres of storytelling existed: the lyric, the epic, and the dramatic, that is: poetry, prose, and theater. As the only audiovisual medium of the pre-industrial age, the picture-frame stage was substantially impaired (especially in comparison to the novel) because its narratives were conveyed in real-time by actors who shared the same physical space as their audience. Stage actors play their parts sequentially, exercising their craft like trade workers, which bears witness to the fact that modern theater as a medium and its dominant narrative form, the drama, originate in mechanical culture. For those of that time, the unity and sequentiality of the action effectively expressed the pre-industrial way of life—that "all the world's a stage"[5]; its perception of space and time, its mentality, its understanding of what it meant to be human, its conception of the world.

The theater employs the curtain as its primary method for manipulating narrational space and time. Like the bridge in pre-industrial networking, it 'bridges' spatial and temporal gaps by covering them.[6] From the subsequent perspective of film, the curtain appears as a rudimentary narrative predecessor of cinematic editing. Advancements in theater technology during the mechanical age attempted to facilitate better and faster changes in space and time—specialized theater buildings with, among others, backdrops, lifting platforms, artificial light, curtains, etc.—but only managed to negotiate these obstacles with limited success.

Thus, the dramatic ideal became the famous (or infamous) unity of space, time, and action: a linear compression of space and time—in contradistinction to epic storytelling, which is characterized by its expansion through space and time, an expansion that is usually linear (but does not have to be). *Before the industrialization of media, audiovisual storytelling was technologically real, i.e., it de-*

---

5 "All the world's a stage, / And all the men and women merely players: / They have their exits and their entrances; / And one man in his time plays many parts ..." (Shakespeare, William: "As You Like It," in: Shakespeare, William (ed.), *First Folio*, 1623)

6 Compare to Freyermuth, Gundolf S.: "NetzWerke. Kommunikative Vernetzung als Basis audiovisuellen Erzählens," in: Wolf, Philipp (ed.), *Medieninnovationen: Internet, Serious Games, TV*, Leipzig: Leipziger Universitätsverlag 2013, pp. 105-150.

pended on the real-time manipulation of real space, and therefore its aesthetic orientation favored the dramatic.

INDUSTRIAL AUDIOVISIONS: FILM AND TELEVISION

Film's ability to record acts that occur in real space and time, and to reorder them *a posteriori* through editing, allows for audiovisual storytelling with greater control of time and space. Its actors do not have to play their roles either live or sequentially. On the contrary, cinematic narratives could be recorded in a multitude of individual scenes (following the model of Taylorism), edited together into a final cut, duplicated, and then distributed by physical transport. Like workers on an assembly line, actors in analog film production worked with machines in fragmented actions. This bears witness to the fact that cinema and its dominant narrative form, the feature film, originate in industrial culture. A medium of mass production and mass consumption, film epitomized industrial life; its perception of space and time, its understanding of what it meant to be human, its conception of the world.

Film so effectively captured industrial life by overcoming spatial and temporal gaps in its audiovisual narratives not by covering them up (e.g. the theater's curtain), but by eliminating them via editing. This facilitated an enhanced and more versatile manipulation of space and time, making it possible to cut back and forth between two or more places/times or to show parallel sequences across several locations, among other techniques. This new freedom allowed film from its inception to experiment with all three traditional modes of storytelling: the lyric, the epic, the dramatic. However, with the introduction of sound, cinematic storytelling concentrated on dramatic structures due not only to technical reasons but also methods of distribution and reception, which followed the classical 'performance' model of the theater.

In the last third of the 20th century—after the rise of television, video cassettes, DVDs, and digital streaming, i.e., increasing privatization in the usage and enjoyment of audiovisions—feature films and television series gradually developed epic storytelling structures in a way that remains infeasible to theater and film productions. The start of epic storytelling in audiovisual media can be seen in the so-called sequel mania that began in the 1980s and the truly epic TV series of the last decade. Today we have, for the first time in the history of culture and media, audiovisual epics whose episodes in their complex narrative structure have become the equivalent of chapters in novels, complete seasons being the equivalent of epics that span many volumes, like Balzac's *Human Comedy*, Proust's *In Search of Lost Time* or Tolkien's *Lord of the Rings*. With the industrialization of media—film and television—, audiovisual storytelling became technologically photorealistic, i.e., it became bound to a manipulation of light and sound stored on film, which takes place a posteriori in postproduction, and a priori, in regard to reception. Further technological advancements led to a privatization of reception, which enabled audiovisual storytelling to develop epic qualities and structures.

DIGITAL AUDIOVISIONS: GAMES

In parallel to this process of audiovisual 'epicization', a new form of audiovisual storytelling arose in the transmedium of software: digital games. On the one hand, they are capable of an even greater manipulation of space and time. On the other hand, their freedom to narrate is restricted by the participation of the players; an interactivity which has been enabled by advancements in media technology. Just as the theater's curtain prefigured cinematic editing, so did the industrial medium of film foreshadow this new action space. The celluloid-based technology of recording and storing audiovisual narratives created a space-time distance that did not exist in the theater: the spatial and temporal gap between the projected actions of moving images on the 'unreal' image space of the screen and the live audience sitting in the darkness of a 'real' movie theater. "Darkness is to space what silence is to sound, the 'interval'", Marshall McLuhan wrote.[7] This analog interval or mediated no-man's-land can be identified as an analog predecessor to the space-time continuum of software-based feedback that digitalization and, particularly, digital networking have opened up, thereby enabling interaction over space and time between games and their users.

For manipulation of their narrative space and time, games rely on software functions, as opposed to the older, hardware-based audiovisual media: theater, cinema, and television. Constituted by the transfer of analog qualities and functions into mathematical values, software can be manipulated arbitrarily. The interface of on- and offline games enables interactivity and constant feedback between audiovisual content and its users (and also between users of the same audiovisual content).

---

7 Quoted from Coupland, Douglas: *Marshall McLuhan: You Know Nothing of My Work!*, New York: Atlas (Kindle edition) 2010, loc. 2047.

Consequently, digital games possess, as is portrayed in chapter *I Games*, three qualities that distinguish them from analog media, and in particular analog games: 1) procedurality and the capability for systematic representation[8]; 2), arbitrary, real-time manipulation of narrative algorithms which empowers the user to interact in and with multi- or nonlinear/hyperepic narratives[9]; 3), real-time generation of near-photorealistic images and cinematically staged 3D storytelling spaces which compel the user to select their own procedural process (from among many), i.e., to 'enter' and navigate the 3D story space.[10] Thus, the audiovisions of games are not prerecorded and assembled in a Tayloristic manner. Of quaternary mediality, digital games enable players to interactively explore, experience, and co-create narrative worlds in a non-linear or multi-linear fashion. Gamers perform in the same fashion that contemporary knowledge workers do: They play out their roles in real-time, in relative independence, in virtual sequences, and in places they arbitrarily chose. This bears witness to the fact that nonlinear audiovisions originate in digital culture and are on the verge of becoming the defining audiovisual medium of the digital age. Digital games express our rapidly changing perceptions of space and time as well as what it means to be human under the conditions of the virtual, i.e., software-based production and communication.

The specific aesthetic consequences of digital game technology might become clearer in comparison to older technologies of space-time manipulation: Theater covers up space-time gaps within its narratives; the cinema eliminates space-time gaps in its narrations, while also causing a new space-time gap separating its prerecorded actions from its live audiences. *Games, however, use the virtual space opened up by their interactive software between the audiovisual content and its users (originally created for communication and virtual transport) as a virtual staging area.* The aesthetic effect is two-fold: a virtualization of space and time and a spatialization and temporalization of virtuality. It is in this new virtual space-time continuum that the unique aesthetic experiences of games emerge—through a fusion of the qualities of their malleable audiovisual worlds and their inherent narrative potential with the many individual choices, reactions, and interactions of its users.

Thus, modern times have been characterized by three variants of audiovisual storytelling:

---

8   See chapter I, part *3 Procedural Turn (since the 1950s)*, p. 53ff.
9   See chapter I, part *4 Hyperepic Turn (since the 1970s)*, p. 63ff.
10 See chapter I, part *5 Hyperrealistic Turn (since the 1990s)*, p. 75ff.

- In pre-industrial culture, the modern theater with its picture-frame stage arose and with it an audiovisual storytelling that was real and followed the ideal of the dramatic.
- In industrial culture, with film and television, new forms of stored audiovisions were created that were photorealistic and gradually moved from dramatic to epic structures.
- In digital culture, with digital games, a new procedurally-empowered variant of audiovisual storytelling is emerging, based on the combinatorics of databases and algorithms which enable systemic and hyperrealistic narrative techniques that produce multi-linear and nonlinear hyperepic stories, open to the user's playful interaction.

COMPLEMENTARITY

This historical comparison demonstrates that the audiovisual media of theater, cinema, and television, as well as the digital transmedium software, radically differ in their ability to manipulate space and time. Consequently, their main aesthetic forms—drama, feature film, interactive game—all offer radically different experiences with regard to narrative space and narrative time. Hypotheticals concerning aesthetic convergence, specifically between film and games, seem to neglect these unique qualities. Cinema is changing profoundly with its digitalization—not in the least under the aesthetic influence of games—and some of these changes seem to make films appear more "gamish." This kind of aesthetic approximation reminds us of the strong impact that cinema itself once had on older media, specifically on theater and literature. However, even the most "cinematic" theater productions of the 1920s or truly "cinematic" novels such as John Dos Passo's *Manhattan Transfer* (1925)[11], James M. Cain's *The Postman Always Rings Twice* (1934),[12] or Raymond Chandler's *The Big Sleep* (1939)[13] never worked as valid substitutes for the experience of watching a film itself; a one to one adaptation was impossible. The same holds true today for the relationship between film and games: Even the most "gamish" and hyperrealistic films cannot replace the experience of actual gameplay.

The fundamental differences between movies and games, particularly in the construction of their narratives, can hardly be resolved. Nonlinear audiovisions

---

11   Dos Passos, John: *Manhattan Transfer*, Boston: Houghton Mifflin Co. 2000 (*1925).
12   Cain, James M.: *The Postman Always Rings Twice*, New York: A. A. Knopf 1934.
13   Chandler, Raymond: *The Big Sleep*, New York: A. A. Knopf 1939.

are characterized by the fact that their storylines are not entirely prescribed but rather are realized only through the interactions of the user with the parameters of a fictional storytelling space. The ideal aesthetic experience emerges; it is not predefined. The possibility of individual experiences remains mostly open within such interactive-narrative structures. The mode of reception, which fixed audiovisual narratives require to achieve their aesthetic potential, is incompatible with rule-based user-actions in a fictional space. Despite all the visual as well as narratological propinquity between games and movies, the inherent tension between narration and interaction in nonlinear audiovisions prevents the same aesthetic convergence we see in the economic and technological spheres. Movies, when they simulate the narrational modes of games, and games, when they try to implement the narrational modes of movies, quickly come up against their limits. Jordan Mechner, who has written games as well as movies (PRINCE OF PERSIA: THE SANDS OF TIME, game 2003, film 2010), summarizes his experience:

"Whereas in a film it's better to show than to tell, in a video game it's better to do than to watch. Give the story's best moments to the player, and he'll never forget them. Put them in a cutscene, and he'll yawn .... Do It, Don't View It."[14]

This mutual tension notwithstanding, both modes of audiovisual expression and the experiences they can create certainly overlap: There are strong elements of convergence in production, distribution, and reception and there are aesthetic qualities that both media obviously share—stories and characters, elements of visual design, mise-en-scène, choreography. Such relationships—partially competing and conflicting, partially collaborative and supplemental—could constitute complementarity (as seen in the theory of sets or in quantum physics). This is characterized by the fact that, despite all overlapping and inner affinity, a total spatial and temporal concurrence of all their elements and properties is impossible. Where the magic circle of play exists completely, the film cannot. And vice versa. This can be illustrated by two Eulerian Circles or a Venn diagram showing the symmetric differences of two sets, one representing the medium of film, the other the medium of games. In such a diagram the overlapping middle section constitutes the common aesthetic and artistic ground of both audiovisual media, while the outer parts represent their unique and incompatible elements.

---

14 Mechner, Jordan: "The Sands of Time: Crafting a Video Game Story," *Electronic Book Review* 2008; http://www.electronicbookreview.com/thread/firstperson/pop-friendly

Summary: The Four Cs

The relationship between digital games and digital movies can, therefore, be summarized by the four Cs: *competition, collaboration, convergence, and complementarity*. Today, competition for audiences and talent, and collaboration through practices of adaptation are still prevalent. Both are slowly giving way to further technological and economic integration and even convergence in production, distribution, and reception. The aesthetic relationship, however, of linear movies and multi-linear games is characterized by complementarity. Both games and movies have unique means of artistic expression at their disposal and can render very different aesthetic experiences, so that one might not ever be able to replace the other. An aesthetic convergence of movies and games, therefore, does not seem very likely.

The driving force of this aesthetic complementarity, I propose, will propel the development of movies and games in the coming decades and, thereby, deeply shape the emerging digital media dispositif—at the very least by opening up a whole new field of intermedial influences and new modes of transmedia storytelling.

II Game Design

Introduction

The development of modern audiovisual media—from theater to film and television to games and transmedia—is characterized by constant differentiation and increasing complexity. The production of digital games stands in clear relation to, and is equally distant from older audiovisual media and arts. The skills, talents, and trades that brought the audiovisual medium of the theater to the forefront of pre-industrial culture—those, for instance, practiced by writers, directors, producers, actors, costume designers, and set designers—were also required by analog film production.

Work in film, the defining audiovisual medium of industrial culture, did not only require significant adaptation efforts of those trades belonging to the theater (a screenplay isn't a drama, movie actors must act for the camera, etc.), it also developed new trades specific to analog film—cinematographers, editors, as well as specialists for optical effects and later for sound recording and sound effects.[1]

By comparison, digital game production embodies a process of even greater differentiation and enhancement in its complexity. Game development requires all those skills and talents already employed in theater and film. It also requires continuous specialist adaptation of prior audiovisual media; for example, the virtualization of dramatic art, scenery construction, and cinematography, or the multi- and nonlinearity of dialogue and sound design.

Completely new challenges have materialized as well, from the development of game mechanics and multi-linear storytelling, to the design of interactively navigable storytelling environments, all the way to the programming of procedural processes. Thus digital game production has ushered in new trades and

---

1 New variants of linear audiovisuality that developed after analog film, particularly analog-electronic television and digital film, added new specializations; for example live-editing and data-wrangling.

specializations which were entirely unknown to film and television—including Game Design[2], Game Arts[3] and Gameplay Programming[4].

The collaborative processes of digital game production hinges upon the categorical difference between linear and nonlinear storytelling. Theater plays are written and performed according to the chronological order of their storylines, comparable to the process of holistic handcraft production. Films are also written, but are mostly shot without regard for the chronological order of their narratives and finally assembled like other industrial products. Digital games, however, do not rely on a screenplay or script; rather, they are created like all other software. This process is also conceived and recorded in writing. The game design document, however, does not include any fixed narratives. Instead it contains all of the physical, functional, and aesthetic details of its storytelling spaces as well as the rules and conditions for possible user interactions. In the development of digital games, the mental (sometimes written) descriptions of singular slices of reality and the specific actions that are supposed to take place therein (which are later staged and recorded) are replaced by the virtual design and procedural construction of complete, hyperrealistic audiovisual worlds. Within these virtual worlds, numerous storylines can be played through—both during the immersive design process itself as well as later by players of the finished product.[5]

With this switch from writing-based conception and linear modes of production to a production process centered on the cyclical iterations of prototypes, lasting consequences arise, particularly for the division of labor among those involved. A central and integrative role thereby falls to the game designer, whose

---

2   Game Designers are responsible for the ludic mechanics and non- or multi-linear stories of digital games; sub-specializations include Author/Content Developer, Concept Author, Level Designer, Stage Director, Game Director, Project Manager.

3   Game Artists support the complete production process of digital games from the creation of objects (Modeling, Texturing), to layout and animation, to the generation of moving image sequences (Rendering); sub-specializations include Concept Artist, Character/World Designer, 2D Animation Artist, 3D Designer, 3D Animation Artist, Level Artist, Storyboard Artist, Art Director.

4   Gameplay Programmers operate at the interface of Game Design, Game Arts, and Game Technology and are responsible for the procedural realization of Game Design and Game Arts; sub-specializations include Front-End Developer, Back-End Developer, User Interface Developer, Tools Developer.

5   For the principle of worldbuilding see below p. 169ff.—There are, of course, also many games whose non-linear narrations are based on linear narratives, specifically adaptations of literary works, movies, and TV series.

function is comparable to that of the director in older audiovisual media,[6] but differentiates itself significantly in regard to content, approaches, and cooperation with other contributors—particularly graphic designers, animators, and programmers. While game design is like directing, the "act of deciding what a game should be,"[7] digital games are not closed, audiovisual narratives. Rather they are "systems of interaction."[8] Game designers conceive of these systems and prefigure their use to an extent that varies from genre to genre. Therefore, game design does not aim to represent storylines in their temporal order but rather to facilitate procedures and assets that find their aesthetic realization only through the act of playing: "The game designer only indirectly designs the player's experience, by directly designing the rules."[9]

Overview

As an aesthetic practice, game design is based on the dual traditions of the analog design of material artifacts and the digital design of software. Procedures and principles of both areas shape the design and production of digital games. This chapter describes the dual prehistory of game design: first the evolution of the practices and theories of industrial design (*II-1 Analog Design*), followed by the digitalization of these design practices as well as of design thinking (*II-2 Digital Design*), and finally the history of game design as well as its most important areas and practices of production (*II-3 A Short History of Game Design, II-4 Areas of Game Design, II-5 Practices of Game Design*).

---

6 See Egenfeldt-Nielsen et al.: *Understanding Video Games*, loc. 687.
7 Schell: *The Art of Game Design*, loc. 265.
8 Salen/Zimmerman: *Rules of Play*, loc. 651.
9 Ibid., loc. 4940.

1 Analog Design

"Design is half of game design."
KATIE SALEN AND ERIC ZIMMERMAN[1]

The Latin verb *designare* means roughly to define and the Italian noun *disegno* means to draw.[2] In the 19th century, templates for cloth patterns were called dessins. In Germany, whoever created these patterns or templates for other products was called a *Mustermacher*—pattern maker—and later renamed, in the context of the Werkbund founded in the early 20th century, to *Formmeister* or *Gestalter*—translated as form master and one who makes a gestalt (form/shape), respectively. Their British and American colleagues described themselves as designers; a word, which the German language adopted after World War II.[3] At that point the idea of designing had long since outgrown the concept of creating patterns and other shapes/forms, encompassing the more general abilities of problem-solving and the production of meaning and significance.[4]

---

1   Salen/Zimmerman: *Rules of Play*, loc. 608.
2   See Berents, Catharina: *Kleine Geschichte des Design: Von Gottfried Semper bis Philippe Starck*, Munich: C.H. Beck 2011, p. 12f. "The 'clear creation and demonstration' follows from the drawing, which Federico Zuccari later differentiated as disegno esterno, a realizing drawing, as opposed to disegno interno, a mental concept. The adoption of the term into English leads then first for several centuries to a narrowing of terminology. Design means drawing, plan, concept, and is mentioned most often in architectural contexts…"
3   Berents: *Kleine Geschichte des Design*, p. 19.
4   In the context of Game Design see Schell, Jesse: *The Art of Game Design*, loc. 1579. "The purpose of design is to solve problems." And Salen/Zimmerman: *Rules of Play*, loc. 634. "Design is the process by which a designer creates a context to be encountered by a participant, from which meaning emerges."

THE EVOLUTION OF INDUSTRIAL DESIGN PRACTICES

The origins of what we today call design, like the theoretical reflection on handcraft-artistic production, date to the early Industrial Age. More exactly, they date to the advent of mass production methods of consumer goods. These origins can essentially be understood as the codification and professionalization of thousands of years of practices surrounding the creation and production of artifacts and social organizations. If we accept Walter Benjamin's claim that photography in the mid-19th century made the optical unconscious visible for the first time,[5] then we can also observe a similar process with the advent of mass production: the awareness of previously unconscious practices in the design of objects and processes. In his *Philosophy of Money*, Georg Simmel wrote that with industrialization a "revolt of objects" would occur, resulting from "the immense abundance, the marvellous [sic!] expediency and the complicated precision of machines, products and the supra-individual organizations of contemporary culture."[6] This was based on the increasing division of labor, which ultimately led to Taylorization, resulting in the separation of design from (mass-)production proper: "The process of development and production now took place," Catharina Berents writes, "in separate work steps."[7]

This separation led to the development of two fundamental practices, particularly in the opposing procedures of rational and agile design that influence both analog and digital design processes to this day. For one, the ancient practice of prototyping was formalized, i.e, the creation of form studies, mock-ups and (partially) functional models in order to help realize and test the overall concept prior to full production and release.[8] This design practice was distinguished by *partiality* and *impermanence*. The most important variations of prototypical incompleteness that have appeared thus far are as follows:

---

5 "It is through photography that we first discover the existence of this optical unconscious, just as we discover the instinctual unconscious through psychoanalysis." (Benjamin, Walter: "Little History of Photography," in: *Selected Writings*, 4 vols., Cambridge, Mass.: Belknap Press 1996, vol. 2, part 2, pp. 507-530, here pp. 511-512) Compare also: "The camera introduces us to unconscious optics as does psychoanalysis to unconscious impulses." (Benjamin: "The Work of Art," p. 266)

6 Simmel, Georg: *The Philosophy of Money*, Abingdon, Oxon, New York: Routledge 2011, p. 525.

7 Berents: *Kleine Geschichte des Design*, p. 32.

8 See Guggenheim, Michael: "The Long History of Prototypes," *limn* Number Zero: Prototyping Prototyping (o. J.); http://limn.it/the-long-history-of-prototypes/

- First, a concentration on horizontality, meaning the prototypes may represent the entire product or process, but at the expense of detail in regard to aesthetics and functionality;
- Second, a concentration on verticality, meaning the prototypes present merely a specific part of the product or process as detailed as possible;
- Third, a concentration on functionality, meaning the prototypes may act as a proof of concept, demonstrating the functionality of the product or process without any consideration for outward aesthetics;
- Fourth, a concentration on aesthetics, meaning the realization of only the external appearance of the product or process, without regard for functionality.

Testing each variation reveals the need to modify the prototypes. Prototype impermanence indicates the second characteristic of the design process: the practice of *incremental iteration*, of step-by-step correction and refinement of the conception and modeling processes. The cyclical nature of design ensures feedback loops and thereby emergent results during each phase: conception, prototyping, interactive testing, analysis, (re-)conception, prototyping, and so forth. Throughout this process, design overrides the exact planning, preparation, and linearity that are typically inherent in industrial production, whether this be in steel or film.[9]

THE EVOLUTION OF INDUSTRIAL DESIGN THINKING

The most successful attempts to theoretically describe and understand past design practices have followed the trial-and-error principle that characterized those very design practices. A hallmark of design theory is not only its tight entanglement with contemporary design practice, but also since its beginning,[10] the ap-

---

9   Thus it seems hardly coincidental that there are certain parallels between these "trial-and-error" design practices and the processes of mutation and natural selection described by Charles Darwin in 1859 almost simultaneously with the origins of industrial design and critical reflection on innovative design processes.
10 The beginning of design theory is characterized by Gottfried Semper's und Christopher Dresser's first theorizations about design, i.e., long before interdisciplinarity became the order of the day. See Semper, Gottfried: *Der Stil in den technischen und tektonischen Künsten, oder, Praktische Aesthetik: ein Handbuch für Techniker, Künstler und Kunstfreunde*, Frankfurt a.M.: Verlag für Kunst und Wissenschaft 1860 http://digi.ub.uni-heidelberg.de/diglit/semper1863/0001, and Dresser, Christopher:

propriation and exaptation of theories of art, communication, and media, which were developed through the analysis of other subjects and fields.[11]

For that reason the history of design theory can be described as a process of selective accumulation and analysis in excess of a hundred years. During this process the approaches borrowed by design theory from poetry and aesthetics in the middle of the 19th century were expanded on by newly arising research prospects that included image theory, pre-structuralist semiotics, photo and film theory, communications theory, information theory, structuralist semiotics, and deconstructivist discourse analysis, among others. Simultaneously and parallel to this process, design theory also formulated its own modern theory, followed by its own post-modern theory.

This list is not just a chronology. It also connects the early development phase of the various approaches and theories relevant to design quite clearly to specific phases of conception, design, and production. This correlation between phases of design and the appropriation of "fitting" theories began in the 19th century with the recourse to traditional poetics and aesthetics, which themselves descended from experience with manual production. The adoption of established theories was followed by the integration of new approaches from art studies and pre-structuralist semiotics. During the second electronic phase of Industrialization—and in the context of the conscious realization of the differences of industrial materials, machines, and media—, modern design thinking discovered the selective analysis of new mass media and their theories, especially mass-print as well as the study of journalism, photography and photo theory, film and film theory. In reaction to the third electronic phase of Industrialization, design turned its attention to reflecting on television and communication theory, as well as information theory and structuralist semiotics, while at the same time developing its own post-modern theories. Finally, with the implementation of digital technology and digital networking in the 1970s and 1980s, deconstructivist discourse analysis as well as actor-network theory and media theory (in its many variations for the humanities and social sciences) began to affect design thinking.

Principles of Decorative Design, London: and New York etc. Cassell, Petter 1873; http://www.gutenberg.org/ebooks/39749

11 See Fallan, Kjetil: *Design History: Understanding Theory and Method*, New York: Berg Publishers 2010, p. 203. "Design history has a long tradition of appropriating theoretical perspectives and methodological approaches from other disciplines, from the heritage from art history, via the more recent romance with material culture studies."

The majority of these theoretical reflections on industrial design practice, from the mid-19th century through the late 20th century, was characterized by its "pre-scientific" nature. Kjetil Fallan writes: "[D]esign history as a distinct, academic field of study in its own right [...] did not emerge until the 1970s."[12] Rather, the analysis of design fundamentals and practices was defined during its first century of existence by numerous artistic-handcraft "movements"—arts and crafts, Jugendstil, art nouveau, life reform, Werkbund, Bauhaus, modernism, art deco, streamline modern, international style, the good form, etc.—and their respective theoretical underpinnings. These movements combined regression and progression, e.g., regression in medieval relations of production and anti-industrial decoration; progression in radical functionalism and machine-worshipping variations of industrialism. In particular this phenomenon manifested itself in the opposition of function and ornament, narrative and nature, typification and individualization. From roughly 1850 through 1950, the interplay of the various ways in which design commonly constructs meaning led to the accumulation of diverse doctrines of anti-industrial decoration and industrial functionality.

This relay race of movements in the context of modern design came to an end only with the transition to postmodern conditions, largely initiated by the proliferation of first analog and then digital electronics. Relative uniformity of style gave way to the postmodern 'anything goes,' blurring and eroding the borders of design. Design moved from the creation of things onto evermore general demands and applications. Just as design had once created artifacts, it now sought to create processes and experiences, as seen in corporate design, communications design, service design, user-experience design, sustainable design, and design thinking. Since then traditional design practices and theories have been called into question through the apparent 'disappearance' of physical artifacts through the process of their virtualization, i.e., the successive replacement of hardware with software and the associated, constant medialization of design processes.

Insofar as industrial design had always reacted to and even sought to mold technological potential, the transition from industrial to digital culture threw it into an inevitable crisis. This affected both the established practices of design as well as its theoretical self-conception.

---

12 Fallan: *Design History*, p. 23.

2 Digital Design

Digital design began in the mid-20th century with the development of commercial software. In order to eliminate uncertainty and chance, an attempt was made to adapt industrial patterns; following a sequential model, roughly in the order of assignment, concept, computation of costs, demand analysis, design, development, testing, and, finally, implementation. This "Waterfall Development Model," during which each step must be completed before the next one can be taken, demands the following: first, the clients must know their own needs, and second, developers must possess enough experience with the (software) product they plan to develop. However, neither of these two requirements were present in most instances of early software development, drawn to transform material processes into entirely new virtual ones.

Repeated failures by this sequential type of software development led to the realization that in the case of digital programs the need to close off each step prior to beginning the next one no longer existed: In mathematical processes, time's arrow only has limited effect. While the materiality of handcraft and industrial production requires a sequential process—of which the iterative processes of design are only an early phase—, software design can be entirely based on the iterative design phase model.

THE DIGITALIZATION OF DESIGN PRACTICE

The difference in the demands placed on analog versus virtual products, and in turn also on their designers, stems from the basic innovation inherent in digital technology: the separation of hardware and software. Material production is tied to specific materials and tools. Virtualization does away with analog variety through the adequate conversion of analog qualities and functions into mathematical values. What used to find its aesthetic form through various devices on mutually incompatible analog media, can now be virtually produced in the transmedium of software and stored digitally. Increasingly, objects of utility became and are becoming von Neumann machines, hybrid hardware and software configurations. This development produces three general conditions of design in digital culture.

First, in comparison to analog design, digital prototypes can be alpha and beta tested to a broader extent because individual usage patterns can be tracked through collected digital data, the product of global networking. This improved accuracy of prototype testing, via automized feedback, can be understood as rationalization. Thus, game designers can determine how their users act and react far more precisely than novelists or filmmakers can determine how their works are received. Jane McGonigal posits:

"Game designers and developers are actively transforming what once was an intuitive art of optimizing human experience into an applied science. And as a result, they are becoming the most talented and powerful happiness engineers on the planet."[1]

Second, the virtualization of content and function renders all hardware arbitrary, i.e., it becomes replaceable. Only stored data is truly indispensable.[2] Hardware's material loss of meaning, unimaginable under analog conditions, does nothing to diminish its economic or aesthetic status. The arbitrariness of hardware—where every laptop could easily be replaced by another—raises the importance of functional as well as optical design during any purchasing decision.

Third, the virtualization of content brought about the demise of fixed form work. Media products, whether text, audio, or image documents, are transformed from analog artifacts, with their unity of content and storage medium, into fluid software. The resulting files are endlessly and interactively changeable both by their producers and, in theory, their users.

From these three general conditions of virtual culture—*datafication, arbitrariness of hardware, and fluidity of software*—arise fundamental consequences for digital design processes. The fluidity of software eliminates the limitations imposed by sequentiality, which characterized analog production and limited in

---

1 McGonigal: *Reality Is Broken,* loc. 657.
2 Anyone who has ever lost a laptop fully understands this premise. The height of the damage lies not with the need to replace the standardized hardware; this can be insured and replaced at anytime and virtually anywhere in the developed world. The same can be said for the equally standardized software programs. The primary objective is the recovery of personal software *data.*

analog design any radical manipulations of the product in defiance of all cyclical iterations. Software data, on the other hand, constantly remains arbitrarily mutable. Its creation is no longer slave to linear processes that in analog production are always defined by the qualities of the materials being used. That which in the real world had to happen sequentially, can happen in the virtual world ahead of time, simultaneously, or even much later.

Although digital design of analog hardware became possible in the late 1950s—first in the auto and aeronautics industries—several decades were to pass before its potential was conceptually realized and put into wide scale practice. Perhaps the most explicit expression of software design thinking arose in 2001 with the "Manifesto for Agile Software Development." The principles of this manifesto oppose the classical "Waterfall Development Model" and emphasize spontaneity and a nonlinear processuality.[3]

Parallel to this transformation, digital design adopted the traditional practices of analog design, namely prototyping and incremental iteration, both of which were deeply transformed through virtualization. This process began in the late 1980s with Computer Aided Design (CAD) software. In comparison to physical production, CAD programs accelerated the traditional process ("rapid prototyping") through the modifiability and reusability of significant elements ("evolutionary prototyping"). The test and feedback phases were accelerated and became more precise through datafication. Thus far, this evolution has brought about the complete virtualization of design processes[4] as well as the advent of entirely new digital design fields, including sound design, interface design, web design, and, of course, game design.

THE DIGITALIZATION OF DESIGN THINKING

Since industrial times, theoretical-aesthetic manifestos and visions of the future have accompanied the crisis of the old and the advent of the new. Typically, they

---

[3] Beedle, Kent Beck Mike/Bennekum, Arie van/Cockburn, Alistair/Cunningham, Ward/ Fowler, Martin/Grenning, James/Highsmith, Jim/Hunt, Andrew/Jeffries, Ron/ Kern, Jon/Marick, Brian/Martin, Robert C./Mellor, Steve/Schwaber, Ken/Sutherland, Jeff/ Thomas, Dave: "Manifesto for Agile Software Development," (2001); http://agile manifesto.org

[4] Of even complex hardware, such as a Boeing 787 ("Dreamliner"), "in which the first full sized realization is made on the series production line." (https://en.wikipedia.org/wiki/Prototype)

feature both regression and progression, i.e., backward-looking and forward-looking perspectives. In their reaction to the constant acceleration of media and aesthetic innovation, these manifestos tend to be part of the crisis and, simultaneously, also part of its solution. During the first decade of the 21st century, a striking accumulation of such manifestos and concepts were produced. Three authors and their perspectives had a formidable impact on the field of design—still primarily as indicators of the crisis and, only secondarily, as contributors to a solution.

In 2005, while teaching at the Art Center College of Design in Pasadena, California, renowned science-fiction author Bruce Sterling wrote *Shaping Things*.[5] The book traces the history of our tools and 'things' from the agricultural through the industrial and into the digital age, predicting the emergence of a completely new type of 'thing' that will be digitally informed and constantly networked. Sterling described these new 'things' with the neologism 'spime'[6] and highlighted their ability to transport their own production and user history through space and time, a result of their additional software components. "This means that in a spime world, designers must design, not just for objects or for people, but for the technosocial interactions that unite people and objects: designing for opportunity costs and cognitive load."[7]

One year later, the Berlin-based cultural theorist Norbert Bolz published *Bang Design*,[8] a short work that he expressly declared as a "design manifesto for the 21st century." 'Bang' is not a neologism like spime, it is an acronym that stands for 'Bit/Atom/Nano/Gene.' Bolz's basic thesis proclaims the end of Industrial era design, clearing the way for an imminent paradigm shift. Following 'decoration,' 'function,' and 'emotion,' 'evolution' will now become a central design task, according to Bolz. In the digital age, man will evolve into the designer of nature, of the environment as well as of his own bodily existence.

"The advance into the core of cell and atom gives man a demiurgic freedom to repeal old European standards and conceptions of man ... Customers of Bang Design develop the normal expectation of a permanent nano-technological upgrading of body and brain."[9]

---

5 Sterling, Bruce: *Shaping Things*, Cambridge, Mass.: MIT Press 2005.
6 Ibid., p. 11ff.
7 Ibid., p. 22.
8 Bolz, Norbert: *Bang Design Design-Manifest des 21. Jahrhunderts*, Hamburg: Trendbüro 2006.
9 Ibid., p. 201 and p. 205.

With that, the designer becomes, in Martin Heidegger's words, the "shepherd of being."[10]

In December 2007, former editor-in-chief of *Wired* and influential member of the digerati, Kevin Kelly, gave a TED talk conceiving the future of the Internet—as a "single global machine."[11] On one hand, it embodies our knowledge and thinking while, on the other hand, it forms a universal nexus in which we can interweave ourselves with our artifacts:

"Every thing will be part of the web. So every item, every artifact that we make, will have embedded in it some little sliver of web-ness and connection. [...] And it will be part of this machine, so that our environment—kind of in that ubiquitous-computing sense—our environment becomes the web."[12]

The future that these three visionaries conceptualize—'things' with history and thus self-awareness (Sterling), nature and man as objects of design (Bolz), the networking of reality and, in turn, virtuality as our new environment (Kelly)—might be viewed by some with skepticism. However, the very existence of these visions indicates a growing awareness of the crisis of Industrial culture and its design practices. What is gradually taking the place of Industrial design practices is significantly impacting game design as well—its practices and its cultural importance.

Firstly, the traditional roles of 'things' and media design are slowly being reversed, as Bruce Sterling anticipated with his utopian "spime" concept. Hardware dominated under analog circumstances. For example, the successively developed elements of book design (type space, cover, cover sheet, table of contents, index, blurb, etc.) are primarily related to fixations in the sense of Hegel's "outer form," the form of being. The design of things once prefigured the design of media. But now the arbitrariness of digital hardware is pushing content—text, audio, still and moving pictures—to the forefront of design efforts.

In addition, the process of virtualization is 'medializing' many artifacts that were previously only perceived as things and not as media. An early, culturally instructive example, extremely popular and profitable since the turn of the century, is the separation of telephone (hardware) and ringtone (software). In analog culture, media design was dictated by the shape of artifacts because their form

---

10 Ibid., p. 207.
11 Kelly, Kevin: "The Next 5,000 Days of the Web," December 2007; http://www.ted.com/talks/kevin_kelly_on_the_next_5_000_days_of_the_web/transcript?language=en
12 Ibid., min. 7 in the interactive transcript.

was the standard for the shape of media. In digital culture, artifacts and media are designed in the same way because the form of—virtualized—media is becoming the model for all that follows: increasingly, media design is shaping the design of things. In this context, digital games are the medium that allow for today's distinct guidelines concerning the design of artifacts, processes, and experiences, as well as the world around us.

A second consequence arises from the fluidity of the digital transmedium. As it permits for interactive modification not only by producers but also by users, digital design can become participatory. With the growth of knowledge-based work and digital culture, those, who in the industrial age were primarily consumers, are now developing an interest in and a readiness for participation—not least of all in the personalization of goods and services. In the Industrial age, the Tayloristic passivity of the individual was the model for work and entertainment design, even in those areas that did not easily lend themselves to a hierarchical division of labor. Similarly in the digital era, open-source practice—with its software architecture oriented towards delocalized, interactive participation, and collaboration as well as virtualized feedback-structures—delivers a universal model for the design of hardware and software alike.[13] One way or another, digital design is interactive and collaborative.

Not limited just to professionals, digital users can become co-designers as well. In addition to "user-centered design," variations of "user-driven design" and even "user-generated design" are being implemented. One reason for the willingness of future users to participate in design processes lies in the fact that digital culture design is no longer merely concerned with the creation of artifacts, but also with the shaping and enhancing of real and virtual experiences;[14] the design of life and the body, though not (yet) in the sense of Norbert Bolz's design manifesto. The long-lasting debates on *gamification*[15] in crucial areas of

---

13 See Freyermuth, Gundolf S.: "Offene Geheimnisse—Die Ausbildung der Open-Source-Praxis im 20. Jahrhundert," in: Lutterbeck, Bernd/Bärwolff, Matthias/Gehring, Robert A. (ed.), *Open Source Jahrbuch 20: Zwischen freier Software und Gesellschaftsmodell*, Berlin: Lehmanns Media 2007, pp. 17-57.

14 See for example Norman, Donald A.: *Emotional Design: Why We Love (Or Hate) Everyday Things*, New York: Basic Books 2004.

15 Defined as "the use of game design elements in non-game contexts" (Deterding, Sebastian/Dixon, Dan/Khaled, Rilla/Nacke, Lennart E.: "Gamification: Toward a Definition," *CHI 2011 Gamification Workshop Proceedings* 2011; http://hci.usask.ca/publications/view.php?id=219). For *gamification* see below p. 224ff.

life such as learning, working, and consuming, indicate the important role of game design in digital culture well beyond the development of digital games.

A third consequence results from the fact that—as Kevin Kelly envisioned—the line between reality and virtuality is becoming more and more permeable. Thus, the task arises to design the integration of real and data spaces. Product design, architecture, and urban planning are melding with the information design of virtual structures and simulated spaces. Reality, or rather, our perception of reality, is cloaked in a shroud of media via digitalization and mobile broadband networking. As the central challenge to industrial design was producing for the masses and creating a standardized public space, the personalization of information perception seems to dictate design in the digital age. Time- and location-based information are becoming accessible on demand. Just as one changes radio stations or personalizes a website simply by interacting with it, guidance systems that can be individualized are establishing themselves in a novel public space, an intermediate realm somewhere between reality and virtuality.

This will completely change how we experience our everyday world. Social and geographical strangers will become instant insiders who move confidently in unfamiliar territory and choose among consumer offers in a well-informed way—something which under analog conditions was only possible after long years of local experience. A main focus of digital design efforts will likely be the creation and shaping of a hybrid reality that is augmented virtually by software. Here again—since the first *pervasive games* and *augmented reality games* were created in the early 21st century—game design plays the crucial role of trend setter and pacemaker.

3 A Short History of Game Design

> "Game design isn't just a technological craft.
> It's a twenty-first-century way of thinking and
> leading."
> JANE MCGONIGAL[1]

THE FIRST 40 YEARS

Historically, four phases can be identified in the creation of digital games. The origins of game design lie in the academic hacker culture of the 1950s and 1960s.[2] The first digital game, SPACEWAR!, written in 1962 by students at MIT,[3] was organizationally produced at the level of handcraft manufacturing, where individuals or small groups produce the entire product. At the same time the source code remained technically, as well as legally, open. The game was not only—as per academic custom—made available free of cost, it could also be extended and improved upon by any player. As Jeremy Parish writes:

"Thus Spacewar was, in effect, the first open-source video game. And it was the first piece of freeware as well; no one responsible for the game's creation profited from it. Ultimately, the code for the game was distributed by DEC for free with every PDP-1 system they sold."[4]

---

1 McGonigal: *Reality Is Broken*, loc. 298.
2 See Freyermuth, Gundolf S.: "Ursprünge der Indie-Praxis. Zur Prähistorie unabhängigen Game Designs," in: Kaminski, Winfred/Lorber, Martin (ed.), *Gamebased Learning. Clash of Realities 2012*, Munich: kopaed 2012, pp. 313-326.
3 See above p. 59f.
4 Parish, Jeremy: "Spacewar!," in: (ed.), *The Essential 50 Archives*, 1UP.com, without year; http://www.1up.com/features/essential-50-part-1-spacewar

In this way the first digital game did not differ from other software innovations, which at that time originated in academia. For example, the infrastructure of global networking was produced by thousands of technically enthusiastic academics following the principles of scholarly research, and published free of patents or copyrights; TCP/IP, Sendmail, Bind, HTTP, Apache, Perl, and Python, just to name a few.

The development of global networking remained tied to academic principles until the 1990s—to habits and behavior that we now associate with the open-source movement.[5] The development of digital games, however, sought other organizational and economic examples. Starting in the 1970s, analog entertainment electronics and the arcade games industry became the role model. With the transition from academic to commercial goals, the second phase of game design began. During this process, the handcraft method of production remained intact for a while, since the first generation of professional game designers continued to conceive of, design, and program games either alone or in very small teams. At this time, digital game design practices oriented themselves both towards the model of analog design, such as the mutually opposing practices of rational and agile design, and the nascent processes of software design.

With the growing medial complexity of digital games, particularly in their narrative and audiovisual design, game design slowly entered its third phase. Over the last three decades a variety of specializations have emerged which concentrate on singular artistic, technical, organizational, and economic aspects of the development of digital games.[6] Thereby, the game industry—like the film industry before it—moved in quick steps from handcraft to industrial modes of organization.[7] The game industry then developed its own big production studios and publishers, which initially followed the example of Hollywood, namely, the

---

5   The term 'open source' itself was only coined in the 1990s. Essential elements of open-source practice, however, can be traced back to the beginning of digitalization. See for the following historical representation, Freyermuth: "Offene Geheimnisse."

6   For example, lead designer, level designer, character designer, technical designer, sound designer, game economy designer, game director, game art director, game artist, concept artist, 3D modeler, asset artist, texture artist, user interface artist, 2D or 3D animator, facial animator, technical animator, engine programmer, gameplay programmer, graphics programmer, tools programmer, data analyst, software tester, quality assurance engineer, localization manager, community manager, project manager, producer.

7   See the description of work processes in Egenfeldt-Nielsen et al.: *Understanding Video Games*, loc. 665.

film industry's extreme division of labor and economic practices, as well as its radical transformation via digitalization.

PRESENT AND FUTURE

However, in the past several years, constant democratization of aesthetic production and global distribution of medial products has resulted in a countermovement: the popularization of indie games.[8] Its advent as well as its stunning success can be understood in the context of the growing crisis of AAA games, i.e., the commercialization of game design and the resulting artistic restrictions. Ideally the designers of indie games focus less on maximizing profits and more on their own artistic inclinations or social agendas. As lone wolves or in small teams, they create games outside of large conglomerates and their established ways of thinking and operating. Despite the popularity of some of their games, indie developers are mostly small entrepreneurs who work in the pre-industrial mode, as is common in literature, the visual arts, or music. Large projects—not only AAA titles like *Grand Theft Auto* or MMOGs like *World of Warcraft*, but also popular software and knowledge projects like Linux or Wikipedia—can hardly be attempted or managed under such conditions.

So the question arises whether indie practices might develop the much-needed competencies which have been restricted by the limitations of minor craftwork, through a—renewed—convergence with the open-source practices from which game design originated. Open-source practices have demonstrated for over two decades how large projects can be managed via global networks of individual or small groups of knowledge-workers—through self-selection, egalitarian collaboration, meritocratic control, and user participation—and even successfully monetized through the dialectic of global cooperation and local competition.

Indie game designers, therefore, could profit from a selective adoption of open-source practices; that is, by overcoming their relapse to handcraft labor practices and by emulating game design practices of big studios in novel ways and on a different level.

---

8   See Freyermuth: "Ursprünge der Indie-Praxis."

4 Areas of Games Design

At the moment game design—understood as the implementation of ludic and narrative conceptions through various divisions of labor—is carried out in highly different ways among the worlds of AAA games, indie games, and so-called serious games. My study largely ignores these differences and concentrates instead on their commonalities.

THE ROLE OF THE GAME DESIGNER

Like the production of theater, film, and television, which require the integration of highly different talents through the aesthetic and practical coordination of the director, so too the design of digital games needs a controlling and integrative element to facilitate the planning, communication, and execution of artistic goals: "Anyone who makes decisions about how the game should be is a game designer," writes Jesse Schell. "Designer is a role, not a person."[1] Tracy Fullerton defines this role as "part engineer, part entertainer, part mathematician, and part social director"[2] and above all as a "universal translator,"[3] who translates the common artistic goal into the technical terminology from the various contributors and the trades they represent.

The history of digital games has so far produced just a hundred noteworthy—primarily male—game designers. A good dozen appear to me particularly influential: on one hand, the *Classic Designers*, Roberta Williams (MYSTERY HOUSE 1980, the KING'S QUEST-Series, 1984-1998), Shigeru Miyamoto (DONKEY KONG, 1981; SUPER MARIO BROS., 1985; THE LEGEND OF ZELDA, 1986),

---

1   See Schell: *The Art of Game Design*, loc. 290.
2   Fullerton: *Game Design Workshop*, loc. 467.
3   Ibid., loc. 649.

Chris Crawford (EASTERN FRONT 1941, 1981; BALANCE OF POWER, 1985), Richard Garriott aka Lord British (ULTIMA series, since 1981), Sid Meier (PIRATES!, 1987; CIVILIZATION, 1991), Will Wright (SIMCITY, 1989; THE SIMS, 2000), Peter Molyneux (POPULOUS, 1989; BLACK & WHITE, 2001; FABLE, 2004), Chris Roberts (WING COMMANDER series, 1990-2007), Warren Spector (WING COMMANDER, 1990; DEUS EX, 2000), David Cage (FAHRENHEIT, 2005; HEAVY RAIN, 2010; BEYOND: TWO SOULS, 2014); and on the other hand, the *Indie Designers*, Jenova Chen (FLOW, 2006; FLOWER, 2009; JOURNEY, 2012), Jason Rohrer (PASSAGE, 2007), and Jonathan Blow (BRAID, 2008).

If during the process of game development, game designers act internally as guardians of the artistic vision, then they also externally represent the players. This begins with the most fundamental decisions: which player-types will primarily be addressed, and how many should compete against whom; single or several players against the game; one player or a group of players against a single player or a group of players, etc.[4] Because games encourage players to put themselves in extraordinary situations and to do things, both good and bad, they would normally never do, game designers are "metacreators of meaning"[5]—in contrast to traditional authors or directors, who create fixed combinations of meaning.

TRIAD, TETRAD, AND THE FUNCTION OF NARRATION

Three attempts have been made to describe the fields of work influenced by game design. A widespread two-layer model distinguishes between 'core' and 'shell', the inner game system and the outer representation system.[6] In contrast, the so-called "MDA" model divides digital games and, thereby their creation, into the trinity of *Mechanics, Dynamics, Aesthetics*.[7] Finally, Jesse Schell places

---

4 See for example the list of player types ibd., loc. 2911.: Competitor, Explorer, Collector, Achiever, Joker, Artist, Director, Storyteller, Performer, Craftsman; also the list of player interaction patterns ibd., loc. 1930-1983.

5 Ibid., loc. 289.

6 See Mäyrä: *Game Studies*, loc. 309.

7 See Hunicke, Robin/Leblanc, Marc/Zubek, Robert: "MDA: A Formal Approach to Game Design and Game Research," *Proceedings of the Challenges in Games AI Workshop, Nineteenth National Conference of Artificial Intelligence* (2004); http://www.zubek.net/robert//publications/MDA.pdf

game design into a tetrad of *Mechanics, Story, Aesthetics, Technology*.[8] The last two approaches have the elements of *Aesthetics* and *Mechanics* in common. The first means simply the outer form—"This is how your game looks, sounds, smells, tastes, and feels"[9]—which corresponds with what the two-layer model describes as the 'shell'. The *Mechanics*, on the other hand, are more part of the 'core' of the game system, as Robin Hunicke, Marc LeBlanc, and Robert Zubek write: "Mechanics are the various actions, behaviors and control mechanisms afforded to the player within a game context."[10]

Viewed from a media-technological perspective, this element of digital games is what connects them to analog games: The *Mechanics* virtualize analog game mechanics, which increases their performance in regard to speed and complexity of processes as well as feedback. The *Mechanics* also cause the most lasting separation from linear audiovisuality, from film and television—the media from which digital games adopted much of their *Aesthetics*.[11]

After *Aesthetics* and *Mechanics*, the triadic model characterizes the remaining qualities of digital games as *Dynamics*, "forces or motions that characterize a system."[12] In contrast, the tetradic model differentiates the same leftover qualities as *Technology* and *Story*. *Technology*, including the central element of the game engine, is understood as the enabling medium: "The technology is essentially the medium in which the aesthetics take place, in which the mechanics will occur, and through which the story will be told."[13]

Story, the most controversial term of the tetrad[14], Schell defines vaguely as "the sequence of events that unfolds in your game. It may be linear and pre-scripted, or it may be branching and emergent."[15] Schell's inclusion of *Story* as the fourth element of game design is striking, since his own definition of games does not include an element of narrative, nor do the definitions from Katie Salen

---

8   See Schell: *The Art of Game Design*, loc. 1200 ff.
9   Ibid., loc. 1217.
10 Hunicke et al.: "MDA: A Formal Approach to Game Design and Game Research."
11 See Schell: *The Art of Game Design*, loc. 1206.
12 Mäyrä: *Game Studies*, loc. 356.
13 Schell: *The Art of Game Design*, loc. 1225. See Egenfeldt-Nielsen et al.: *Understanding Video Games*, loc. 644: "Thus, a game engine is loosely comparable to a word processor which enables an author to write words of her choosing or to a theatre with props which enable a director to stage plays without building everything from scratch."
14 For the conflict between ludologists and narratologists see p. 203ff.
15 Schell: *The Art of Game Design*, loc. 1210.

and Eric Zimmerman, or Jane McGonigal.[16] That Jesse Schell claims *Story*—next to *Aesthetics, Mechanics*, and *Technology*—as the fourth task and work field of game design is what distinguishes his tetradic model. In contradistinction to his own definition of what makes a game, here Schell recognizes, from practical game design experience, the crucial significance of narration for digital games. Only in their narrative form do game mechanics arouse deeper interest and emotions, as Tracy Fullerton states:

"Imagine playing a game in which you are a set of data. Your objective is to change your data to increase its values. To do this, you engage other sets of data according to complex interaction algorithms. If your data wins the analysis, you win. This all sounds pretty intangible and rather boring, but it is a description of how a typical combat system might work from a formal perspective. To connect players to the game emotionally, the game designer creates a dramatic premise for the interaction that overlays the formal system. [...] [L]et's imagine you play a dwarf named Gregor rather than a set of data. You engage an evil wizard, rather than an opposing set of data, and you attack him with your broadsword, rather than initiating that complex interaction algorithm. Suddenly, the interaction between these two sets of data takes on a dramatic context over and above its formal aspects."[17]

On the other hand, digital games that want to tell specific stories must develop storytelling mechanics that make these narratives possible. This interdependent relationship constitutes the special role played by narration in digital games.

This relationship further reveals itself in the shaping of characters. As a central element of every narrative, characters help readers, viewers, and players to identify with the story being told. For example, as types they can embody demographic groups, their values and ways of life, or as individuals they may stand for specific qualities, desires, fears. In regard to their function within the narrative, the protagonist and antagonist are distinguished from one another by their distinct needs and desires.

This diegetic relationship (inherent in narratives of literature, theater, film, and television) is complicated in digital games by a second relationship: the one that exists between the protagonist of the narrative and the player. This relationship can be categorized according to the amount of control—so-called 'agency'—that players have over 'their' characters. Above all, game design must decide two things in regard to plot and characters:

---

16 For these definitions see p. 31ff.
17 Fullerton: *Game Design Workshop*, loc. 2947.

1) To what degree should characters be defined by the player, i.e., to what degree should the player be able to develop and change characters in regard to their looks, their characteristics, their histories and goals;
2) Should characters be completely under the control of the player or have some degree of autonomy in their actions, i.e., should characters have their 'own life' through programming of applicable artificial intelligence.

These specifics of nonlinear, interactive narration demonstrate that digital games are producing fundamentally new forms of storytelling. No longer are singular stories told, but rather open worlds rich in narrative are produced procedurally, hyperepically, and hyperrealistically: navigable and mutable in real-time, multi-linear and open spatially, increasingly photorealistic without indexical reference to reality.

5 Practices of Game Design

The development of digital games can ideally be outlined in three phases: *conception, design, production*. Of course, in practice such a clear division rarely exists.

THE PROCESS OF GAME DEVELOPMENT

It always starts with an idea. The question, where it might come from, can rarely be answered, and if it can, then only on an individual basis. Like artists and musicians, writers and filmmakers, game designers report two scenarios: sudden inspiration and targeted brainstorming in teams. Game design handbooks offer more or less helpful recommendations for both the opening up of new perspectives for the individual and the collective organization of creative processes.

Two sources for game ideas are mentioned again and again. First, the creation of digital games is similar to that of literature or film in that—just as poems are made from poems and movies from movies—older games often provide the raw material for new ones. This is especially true when designing for a particular genre. Someone who wants to design games, should first play a lot.

Second, ideas for innovative games also spring from utterly diverse sources, from intermedial engagement with other forms of art and from experiences made in 'the real'. "Ideas can come from anywhere—books, movies, television, and of course other games are frequent sources," says the developer Noah Falstein, who has worked in the game industry for 30 years, "but I've had ideas spawned from personal relationships, from dreams, from scientific principles, from art, from music theory, and from children's toys."[1]

---

1   Quoted after ibid., loc. 4909.

After the conceptual phase, game designers move on to the iterative processes of horizontal, vertical, functional, and aesthetic prototyping—characteristic of analog as well as digital design.[2] Therefore, the testing and improvement of game mechanics is of particular importance. Game design literature classifies the elements of game mechanics in many different ways. Jesse Schell, for instance, names:[3]

- The *functional space* of the game: its dimensions, characteristics, boundaries, etc.;
- The *objects* that can be found in this space: their attributes, their states, their dynamics, etc.;
- The *actions* that are possible in this space: the possibilities for navigation, acting, communicating, manipulating objects, etc.;
- The *rules* of the game that superordinately control the sub rules of space, objects, and action: for instance, the time relations of the actions or the relation between skill and chance in the course and outcome of the game;
- The *goals* of the game: their concreteness, their achievability, the rewards offered, and so on.

Schell understands the objects as the nouns of game mechanics, their attributes as adjectives,[4] and their actions as verbs: "A game without actions is like a sentence without verbs—nothing happens."[5] Schell sees the artistic shortcomings of digital games as primarily resting on an alarming shortage of verbs. Though possessing extraordinary physical abilities (such as walking, jumping, and shooting), characters are often times psychologically as well as intellectually underdeveloped, i.e., thus far it has been nearly impossible for them to feel, reflect, or argue: "Videogame characters are severely limited in their ability to do anything that requires something to happen above the neck."[6]

Tracy Fullerton categorizes the elements of game mechanics, which have to be tested in prototypes, according to other criteria. For example, she differentiates rules from computer-controlled procedures and provides procedural definitions for not only objects but many other resources, including 'lives', health, raw materials, and currency. Likewise she speaks of characters rather than actions,

---

2   For prototyping see p. 144ff.
3   Schell: *The Art of Game Design*, loc. 2900-3500.
4   Ibid., loc. 3027-3036.
5   Ibid., loc. 3213.
6   Ibid., loc. 5606. See Schell: "Die Zukunft des Erzählens."

mentions narration as an important element, and sets aside a special category for conflicts—obstacles and resistance, opponents and dilemmas:

"Traditional dramatic conflict can be broken down into categories such as character versus character, character versus nature, character versus machine, character versus self, character versus society, or character versus fate. As game designers, we might overlay another group of categories, which are player versus player, player versus game system, player versus multiple players, team versus team, etc."[7]

THE PRINCIPLE OF WORLDBUILDING

Another central method of game design is world building. Game designer David Jones, for instance, reports on creating GTA: "GRAND THEFT AUTO was not designed as GRAND THEFT AUTO. It was designed as a medium. It was designed to be a living, breathing city that was fun to play."[8] Only once this 'game-scape' was finished and one could play with it in every sense of the word, only then were the hyperepic narratives developed that are now associated with GTA. Tom Chatfield thus describes the "aesthetics of world-building" as a central moment of digital culture.[9]

Worldbuilding is certainly not an entirely new practice in the history of the arts. Epic storytelling strove to capture dying worlds, as, for example, Honoré de Balzac undertook with the *Comédie Humaine*. Others attempted to invent entirely new fictional worlds, like J. R. R. Tolkien with *Lord of the Rings*. Dramatic storytelling, however, bound to audiovisual representation in time and space, was largely barred from such worldbuilding—mostly for media-technological reasons; both the production requirements and the circumstances of reception in the theater and cinema. Only with the transition to virtual, i.e., software-based audiovisuality, did the construction and reception of complete audiovisual worlds move into the realm of possibility.

In audiovisual 'story worlds' or 'story universes' three-dimensional areas for action may not completely replace linear storylines, but they certainly start to compete with them. These three-dimensional action areas have to be designed rather than simply described. Thus Henry Jenkins speaks of the "story architec-

---

7   Fullerton: *Game Design Workshop*, loc. 3206.
8   Schell: *The Art of Game Design*, loc. 2212.
9   Ibid., loc. 2188-92.

ture" of narrative transmedia worlds.[10] Game designers, who develop this kind of 'environmental storytelling', work as "narrative architects [...] privileging spatial exploration over plot development."[11]

Aesthetically, the construction of these virtual worlds follows the principles of theming.[12] Theming has been in development since the 1950s in the context of Disney's theme parks, which can be seen as analog anticipations of virtual worlds. Theming connotes design processes of selection, compression, and unifying stylization—the filtering of the audiovisual 'noise' of complex realities or fictions—for the purpose of a more controlled production of experiences.

In the same way that theme parks create fictions into which people can enter, worldbuilding turns digital images from framed windows, through which other worlds can only be viewed (as in the theater or the movies) into interactive portals. They not only allow entrance to fictional narratives, as theme parks do, but also interactive participation and, in turn, new audiovisual experiences. The audiovisual worldbuilding of digital games is therefore different from all previous analog attempts because the resulting storytelling spaces are procedural systems: "a group of interacting, interrelated, or interdependent elements forming a complex whole."[13]

Like all systems, audiovisual game worlds contain objects with specific characteristics and potential ways of interacting with one another. Virtual systems, which are the foundation of all audiovisual worldbuilding for games, simulate biological, social, cultural, and economic conditions, while simultaneously enabling interaction with these simulations. Through these playful interactions users tend to build mental models: "The computer is just an incremental step," says Will Wright, "an intermediate model to the model in the player's head."[14]

For systematic simulations, it is fundamentally important that they concern themselves—independent from any degree of realism—with simplified abstractions of real-world role models: "A simulation does not attempt to simulate every aspect of its referent, but instead focuses on those elements necessary to the game."[15] Different principles can underlie these abstractions, from the produc-

---

10 See p. 72f.
11 Chatfield, Tom: "Bridging the Gap," *Prospect* 2011; http://www.prospectmagazine.co.uk/arts-and-books/bridging-the-gap
12 See Jenkins: "Game Design as Narrative Architecture."
13 Gottdiener, Mark: *The Theming of America: Dreams, Visions, and Commercial Spaces*, Boulder Colo.: Westview Press 1997.
14 Quoted after Fullerton: *Game Design Workshop*, loc. 4092.
15 Salen/Zimmerman: *Rules of Play*, loc. 785.

tion of specific experiences to the teaching or training of specific skills: "Ultimately, of course, we don't care about creating either stories or games—we care about creating experiences. Stories and games can each be thought of as machines to help create experiences."[16]

It is in the mechanics of these systems—the result of the necessary abstraction processes—where one finds not only the functionality of simulations, but also their message, their ideology. Ian Bogost speaks, therefore, of the "inherent subjectivity" of the world model that digital games offer.[17] Frans Mäyrä demonstrated this fact with the example of Sid Meier's CIVILIZATION:

"[T]he rules of the simulation are built on a particular vision of history, crystallized by historian Arnold J. Toynbee in *A Study of History* (1934-1961, 12 volumes). According to this view, civilizations can be seen as units with life cycles, similar to those that organisms have (a view influenced by the German philosopher Oswald Spengler)."[18]

AUTHORSHIP IN GAME DESIGN

The steady interdependence between (1) audiovisual systems that are created by game designers—where worldviews, as well as intentions and expectations of how these worlds should be used, unfold—and (2) the actual realization of the potential actions by the players (individuals as well as groups), poses a longstanding question anew for our digital age: How should creative authorship, and in turn author's rights, be defined?

Digital games have created conditions and possibilities for the control of aesthetic meaning incomparable to all that has preceded them: authorship not only by producers but also by users, i.e., players—by individuals, collaborating groups, but also by contributors in distributed networks who hardly know each other. The degree of authorship on the part of the player may vary from genre to genre and game to game, but even the most simple gameplay in virtual worlds generates co-authorship, irrespective of whether players document their actions

---

16 Schell: *The Art of Game Design*, loc. 5474. Also McGonigal: *Reality Is Broken*, loc. 595: "A good game is a unique way of structuring experience and provoking positive emotion."
17 Quoted after Fullerton: *Game Design Workshop*, loc. 2020.
18 Mäyrä: *Game Studies*, loc. 1454.—See Salen/Zimmerman: *Rules of Play*, loc. 5525: "Games are systems of meaning."

(in so-called *Let's Play* videos) or whether they become co-designers, in a more traditional sense, of their experiences through *mods*.

The specific 'distributed' form of authorship in digital games as well as the specific nature of their dramatic conflict point to a specific sequence of the iterative prototyping process. At its heart lie numerous variations of play testing—by the designers or the team itself, by chosen individuals and diverse focus groups.[19] Concerning play testing, most handbooks on game design stress two requirements. First, the necessity of posing clear questions: "You should be able to state the questions clearly. If you can't, your prototype is in real danger of becoming a time-wasting boondoggle, instead of the time-saving experiment it is supposed to be."[20] Second, the necessity of working initially with analog prototypes: "[I]t allows you to focus on gameplay rather than technology."[21]

Playtesting as a part of prototyping gains an enhanced significance in digital game design when compared to the design of analog objects, where the process of prototyping was developed. Eric Zimmerman writes: "The behavior of complex, interactive systems—like games—is incredibly difficult to predict. You generally cannot know exactly what players are going to do once they start playing your game."[22] This also forms the divide between digital games and linear audiovisions. Unlike theater plays, feature films, or television series, games are not written. As Tracy Fullerton claims: "No one, no matter how smart they are, can conceive and produce a sophisticated game from a blank sheet of paper and perfect it without going through this process," i.e., the process of prototyping and play testing.[23]

---

19 Vgl. Zimmerman, Eric: "How I Teach Game Design. Lesson 1: The Game Design Process," *Gamasutra*, October 19, 2013; http://www.gamasutra.com/blogs/EricZimmerman/20131019/202710/How_I_Teach_Game_Design_Lesson_1_The_Game_Design_Process.php. More detailed descriptions give Schell: *The Art of Game Design*, loc. 3213, and Fullerton: *Game Design Workshop*, loc. 873.
20 Schell: *The Art of Game Design*, loc. 2104.
21 Fullerton et al.: *Game Design Workshop*, loc. 5218.
22 Zimmerman: "How I Teach Game Design. Lesson 1."
23 Fullerton: *Game Design Workshop*, loc. 603. See Freyermuth, Gundolf S.: "Lesen wird in vielen Computerspielen zu einer Überlebensfähigkeit," in: Böhm, Thomas (ed.), *New Level: Computerspiele und Literatur*, Berlin: Metrolit 2014, pp. 115-144.

DON'T FOLLOW THESE RULES! A PRIMER FOR PLAYTESTING
By Nathalie Pozzi and Eric Zimmerman[24]

What is playtesting?
Playtesting is a *methodology* borrowed from game design where unfinished projects are tested on an audience. A playtest happens when people come together to try out a work in progress. The next steps for changing the project are based on the results of the playtest.

Playtesting is also an *attitude* towards the creative process, an approach that emphasizes problem-solving through iteration and collaboration with members of your audience.

When is playtesting useful?
Playtesting can help develop any kind of work that involves interaction between a created experience and a participatory audience. Although many of the ideas of playtesting come from game design, they can be applied in any field.

What does playtesting look like?
Playtesting can look like any number of things. At the University of the Arts, we met as a group on a regular basis and shared works in progress. We would spend about 30-60 minutes interacting with and discussing one project—perhaps in a studio space, perhaps outdoors in a park or on the street—and then move on to the next.

Isn't playtesting the same as user testing / editing / rehearsal / critique?
Yes and no. Playtesting is not discipline-specific and versions of it can be found in many practices. The style of playtesting we outline here comes from game de-

---

24 Nathalie Pozzi is an architect and artist, who explores the critical intersection of space, light, material and culture. Eric Zimmerman is a professor at the Game Center of the New York University and co-author with Katie Salen of *Rules of Play*. Eric and Nathalie have collaborated on the design of several playable installations that have been exhibited at the Museum of Modern Art in New York City, the Smithsonian American Art Museum in Washington, D.C., as well as all over the world.—This essay was originally written for and published in De Campo, Alberto/Hentschel, Ulrike/King, Dorothee/ Kufus, Axel (ed.): *Play: Test*, Revolver: Berlin 2013. It was also republished in Fullerton: *Game Design Workshop*.

sign and is particularly relevant for projects that involve direct audience interaction.

THE "RULES" ... before you playtest

A. Playtest before you think you are ready
You always playtest a work in progress, not a finished design. That means you should playtest as early as you possibly can—usually much earlier than you think you should. It is much better to playtest your ugly prototype than to wait and playtest a more polished project. A playtest is not a presentation. If you feel ready and comfortable to present and playtest your design, you have waited too long—it is probably too late to make substantial changes. Train yourself to overcome your discomfort and playtest as early in the process as you possibly can.
 Is it too early for you to playtest? If the answer is yes, then playtest anyway.

B. Strategize for early playtesting
Figure out how to create a working prototype far in advance of any final deadline. This is often a question of tactical implementation. Can you make a paper prototype of a digital project? Can you scale down a work meant for 100 participants to something you can playtest with a dozen? Rather than plan your entire project in advance, focus instead on what is needed to enable the next playtest.
 Simplify your project so that you can playtest today.

C. Know why you are playtesting
Enter into every playtest with a concrete idea about what you want to learn and what questions you hope the playtest will answer. Narrowing what you want the playtest to investigate can help you simplify your project and playtest sooner. Generating research questions in advance will also help you structure the playtest itself. If you are doing things right, your playtest will raise issues and questions that you did not anticipate. However, you should still go into every playtest with a clear agenda.
 What is the one key question that you want your playtest to answer?

D. Prepare variations
Go into a playtest with different versions of your project to try out. This allows you to make the most out of the playtest session and it also helps you to improvise and try out new ideas during the playtest. Variations might mean different sets of game rules to play, software settings to cycle through, or contexts for a performance. Variations give you options if something breaks down, and they let you do comparisons to see which variation works best. One tip: change as little

as possible each time (only one element) so that you can understand better the exact effects of your change.
What can you change to try out different variations of your project?

E. Be grateful to your playtesters
Whoever is playtesting your project is doing you a big favor. They are donating their time and attention for the sole purpose of helping you with your unfinished project. Playtesting is hard. But no matter how much stress and uncertainty you might have about the project, try and maintain a feeling of gratitude towards your playtesters. Be happy they are there and be sure to let them know how thankful you are for their time.
Take a deep breath and say thanks.

F. Design the learning experience
Remember to design the way that people will learn about your project. If you are creating a complicated interactive system, the experience of learning how to understand and interact with the system is an important part of the overall design problem.
Does your playtest address the learning process?

G. Blame yourself, not your playtesters
Remember to warn your playtesters that they will be interacting with an unfinished, rough version of what will at some later point be a smoother experience. Be sure to tell them that if they are frustrated or confused, it is not their fault—it is your fault for not designing a better experience for them. It's OK for them to be confused—after all, the most valuable part of the playtest is not what they do understand, but what they don't.
Never make your playtesters feel foolish.

H. Know your testers
What do you need to know about your playtesters before the playtest begins? If you are meeting them for the first time or don't know them very well, talk with each person and take notes that will help put their reaction to your project in context. Playtesters come in many varieties. For example, the learning curve of a hardcore gamer is very different than someone without deep experience in a particular game genre.
Do you know who your playtesters are?

I. Don't explain
Put the project ahead of the theory. Resist the temptation to explain the ideas and intentions behind your project to your playtesters. Instead, let them interact with

the LEAST possible explanation from you in advance. By explaining your ideas beforehand, you are ruining the chance to see the authentic reactions that your project provokes. It is hard to hold back and not explain. But by forcing your project to carry your ideas (rather than your explanation), you are challenging your work to be better.
Is it possible to not say anything before the playtest starts?

J. Take notes
In game design, we often prepare a sheet of paper for each playtester, with questions written out and room to take notes. The notes page is structured to facilitate what you need to know BEFORE, DURING, and AFTER each playtest. During a discussion, taking notes will help to elicit better feedback—if your testers see you taking notes they will be more likely to give you detailed and thoughtful answers.
Prepare a notes sheet and use it. It is worth the extra effort.

... during a playtest

K. Be selfish
The purpose of your playtest is not for your playtesters to have fun. It is for you to learn what does and does not work about your project. If you try too hard to give playtesters a good time, you will lose the opportunity to get the hard truth from them. Don't be afraid to show your playtesters something broken and half-finished. That is in fact the entire premise of the playtest.
Don't worry about being entertaining.

L. Encourage your playtesters to talk aloud
If it is possible for your project, ask your playtesters to talk out loud about their thoughts and feelings as they interact with your work. A "think-aloud" playtester can give you valuable insight into how they are perceiving and interpreting the details of your project. Let your playtesters tell you why they are doing what they are doing and what they think is happening as a result. This may require that you periodically remind them to vocalize.
Don't be shy about reminding your playtesters to think aloud.

M. Notice everything
Prepare on your notes sheet the categories of the main things you want to observe, such as when players seemed frustrated, what make them laugh, or how many times they tried and failed before they gave up. Keep track of how long it

took to run the playtest, which variations your testers preferred, and any other important information. Try to take notes on everything that you can—otherwise, you will be at the mercy of your selective memory, which will cast everything in the best possible light.

Are you noticing everything—or just what you want to see?

N. Shut up

While you are observing the playtest, say as little as possible. You will feel an overwhelming urge to help out your playtesters, to tell them what to do and what they are doing wrong. But you must do everything you can to not interfere. Their mistakes and misunderstandings are extremely useful: you must let them explore the project on their own. If they are completely confused, step in and assist them, but in general you should do everything you can to shut up. If you tell them what to do, you lose the main purpose of the playtest, which is to see how OTHER people react to your project. Learning to shut up during a playtest requires discipline.

Can you shut up—not just a little, but really, completely, shut up?

O. See the big picture

As your playtesters interact with your project, remember to not just focus on the workings of your designed system. Try to see the human element at play. What are the emotional responses of your playtesters, what is their body language, how are they interacting with each other? Seeing the bigger picture can help you understand when your audience is engaged and when they are bored. It is easy to focus too much on what you designed, rather than on the effect it is having.

Stay focused on the impact of the project, not just the project itself.

P. Don't be afraid of data

One way to get objective about your playtest is to record data and put it in a spreadsheet. Every project has data to collect: At what moments did everyone fall silent? How many steps did each participant take as they walked through the space? If you are working in software, the program can record important user input, such as time spent in different areas of the experience. Otherwise, just remember to record the data in your notes. Too much data can be overwhelming to interpret, but tracking the right data can be incredibly valuable.

What is the data that will answer your key questions?

Q. Answer a question with a question

When playtesters ask you how something works, or what something means, it is probably because they are confused. Rather than explain it to them, you can answer their inquiry with a question of your own. Don't tell them what the blue button does—instead, ask them what they think it does, or even better, what they think it SHOULD do. It's more important to get them to speculate about your project than for you to explain it to them. Their opinions are more valuable than yours.

Every time a playtester asks you something, ask them something back.

R. Hunger for failure

One of the attitudes that helps with playtesting is to yearn for your project to fail. Of course we all want successful results, but unsuccessful moments are much more useful. If you are only looking for the successes, you will remember the smiles and laughter and think that your project is in perfect shape (we call this the "happy face syndrome"). But you need to cultivate a desperate hunger to focus on what is not working properly. Otherwise, your project will never get better.

Are you enjoying the successful moments too much and ignoring the failures?

... after a playtest

S. Discuss what happened

After the playtest, talk about the experience with your playtesters. Use your notes sheet to structure the conversation. Begin with very specific questions, such as what was most difficult for them to understand about the project, or why they reacted to a particular aspect of the design. Finish with more general questions, such as what they liked best about the experience or what they would change to make it better.

The more concrete your questions, the more useful answers you will get.

T. Put feedback into context

It can be useful to distinguish between expert and non-expert testers. Experts are familiar with what it means to make a project like yours. Non-experts aren't.

When getting critical feedback from non-experts, remember that they are the patient and you are the doctor—you can take their suggestions as symptoms of what is and isn't working in the project, rather than as directions for the next steps in your design. If someone tells you to tear down a room and make it bigger, they are really telling you that it feels small. Rather than take their advice, perhaps just rearrange the furniture. Don't expect your players to understand all of the ramifications of every suggestion they make.

Ask for feedback, but don't take suggestions literally.

U. Collaborate with your playtesters

One of the most thrilling moments of playtesting is collaborating with your playtesters—brainstorming with them, trying out their ideas, and seeing how the changes impact your project. Plan your playtest session so that you have time to experiment with new ideas as they emerge through the playtesting itself. They are seeing the project with fresh eyes and so their ideas are often better than yours.

Embrace shared authorship with your playtesters.

V. The cruelly honest playtest

Playtests represent moments of truth—when your brilliant ideas may all come crashing down. Playtests are truthful because they are a safe place to simulate your final context. When your project is completed, you probably won't be there to explain away all of the problems and defend your intentions. In a playtest, you get to cruelly see whether or not your ideas actually work in practice. Part of the playtest attitude is building up your pain tolerance and coming to enjoy the hard truth of the playtest.

Face the truth of your playtest, even if it hurts.

W. Embrace the unexpected

Never forget that *play* is half of *play*test. Being playful means being open to unexpected, happy accidents. Let go of the way you *want* your work to be used or interpreted. Be open to the strange new things people do with your project. Accidents are for those who are ready to take advantage of them.

If things don't go as planned, you may be on to something better.

X. The playtest's the thing

The playtesting process is as important as the actual project you are making. If you can manage to get the process right, then you will find that the problems in your project begin to solve themselves.

Forget what you are making. Focus on how you make it.

Y and Z. Break these rules

There is no single magic solution that will solve every problem you encounter. So you need to create the process that works for you. Don't follow these "rules." They are not meant to be followed—they are meant to be twisted, modified, broken, and refashioned into something new. The best playtest is the one you invent yourself.

III Game Studies

Introduction

As media and the arts evolve over time, corresponding theoretical analysis and debate do as well.[1] Academic studies also have a history. In this respect, the relevance and meaning of theories differ in genesis and validity. In Western modernity, theoretical reflection on the arts came into existence as a sedimentation of aesthetic practices—that holds true from Leon Battista Alberti's *De Pictura* (1435)[2], to Jesse Schell's influential *The Art of Game Design* (2008).[3] Historically, aesthetic practices were always analyzed and codified through scriptualization or textualization in increasing levels of abstraction.

Thus, theoretical reflection on media and the arts begins as the sedimentation of artistic practices and evolves from these praxis-oriented theorems into others that are more theoretically or historically-oriented. This process is demonstrated by the evolution of film theory. In the early 20th century, the examination of the defining medium of the industrial age began with theoretical deliberations that I will call *theories of the practitioners*, in particular the writings of avant-garde directors like Sergei Eisenstein or Vsevolod Pudovkin, who explored the techniques and the aesthetic potential of filmmaking. Their main focus was practical

---

1 The prolog extends and systematizes thoughts that I first approached in the context of film education. See Freyermuth, Gundolf S.: "Angewandte Medienwissenschaften. Integration künstlerischer und wissenschaftlicher Perspektiven in Lehre und Forschung," in: Ottersbach, Beatrice/Schadt, Thomas (ed.), *Filmlehren. Ein undogmatischer Leitfaden für Studierende*, Berlin: Berta + Fischer 2013, pp. 263-278.
2 Alberti, Leon Battista. *On Painting. Translated with Introduction and Notes by John R. Spencer.* New Haven: Yale University Press 1970 (*1956); http://www.noteacce ss.com/Texts/Alberti/
3 Schell: *The Art of Game Design.*

as well as artistic: "How can we develop film as an art form, as a significant medium of expression?"[4]

These *theories of the practitioners* were followed shortly thereafter by *theories of the theoreticians*. Early theoreticians came to film from older and established fields of academic research, particularly from philosophy, the theory of fine and visual arts, literature and theater studies, sociology, psychology and pedagogy. Consequently, the writings of these early theoreticians of film remained highly committed to the perspectives and preferences of their 'native' disciplines. The most important examples were, Rudolf Arnheim's book *Film as Art* (1932)[5] and Walter Benjamin's essay "The Work of Art in the Age of Mechanical Reproduction" (1936).[6] This first phase of theory-oriented reflection on the new medium of film from 'external perspectives' can be understood as an example of 'exaptation'[7]: Certain theoretical ways of thinking and academic practices developed within the context of different research subjects were extended beyond their original context and applied to film.

The next phase, beginning by the middle of the 20th century and originating mainly in film criticism, saw the formation of genuine theories of film. Two of the most important examples are André Bazin's *Qu'est-ce que le cinéma?*[8] (c. 1958-1962) and Siegfried Kracauer's *Theory of Film: The Redemption of Physical Reality* (1960)[9]. In the wake of these first *theories of film theoreticians*, i.e.,

---

4   See Eisenstein, Sergei/Jay Leyda: *Film Essays and a Lecture*. Princeton, N.J.: Princeton University Press 1982; Pudovkin, Vsevolod Illarionovich, et al.: *Selected essays*. London, New York: Seagull Books 2006.—Both authors had connections with the world's first film school, founded 1919 in Moscow; Pudovkin studied there starting 1920, Eisenstein became a professor in 1928.—For this observation I have Lisa Gotto to thank.

5   Arnheim, Rudolf: *Film as Art*, London: Faber 1969 {*1932}.

6   Benjamin, Walter, et al.: *The Work of Art in the Age of its Technological Reproducibility, and Other Writings on media*. Cambridge, Mass.: Belknap Press of Harvard University Press 2008.

7   This term that Stephen Jay Gould introduced into the theory of evolution 30 years ago describes a process of appropriation and conversion in which certain traits gain a new function. See Gould, Stephen Jay/Vrba, Elizabeth S.: "Exaptation: A Missing Term in the Science of Form," *Paleobiology* 6, 1 (1982).

8   Bazin, André/Hugh Gray. *What Is Cinema?*, Berkeley: University of California Press 1967.

9   Kracauer, Siegfried. *Theory of Film: The Redemption of Physical Reality*. New York: Oxford University Press 1960.

theories of expert theoreticians, film studies was able to establish itself in more and more universities around the world as an academic discipline. This third phase in the theoretical reflection on film from 'internal perspectives' can be understood with another term from the theory of evolution: the successful 'adaptation' of academic thinking and practices to a new subject and new medium of aesthetic expression, namely film.

Thus, the process whereby new media and art forms were theoretically explored and evaluated was divided into three qualitative steps:

- Practitioners described and analyzed the evolving artistic practices. The goal of their theoretical writings was to systematize and guide aesthetic production. These *theories of the practitioners* resulted in a *sedimentation* of practice, i.e., *abstractions of the first order*.
- Studies of new media advanced to theories that no longer exclusively served artistic practice. This was accomplished by importing existing theories and academic practices from older disciplines. These *theories of external theoreticians* appropriated and applied existing theories and academic or scientific practices to the new field, thereby working from an external perspective and with *abstractions of the second order*, i.e., *exaptations*. Their works initiated an academic analysis of the new object, while remaining largely bound to the perspectives of their original disciplines.
- Through direct engagement with new media and its artistic practices, these exaptations of theories finally led to *theories of expert theoreticians*— meaning genuine theories of photography, film, or design. These were then *abstractions of the third order*, theoretically oriented reflections from mostly internal perspectives. This third step can also be understood with a term from evolutionary theory: theoretical ways of thinking and academic practices successfully *adapted* to the new subject field. This third step alone led to the establishment of a new academic discipline.

Sedimentation, exaptation, and adaptation—the development of Game Studies has so far followed this three-step process, through which new media and aesthetic practices have been theoretically understood and researched since the start of the industrial revolution:

- The existing theories of game design are abstractions of the first order, *theories of practitioners*, trying to develop a systematic understanding of the artistic practice in order to guide it more effectively.

- To date, Game Studies work primarily with *theories of external theoreticians*; i.e., with *abstractions of the second order*, exapted from other disciplines and subjects in order to initiate a theoretical debate of the new subject, digital games.
- The third and final step of this process has not yet been taken: the development of adaptative abstractions of the third order, that is, *theories of game theoreticians* (resulting from the historical-theoretical analysis of digital games and describing them sui generis).

Overview

The essential purpose of this introduction into Game Studies, i.e., the academic discipline that researches digital games, is to describe the prevailing conditions for a transition from exaptive to adaptive theories. First, I will sketch the prehistory of digital games, as well as central approaches of the theoretical and academic occupation with analog games (*III-1 Theories of Analog Games vs. Theories of Digital Games*). In the second step I will portray the dominant positions that have arisen from the three contemporary variations of Game Studies (*III-2 The Schisms of Game Studies*).

The observation and description of the cooperation and even the parallel existence of these approaches will lead to the conclusion that the existing schisms could and should be overcome by transferring current disputes into interdisciplinary debate and analysis. Rather than relying on imported perspectives and methods, this analysis should originate from interests and approaches that are developed through the direct study of digital games (*III-3 Desideratum: Overcoming the Schisms*).

Finally, I will develop perspectives for research which could further the formation of such adaptive, genuine theories; both for the study of digital games generally (*III-4 Perspectives of Research 1: Digital Games*) as well as for the important sub-segment of serious games specifically (*III-5 Perspectives of Research 2: Serious Games*).

1 Theories of Analog Games vs. Theories of Digital Games

> "As the history of the video game invokes a history of non-electronic games, video game studies must admit a debt to the study of non-electronic games."
>
> JESPER JUUL[1]

PRE-INDUSTRIAL THEORIES OF PLAYING AND GAMES

In order to investigate the study of digital games as an academic discipline, its prehistory must first be investigated. In becoming digital, games pass through a kind of accumulative media shift comparable to earlier changes in the realm of visual and audiovisual representation.[2] I have already described this process as "the double alterity of digital games."[3] Consequently, the theoretical analysis of games—following the examples of theater and film studies—is divided into two parts: the study of analog games and the study of digital games.[4]

---

1 Juul: *Half-Real*, loc. 106.
2 With the advent of photography, most aesthetic and cultural functions of painting shifted to the new industrial medium of semi-automatic reproduction. Something similar happened with the advent of cinema: Most aesthetic and cultural functions of the theater shifted to the new industrial medium of mass entertainment.
3 See chapter I, part 6 *The Double Alterity of Digital Games*, p. 87ff.
4 Part of the philosophical and theoretical prehistory of digital games are not only debates about analog games, but also about other popular forms of entertainment, for example fairs and their rides, mirror cabinets and shooting stands, panoramas, dioramas, arcades, and theme parks, also with rides and other attractions.

Theoretical analyses of human play and games run like a clear thread through Western culture since antiquity. As Jesper Juul writes, "it seems that almost every well-known philosopher has theorized on play."[5] In the context of Game Studies, the philosophical reflections of three thinkers on analog games have been and continue to be relevant: Gottfried Wilhelm Leibniz (1646-1716), Friedrich Schiller (1759-1805), and Friedrich Nietzsche (1844-1900).

Leibniz understood games in the context of the Enlightenment "as an expression of the free inventive spirit under regulated conditions."[6] As a mathematician and philosopher he laid decisive academic groundwork for a variety of areas that impact digital games. Theoretical as well as practical research on mechanical calculators allowed him to, as George Dyson writes, invent the binary shift register as the central element of digital computers 270 years before its technical realization.[7] His interest in the mathematical calculation of probabilities and his occupation with games of chance made him, as Gilles Deleuze formulated, "one of the great founders of game theory."[8] Above all, Leibniz understood games as a central method for knowledge production and transferring knowledge and skills. He approved the use of war games—which could simulate historical battles—for officer training[9] and supported the opinion "that many new games could be thought up to expand the abilities of the soul and even practice the virtues themselves."[10] In his 1675 text written in Paris "Drôle de Pensée, touchant une nou-

---

5   Ibid., loc. 935.
6   Loemker, Leroy E.: "Introduction: Leibniz as Philosopher," in: Leibniz, Gottfried Wilhelm/Loemker, Leroy E. (ed.), *Philosophical Papers and Letters*, Dordrecht, Holland ; Boston: D. Reidel Pub. Co. 1976, pp. 1-69, here p. 61, note 39.
7   Dyson, George: *Turing's Cathedral: The Origins of the Digital Universe*, New York: Vintage Books (Kindle edition) 2012, loc. 2378: "In the shift register at the heart of [...] all processors and microprocessors [...] voltage gradients and pulses of electrons haven taken the place of gravity and marbles, but otherwise they operate as Leibniz envisioned in 1679."
8   Deleuze, Gilles: "Leibniz," *Les Cours de Gilles Deleuze—webdeleuze.com*, April 15, 1980; http://www.webdeleuze.com/php/texte.php?cle=50&groupe=Leibniz&langue=2
9   See Hilgers, Philipp von: "Vom Einbruch des Spiels in der Epoche der Vernunft." in: Bredekamp, Horst/Schneider, Pablo (ed.), *Visuelle Argumentationen: die Mysterien der Repräsentation und die Berechenbarkeit der Welt*, Munich: Fink 2006, pp. 205-224.
10 Leibniz, Gottfried Wilhelm: "Zufällige Gedanken von der Erfindung nützlicher Spiele aus dessen mündlicher Unterredung aufgezeichnet von F. F. F." in: Leibniz, Gottfried

velle sort de REPRESENTATION" he even invented a "game palace," reminiscent of modern arcades. He conceived of it as not only a place of enjoyment and business but also as one of—panoptic—recognition:

"Leibniz goes on to name the native and foreign games to be played in the individual rooms of the play-palace, in order to explain, concerning the internally valid currency, that the visitor must exchange play money at the entrance. [...] Leibniz closes this passage with an eulogy on his academy of play, which should increase the profit, which should burst at the seams, and where dangerous passions would be transformed into useful training of thought and imagination."[11]

If Leibniz analyzed games as a method for the production and distribution of knowledge from an Enlightenment perspective, then Friedrich Schiller understood games as a central antidote to rationality and domination over nature. For Schiller games promised to heal the wounds he believed were inflicted on modernity by Enlightenment rationality: the fragmentation of life, work, and. thereby, personality. In this way Schiller shifted the focal point of the philosophy of knowledge, which Leibniz and Immanuel Kant were most concerned with, to a philosophy of holistic human education: "The human being plays only where he is human in the fullest meaning of the word, and he is only human where he plays."[12]

Schiller wrote his letters "On the Aesthetic Education of Man" in 1793/94 under the impression of the French Revolution, which he understood as the political realization of Enlightenment efforts. Disappointment over its development clearly shaped his thoughts. He projected two steady, contradicting drives throughout world history: an outward sensory substance drive—human desire and other irrationalities—would stand across from an inner, rational drive based on form, among other moral norms and rational behavior. These two drives would be reconciled by a third one, the play drive, in which the two poles, gratification of lower instincts and morality, come together and interact dynamically:

Wilhelm/Guhrauer, Gottschalk E. (ed.), *Leibnitz's deutsche Schriften*, Berlin: Veit 1840, pp. 491-493, here p. 493.

11 Bredekamp, Horst: "*Kunstkammer*, Play-Palace, Shadow Theatre: Three Thought Loci by Gottfried Wilhelm Leibniz," in: Schramm, Helmar, et al. *Collection, Laboratory, Theater: Scenes of Knowledge in the 17thCcentury*. Berlin, New York: Walter de Gruyter 2005, pp. 266-283, here p. 269.

12 Schiller, Friedrich: "Letters on the Aesthetical Education of Man," http://www.guten berg.org/files/6798/6798-h/6798-h.htm

"In the midst of the formidable realm of forces, and of the sacred empire of laws, the aesthetic impulse of form creates by degrees a third and a joyous realm, that of play and of the appearance, where she emancipates man from fetters, in all his relations, and from all that is named constraint, whether physical or moral."[13]

With this construction Schiller lent "his play concept an anthropological dimension, by leading playful behavior back genealogically to natural animal excess behavior."[14] However, Schiller also positioned the game as a thoroughly subversive corrective to Enlightenment rationality and the logic of purpose-oriented domination of nature. "The freedom from instrumental goal-setting [...] is supposed to open up the possibility for the human being to finally become that, which he should be, according to his nature."[15] The concept of equating human play with liberation from alienated circumstances was realized once again one-and-a-half centuries later through Herbert Marcuse's Schiller reception—not coincidentally around the same time a new ethics of games was developing: "In a genuinely humane civilization, the human existence will be play rather than toil, and man will live in display rather than need."[16]

Friedrich Nietzsche's understanding of the game enhances this perspective: an expression and practice of childish freedom, the game represents a disruptive force that seeks to undermine established ways of behaving, procedures, and hierarchies. For example, Nietzsche describes the Greek tragedy as a game between Apollonian and Dionysian forces.[17] Furthermore, he sees in the game and its mechanics of the "infinite return of the same," the fundamental principle with which to grasp the running of the world, i.e., the divine world-game:

"[T]he doctrine of the eternal recurrence of the same expresses the play-character of the world. [...] This does not mean that the content of each and every moment must be the

---

13 Ibid.
14 Krämer: "Ist Schillers Spielkonzept unzeitgemäß? Zum Zusammenhang von Spiel und Differenz in den Briefen 'Über die ästhetische Erziehung des Menschen,'" p. 158.
15 Neuenfeld, Jörg: *Alles ist Spiel: zur Geschichte der Auseinandersetzung mit einer Utopie der Moderne*, Würzburg: Königshausen & Neumann 2005, p. 41.
16 Marcuse, Herbert: *Eros and Civilization: Philosophical Inquiry Into Freud*, Boston: Beacon Press 1955, p. 188.
17 See Nietzsche, Friedrich. *Birth of Tragedy*, Arlington, VA: Richer Resources Publications 2009 (*1872); http://records.viu.ca/~johnstoi/Nietzsche/tragedy_all.htm

same, but rather that the structure of each moment is the same insofar as each moment is a moment of play."[18]

Nietzsche understands playing—which occurs innocently and beyond morality—as both the force that moves the world as well as ever-passing life, and as the driving force behind the origin of art. His thinking also marks the point at which specialized academic disciplines—split-off from philosophy during the Enlightenment and Industrialization—discover the phenomenon of games and playing games for themselves.

INDUSTRIAL THEORIES OF PLAYING AND GAMES

Since the middle of the 19th century, groundbreaking works in the new research fields of psychology, sociology, pedagogy, ethnology, and anthropology were published. Many of them addressed the phenomenon of play. Jesper Juul divides these into two categories: Theories that only concern themselves with games for specific knowledge purposes of their respective disciplines and theories concerned with games and the phenomenon of play themselves.[19] Among the first group, four influential works are worthy of note.

In *The Principles of Psychology* Herbert Spencer (1855-1880) defines play as a result of excess energies that are not immediately necessitated by the fight for survival. In *Mind, Self, and Society From the Standpoint of a Social Behaviorist* (1934) George Herbert Mead analyzes the meaning of play for identity formation.[20] He distinguishes open play *(play)* from *role play*, which he describes as the first phase of childlike identity formation. In rule-governed play *(games)*, however, the child not only sees another player as the "significant other", but also sees the group as well as the rule system as the "generalized other."[21] According to Mead, playing takes on a central role in the internalization of social control, especially in the development of self-consciousness.

---

18 Hinman, Lawrence M.: "Nietzsche's Philosophy of Play," *Philosophy Today* 18, Summer (1974), pp.-119-120.
19 Juul: *Half-Real*, loc. 108.
20 Mead, George Herbert/Morris, Charles W.. *Mind, Self & Society From the Standpoint of a Social Behaviorist*, Chicago, Ill.,: The University of Chicago Press 1934; https://www.brocku.ca/MeadProject/Mead/pubs2/mindself/Mead_1934_toc.html
21 Ibid.: "The organized community or social group which gives to the individual his unity of self may be called 'the generalized' other."

In *The Presentation of Self in Everyday Life* (1956), Erving Goffman, from a sociological perspective, interprets social behavior as play, following the theater model (stage, actors, masks, props, audience).[22] Gregory Bateson also examines social communication, especially its framing, as game or non-game in *A Theory of Play and Fantasy* (1972).[23] Further research on playing has been performed since the 1920s in the areas of cybernetics and mathematical game theory,[24] since the 1940s in the area of artificial intelligence,[25] and since the 1960s in the context of—first analog and then digital—simulation.[26]

A second, smaller group of academic texts in the 20th century was devoted exclusively to analog games. Of major importance were publications by three authors: Johan Huizinga, Roger Caillois, and Brian Sutton-Smith. In *Homo Ludens* (1938)[27] Johan Huizinga uses a cultural-historical perspective to contrast the playing man with the type *Homo Faber*, described by Max Scheler as the workingman.[28] Huizinga defines play as a phenomenon of freedom that came into being prior to any human culture and is at the same time a primary reason thereof.[29] The activity of playing characterizes voluntariness, regularity, and order, as it takes place apart from daily and working life:

"Summing up the formal characteristics of play we might call it a free activity standing quite consciously outside 'ordinary' life as being 'not serious', but at the same time absorbing the player intensely and utterly. It is an activity connected with no material inter-

---

22 Goffman, Erving: *The Presentation of Self in Everyday Life*, Edinburgh: University of Edinburgh 1956.
23 Bateson, Gregory: "A Theory of Play and Fantasy," in: Bateson, Gregory (ed.), *Steps to an Ecology of Mind: Collected Essays in Anthropology, Psychiatry, Evolution, and Epistemology*, San Francisco: Chandler Pub. Co. 1972, pp. 138-148.
24 See Von Neumann, John/Morgenstern, Oskar: *Theory of Games and Economic Behavior*, Princeton: Princeton University Press 1944; https://archive.org/details/theoryofgamesand030098mbp
25 See chapter 1, part *3 Procedural Turn (since the 1950s)*, p. 53ff.
26 See Rolfe/Staples: *Flight Simulation*.
27 Huizinga: *Homo Ludens*.
28 Scheler, Max/Manfred S. Frings. *The Human Place in the Cosmos*. Evanston, Ill.: Northwestern University Press 2009 (*1928).
29 Huizinga: *Homo Ludens*, loc. 105: "In culture we find play as a given magnitude existing before culture itself existed, accompanying it and pervading it from the earliest beginnings right up to the phase of civilization we are now living in."

est, and no profit can be gained by it. It proceeds within its own proper boundaries of time and space according to fixed rules and in an orderly manner."[30]

That said, Huizinga introduces the influential concept of the "magic circle": a separate realm of play, marked by the establishment of separated places (stage, playground, game table, game board, screen, etc.):

"We found that one of the most important characteristics of play was its spatial separation from ordinary life. A closed space is marked out for it, either materially or ideally, hedged off from the everyday surroundings. Inside this space the play proceeds, inside it the rules obtain."[31]

Huizinga recognizes competition and representative presentation as the two fundamental manifestations of games: "a contest for something or a representation of something."[32]

Two decades later Roger Caillois wrote *Les jeux et Les Hommes* (1958) with the expressed intention of continuing Huizinga's thoughts.[33] His six fundamental rules of games differ from Huizinga's only slightly (voluntariness, unproductivity, spatial and temporal boundaries, regularity, other reality, i.e, magic circle). New, however, are two insights. First, the distinction between the unregulated, instinctive play of individuals (*paidia*) and the rule-governed, codified (social) games that require skill or practice (*ludus*).[34] In progressing from *paidia* to *ludus*, Caillois sees a process of civilization, i.e., individual and social evolution. According to Caillois, forms of play dictate social forms. Second, he distinguishes four fundamental elements of games. The first two correspond to the type of interaction: competition (*agon*) vs. chance (*alea*). The other two characterize the experience of the player: affectation through roleplaying and disguise (*mimicry*) vs. exhilaration through the sensations of physical movement (*ilinx*).[35]

Caillois' claim that ludic progression correlates with societal progression was taken up in two works by Brian Sutton-Smith: *The Study of Games* (1971) and

---

30 Ibid., loc. 278.
31 Ibid., loc. 397.
32 Ibid., loc. 284.—This difference already points towards the later debate between ludologists and narratologists.
33 Caillois, Roger: *Man, Play and Games*, Urbana: University of Illinois Press 2001 (*1958).
34 See ibid., p. 27.
35 Ibid., p. 71f.

The Ambiguity of Play (1997).³⁶ Egenfeldt-Nielsen et al. summarize Sutton-Smith's insights as follows: "the more complex a social system, the more advanced its games."³⁷ Historically Sutton-Smith differentiated between antique and modern rhetoric, i.e., how games are talked and thought about in society. Discourses about games as representations of fate (luck, will of the gods) and power (war games, sports), as an expression of communal identity and of frivolity (subversion of non-playful order) dominated throughout antiquity. In modern times, prevalent discourses are concerned with games as progress (learning), as an expression of the imaginary (art) and as the realization of the self (fun, self-development).³⁸

However, what differentiates these industrial theories of games and play from their pre-industrial predecessors is the striking disregard for aesthetic matters. An early attempt at a theory of games as a medial form can be found in Marshal McLuhan's *Understanding Media* (1964).³⁹ McLuhan maintains that games, like all media, are enhancements of human senses and capabilities: "Any game, like any medium of information, is an extension of the individual or the group."⁴⁰ No different than art, games aesthetically oppose industrialization:

"[A] man or society without games is one sunk in the zombie trance of the automation. Art and games enable us to stand aside from the material pressures of routing and convention [...] In games we devise means of non-specialized participation in the larger drama of our time."⁴¹

Games fulfill this function only when they stay in close touch with reality. "For fun or games to be welcome, they must convey an echo of workaday life."⁴² As a consequence McLuhan classifies games as historical indicators: "When cultures change, so do games."⁴³

The games that McLuhan could relate to at the start of the 1960s were exclusively analog. A decade later, however, the popularization of digital games began. This was first documented by and analyzed in essayistic and journalistic re-

---

36 Avedon/Sutton-Smith: *The Study of Games*; Sutton-Smith: *The Ambiguity of Play*.
37 See the overview in Egenfeldt-Nielsen et al.: *Understanding Video Games*, loc. 926.
38 Sutton-Smith: *The Ambiguity of Play*, pp. 7-12.
39 McLuhan: *Understanding Media*.
40 Ibid., loc. 3459.
41 Ibid., loc. 3388-3393.
42 Ibid., loc. 3388.
43 Ibid., loc. 3412.

flections, such as Stewart Brand's now classic *Rolling-Stone* article "Spacewar: Fanatic Life and Symbolic Death Among the Computer Bums" (1972).[44] In the early 1980s, theoretical texts were published that concerned themselves directly and exclusively with digital games; these were among the first Game Studies texts.

---

44 Brand, Stewart: "Spacewar: Fanatic Life and Symbolic Death Among the Computer Bums," *Rolling Stone*, December 7, 1972; http://www.wheels.org/spacewar/stone/rolling_stone.html

2 The Schisms of Game Studies

The ongoing theoretical debate on digital games is still roughly divided into the three aspects that Katie Salen and Eric Zimmerman listed in 2003: "Rules, Play, Culture," where (1) "rules" concern the "organization of the designed system," (2) "play" entails the "human experience of that system," and (3) "culture" constitutes the "larger contexts engaged with and inhabited by the system."[1]

This threefold division reflects the existing schism of Game Studies. Humanist research concentrates on "culture," i.e., "larger contexts." Social science research is concerned with "play," i.e., "human experience." Finally, theoretical texts on game design focus on "rules," i.e., the organizing principles of games. Around 1980, the emergence of the first writings on game design signaled the beginning of Game Studies.

SEDIMENTATIVE APPROACHES: GAME DESIGN THEORIES

The point of departure and arrival for all game design theory is artistic practice. Game design theorists often pose the two-sided question: "What makes a good game?" and "How are good games made?" The answers to these questions have varied over the last three decades of game design theory: From the first important publication, Chris Crawford's *The Art of Computer Game Design* (1984)[2], to the trio of books that are probably most influential in contemporary game design and education: Katie Salen and Eric Zimmerman's *Rules of Play: Game Design Fundamentals* (2003)[3], Jesse Schell's *The Art of Game Design: A*

---

1 Salen/Zimmerman: Eric: *Rules of Play*, loc. 186.
2 Crawford, Chris: *The Art of Computer Game Design*, Berkeley, Calif.: Osborne/McGraw-Hill 1984.
3 Salen/Zimmerman: *Rules of Play*.

Book of Lenses (2008)[4], and Tracy Fullerton's *Game Design Workshop: A Playcentric Approach to Creating Innovative Games* (2008).[5] Despite the differences in their analyses, which led them to derive various and divergent design principles, almost all game design theories share one important commonality: working on theories of the first order, they are not interested in their improvement as standalone research—i.e., they are not engaging in any systematic academic research—, but rather they are exclusively concerned with the improvement of their object of study: "[T]he main emphasis in game design is on producing games rather than research papers."[6]

Most authors of game design studies seem to find a codification of existing practices crucial to the optimization of game development and production. Consequently, they strive for two elements:

- A systematic analysis and argument-based justification for the existing procedures of production, which originate and evolve spontaneously, i.e., unplanned and without systematic research or reflection.
- The development of a clear and reliable terminology for game design, whose practitioners have had to make do without a defined and shared technical language.[7]

The *conditio sine qua non* for both the codification of procedures and terminology is theorizing and theoreticization, a process of abstract transcendence of concrete practices. However, this is precisely something that most praxis-oriented authors and readers wish to avoid. As a result, game design theory should be classified as *accidental theory*, which often fails to satisfy its own claims or the demands of academia.

From the perspective of aesthetic theory, the best theoretical game design texts are descriptive and normative. They search for answers to their double-

---

4 Schell: *The Art of Game Design*.
5 Fullerton: *Game Design Workshop*.
6 Mäyrä: *Game Studies*, loc. 2430.
7 This situation continues: "The lack of a single vocabulary is one of the largest problems facing the game industry today." (Fullerton: *Game Design Workshop*, loc. 1704) And: "In the past 30 years, video games have become more beautiful, more intricate and more intense—but we still lack a critical language to evaluate them." (Lewis, Helen: "Why Are We still so Bad at Talking about Video Games?," *New Statesman*, November 20, 2012; http://www.newstatesman.com/culture/2012/11/why-are-we-still-so-bad-talking-about-video-games)

question from the perspective of practical insight, which takes the shape of recipe-like prescriptions or rules-of-thumb. Aristotle first established both perspectives in his *Poetics*. Since Hegel and his founding of historical aesthetics, timeless norms have been called into question: "No man can overleap his time, the spirit of his time is his spirit also; but the point at issue is, to recognize that spirit by its content."[8] The diverse aesthetic theories of modernity[9] preserve Hegel's insight into the historicity of art, as well as its analysis. In order to conceptually grasp the complexity and fluidity of aesthetic artifacts and processes, aesthetic theory must progress from the normative and systematic to the historical. Free from the shackles of religion and tradition, the aesthetic production of modernity faces the challenges and contradictions of its time in ever-changing ways: leaving no room for exemplary rules or guidelines.

Caused by its goal of codifying practice, the theoretical "backwardness" of game design theory characterizes its very essence and is hardly rescindable. Other deficits, such as the analysis of individual and societal use, result from an eclectic knowledge of respective research circumstances, i.e., a lack of contact with other areas of Game Studies. Jesse Schell recognizes this deficiency when he writes, "there is no 'unified theory of game design.'" Looking for a "simple formula that shows us how to make good games," he places his hopes not on the social science or humanistic approaches of Game Studies, but on the discovery of a set of timeless rules that only the natural sciences could provide. Schell writes: "Game designers await their Mendeleev. At this point we have no periodic table. We have our own patchwork of principles and rules, which, less than perfect, allows us to get the job done."

The gap between game design theories—theories of the practitioners—and the rest of Game Studies—theories of external theoreticians—, is still quite small in comparison to the divide in older media and arts.[10] Nonetheless, the separation of game design theory from the rest of Game Studies constitutes the first schism. As Dmitri Williams suggested a few years ago, the second schism exists between

---

8   Hegel, Georg Wilhelm Friedrich: *Lectures on the History of Philosophy*, vol. 2: *Plato and the Platonists*, Lincoln: University of Nebraska Press 1995, p. 96.
9   From George Lukács to Walter Benjamin, Theodor W. Adorno, Peter Szondi, and Marshal McLuhan all the way to Michel Foucault or Roland Barthes.
10 For example in comparison to the distance between literature and literary studies or film and film studies where "the distance between scholars and practitioners can loom large, and it seems at times that the two groups barely speak the same language." (Egenfeldt-Nielsen et al.: *Understanding Video Games*, loc. 355)

the approaches imported and exapted from social sciences and the approaches imported and exapted from the humanities.

EXAPTATIVE APPROACHES 1: THEORIES FROM SOCIAL SCIENCES

The core question of the social science approach to digital games is: "What are the effects of digital games?"[11]—on gamers, whether children or adults, on society and culture. This principal orientation determines the research focus on possible transfers between game experiences and reality, i.e., between experiences gained within the so-called "magic circle of play" and the everyday world. For many years now, this part of Game Studies has concentrated on games and socially undesired behavior, particularly violence, or games and socially desired behavior, particularly learning.

In the first branch of research, numerous studies developed competing theories of *inhibition, stimulation, habituation,* and *catharsis* by importing psychological, sociological, and (media) pedagogical methods into Game Studies. A current research trend to renounce simple cause-and-effect relationships between media consumption and everyday behavior is underway. However, this shift affects the second branch of research as well, the cause-and-effect relationship with regard to learning.

In recent years, the most important publications dealing with Digital Game-Based Learning or Digital Media Learning have been Marc Prensky's *Digital Game-Based Learning* (2001) and *Don't Bother Me Mom—I'm Learning* (2006)[12], as well as James Paul Gee's *What Video Games Have to Teach Us About Learning and Literacy* (2003).[13] These texts suggest transfer effects of learning games, which other research, particularly concerning violence, failed to find. The contradiction is an unresolved problem, central to Game Studies, which is grounded in social sciences research methodology: quantitative and

---

11 Williams, Dmitri: "Bridging the Methodological Divide in Game Research," *Simulation and Gaming* 36, 4 (2005), p. 1; http://www.dmitriwilliams.com/GameMethods.pdf
12 Prensky, Marc: *"Don't Bother Me Mom, I'm Learning!": How Computer and Video Games Are Preparing Your Kids for Twenty-First Century Success and How You Can Help*, St. Paul, Minn.: Paragon House 2006, and *Digital Game-Based Learning*, New York: McGraw-Hill 2001.
13 Gee, James Paul: *What Video Games Have to Teach Us About Learning and Literacy*, New York: Palgrave Macmillan 2003.

qualitative data collection by means of structured interviews and participatory observation, usually under laboratory-type conditions. The questionable value of such empirical research has been discussed since the 1960s, since the so-called positivism dispute; i.e., the notorious unreliability of empirically gathered data and the dubious process of generalization from small-group experiments. The trend to combine quantitative and qualitative research seems to be helpful, but it cannot solve the fundamental problematic nature of both approaches.

Another important area of social science-inspired research is ethnographical studies that use participatory observation and biographical documentation. Sherry Turkle's *Life on the Screen: Identity in the Age of the Internet* (1995)[14] establishes the definitive rules for this kind of approach just as Edward Castronova did for the socio-economic exploration of digital game worlds since 2000.[15] Furthermore, communication science studies concern themselves with the question of how digital games create fun and fascination for users.[16]

Borrowing objectives and approaches from social sciences—sociology, psychology, pedagogy, ethnology, or economics—, this variant of Game Studies concentrates on players and gamers, individuals and collectives, on observable behavioral patterns and experiences. Thus the social science approach reveals little about games themselves. The content and aesthetic forms of games are researched by a second group of imported theories.

EXAPTATIVE APPROACHES 2: THEORIES FROM THE HUMANITIES

Research that takes its cue from the humanities tends to center on games as aesthetic and cultural artifacts and, therefore, asks two related questions: "What are the meanings of digital games?" and "What cultural meanings can be made

---

14 Turkle, Sherry: *Life on the Screen: Identity in the Age of the Internet*, New York: Simon & Schuster 1995.

15 Castronova, Edward: "Virtual Worlds: A First-Hand Account of Market and Society on the Cyberian Frontier." *CESifo Working Paper Series* 618 (2001); http://papers.ssrn.com/sol3/papers.cfm?abstract_id=294828; Castronova, Edward: *Synthetic Worlds: The Business and Culture of Online Games*, Chicago: University of Chicago Press 2005; Castronova, Edward: *Exodus to the Virtual World: How Online Fun is Changing Reality*, New York: Palgrave Macmillan 2007.

16 See Klimmt, Christoph: *Computerspielen als Handlung: Dimensionen und Determinanten des Erlebens interaktiver Unterhaltungsangebote*, Cologne: Halem 2006.

through digital games?"[17] Importing and exapting methods of research mostly from art history, literary studies, film studies, and media studies, this variation of Game Studies explores digital games as expressive or aesthetic forms, trying to determine their cultural reception and usage. Two prevalent lines of inquiry are:

- Hermeneutical interpretations query the content and aesthetic forms of digital games and genres by analyzing their constitutive elements and the rules of their combination;
- Games or game genres are studied with regard to their cultural importance by analyzing them from different perspectives—sociology, psychoanalysis, formalism, structuralism, post-structuralism, discourse theory, gender theory, reception research, and many more. The primary objective of these studies is to discover the numerous connections among the inner forms of these artifacts, their genesis, their social use, and the specific cultural conditions in which games and genres are created, of which they are representations and which they affect, willingly or unwillingly.

The first key Game Studies texts of the humanist variation were published in the last decade of the 20th century. Three books have had a particularly lasting impact: Brenda Laurel's *Computer as Theatre* (1991)[18], Espen Aarseth's *Cybertext: Perspectives of Ergodic Literature* (1997)[19], and Janet H. Murray's *Hamlet on the Holodeck: The Future of Narrative in Cyberspace* (1998).[20] Clearly, the inspiration for these works on digital games was drawn from examples set by older media—theater, movies, and television—, but also from hyper-textual narration and analog games. Aarseth develops a "typology of cybertexts," categorically separating narrative media from digital games: Literature, theater, or film call for interpretation, whereas digital games call for configuration.[21] In contrast, Murray sees the computer as a fundamentally representational and narrative medium due to its procedural, participatory, spatial, and encyclopedic properties.[22]

---

17 See Williams: "Bridging the Methodological Divide in Game Research."
18 Laurel, Brenda: *Computers as Theatre*, Reading Mass.: Addison-Wesley 1993.
19 Aarseth, Espen J.: *Cybertext: Perspectives on Ergodic Literature*, Baltimore Md.: Johns Hopkins University Press 1997.
20 Murray: *Hamlet on the Holodeck*.
21 Aarseth: *Cybertext*, pp. 62-65.
22 Murray: *Hamlet on the Holodeck*, p. 71f.

This disagreement, which formed itself in 1997/98 between two literary scholars, can be seen as a prefiguration of the coming conflict between ludology and narratology, as Frans Mäyrä suggested.[23] In 1999, this internal schism within humanist Game Studies deepened when Gonzalo Frasca introduced the term "ludology" for "the yet non-existent 'discipline that studies game and play activities.'"[24] At this time, Jesper Juul also insisted on the incompatibility of play and narration in his Master Thesis *A Clash Between Game and Narrative*: "Computer games are not narratives, but phenomena whose qualities are in exploration and repeatability."[25]

Looking back on the subsequent development of digital games as well as Game Studies, we can see that play and narration were not as incompatible as ludologists once assumed. However, it is now clear, as Egenfeldt-Nielsen et al. write, that the historical function of ludology was "to define the new discipline of Game Studies, beyond the dominant paradigms—the hypertextual (Landow, 1992) and the cinematic (Manovich, 2001)."[26] The long-lasting ludology vs. narratology debate in humanist Game Studies[27] finally prompted, if nothing else, one central insight: the radical otherness or alterity of the digital transmedium generally and more particularly of digital games.

Thus, the years of the early 21st century can be considered the foundation period of humanist Game Studies.[28] Next to a rising number of book and magazine

---

23 Mäyrä: *An Introduction to Game Studies*, loc. 180: "Together, these two works also function as symbols for the two alternative approaches which collided in the first major debate animating the young game studies community a few years later."

24 Frasca, Gonzalo: "Ludology Meets Narratology: Similitude and Differences Between (Video)Games and Narrative," *ludology.org* (*1999); http://www.ludology.org/articl es/ludology.htm

25 Juul, Jesper: "A Clash Between Game and Narrative: A Thesis on Computer Games and Interactive Fiction," (1999); http://www.jesperjuul.net/thesis/

26 Egenfeldt-Nielsen et al.: *Understanding Video Games*, loc. 4965. See reference to Landow: Landow, George P.: *Hypertext: The Convergence of Contemporary Critical Theory and Technology*, Baltimore: Johns Hopkins University Press 1992. See reference to Manovich: Manovich, Lev: *The Language of New Media*, Cambridge Mass.: MIT Press 2000.

27 That is, the debate between a point of view that essentially originated in the engagement with analog games and another point of view that essentially originated in the engagement with analog narrative media.

28 See for example Egenfeldt-Nielsen et al.: *Understanding Video Games*, loc. 340 and Juul: *Half-Real*, loc. 148.

publications[29], which point to the increasing breadth of research, Game Studies began to establish a place at the university level—first in the Anglo-Saxon system then the Scandinavian. Graduate and post-graduate courses of study were offered; the first professorships for Game Studies were created.[30] Simultaneously the conflict between the ludologists and the narratologists diminished, not least under the influence of Henry Jenkins' concepts of narrative architecture and transmedial storytelling.[31] In 2005, even Jesper Juul described "the denial of fiction" as an "alluring position that I have also previously taken"[32] and corrected his view of digital games:

"To play a video game is therefore to interact with real rules while imagining a fictional world [...] The interaction between game rules and game fiction is one of the most important features of video games"[33]

---

29 The *Digital Games Research Association* (DIGRA; http://www.digra.org/) was founded in 2003; the journal *Game Studies* is publishing since 2001 (http://gamestudies.org), *Games and Culture* since 2006 (http://gac.sagepub.com/).
30 On the current situation see Epilog p. 231ff.
31 See Egenfeldt-Nielsen et al.: *Understanding Video Games*, loc. 4811; Jenkins: "Game Design as Narrative Architecture"; Jenkins, Henry: "Transmedia Storytelling: Moving Characters From Books to Films to Video Games Can Make Them Stronger and More Compelling," *Technology Review*, January 15, 2003; http://www.technologyreview.com/news/401760/transmedia-storytelling/
32 Juul: *Half-Real*, loc. 178.
33 Ibid., loc. 43-51.

3 Desideratum: Overcoming the Schisms

Despite progress in recent years, Game Studies is still marred by its dual schism: (1) the significant difference in the approaches borrowed from social sciences and those borrowed from the humanities; (2) the growing separation between humanist and social science theories of the second order and practice-oriented game design theories of the first order, which is perhaps even more detrimental. In 2005, Dmitri Williams proposed reconciliation through interdisciplinarity:

"There is a solution: social science needs context, and humanists need generalizability. Modern scholarship is filled with calls for interdisciplinary work, with moderate success. We are scholars of a new medium and we need to think differently."[1]

LONGING FOR SYNTHESIS

In my view, the above advice was hardly considered. It only applied to theories of the second order anyhow. In the same year, Jesper Juul attempted "to integrate these disparate perspectives into a coherent theory of video games."[2] Shortly thereafter, two fundamental Game Studies texts repeated the same desire for a multidisciplinary synthesis: *Understanding Video Games* (2008) by Egenfeldt-Nielsen et al. and *An Introduction to Game Studies* (2008) by Frans Mäyrä. For example, Mäyrä writes:

"The vision of game studies informing this book can be described as multidisciplinary and dialectical; if and when we understand anything, it is by making connections that open up new directions for thinking about games. Bringing into contact existing but previously

---

1 Williams: "Bridging the Methodological Divide in Game Research," p. 10.
2 Juul: *Half-Real*, loc. 59.

separate ideas, concepts, and frames of thought, we can proceed to create a synthesis of them, and see our grasp of things evolve."[3]

The first pertinent German language contribution, published four years later, brought doubt to the possibility of such a synthesis: "The long overdue consolidation of the research field renders any study striving for completeness impossible..."[4] However, before making an attempt at "synthesizing the work that has been done so far in game studies,"[5] we should ask ourselves whether this is a meaningful endeavor and a worthy aspiration in the first place.

There seems to be a gulf of indifference and even suspicion between the theories of the first and the second order—and their representatives. Due to their low level of abstraction, theories of game design are regarded with a certain condescension by social scientists and humanists. Vice versa, many game designers and theorists of game design doubt the general 'value' of any theories with a higher level of abstraction. The gulf between both of these groups of game scholars is probably wider in German speaking countries than in other regions with education systems where there are closer relationships between theoretical and artistic or vocational instruction. All in all, however, this gulf is global, as theories of the first and second order pursue different epistemic interests.

Theories of the first order make practice (rather than theory) their starting point, sticking close to production. Their main objective is to intervene in, and positively influence, the design of games. Theories of the second and third order, on the other hand, strive for abstraction and greater systematic and historical insights. In order to achieve these goals, theoretical reflection has to remove itself (at least partly) from the everyday processes and challenges of artistic creation. Liberated from practice-related constraints, scholars can develop wider and more historical perspectives, enabling them to connect the essence of the medium with its past, and also the past of all other media and art forms. Distance from practice also affords a scope beyond the limits of the medium and all media, i.e., research that integrates Game Studies with other fields of knowledge—knowledge of other media and art forms, of one's own culture and other cultures, of psychology and pedagogy, of society, economy, and the sciences.

In a postmodern reality, both historical perspective and close relationships to other fields of knowledge have become essential preconditions for original artis-

---

3   Mäyrä: *An Introduction to Game Studies*, loc. 86.
4   GamesCoop: *Theorien des Computerspiels zur Einführung*, p. 11 and Beil: *Game Studies*, p. 2.
5   Egenfeldt-Nielsen et al.: *Understanding Video Games*, loc. 310.

tic creation that strives to go beyond constant repetition of the familiar, the proven, and the popular. As digitalization strips artistic practices of their relevance, new methods have to be found on a timely basis or even just in time. Thus, historical knowledge and theoretical reflection acquire a new degree of significance. It is essential to have a thorough understanding of traditional procedures of visual, auditory, and audiovisual production—that is, an adequate familiarity with traditional forms of narration and representation as they were developed historically in literature, the fine arts, theater, film, television, video, and, of course, particularly in analog games. Only such knowledge will enable game designers to recognize traditional patterns and to adroitly modify, or even defy, artistic conventions in their digital or transmedia productions.

Thus, it is not too difficult to demonstrate the 'value' and even the 'use value' of theoretical knowledge for creative practice. On the other hand, theoretical attempts to understand aesthetic artifacts, processes, and experiences, need to be informed by artistic practice. The distance from praxis that characterizes approaches from the social sciences and humanities seems to have produced some less than convincing research results. This distance might also be one reason behind the much-lamented lack of synthesis in Game Studies.

"[R]elying too heavily on existing theories will make us forget what makes games games," Jesper Juul wrote more than a decade ago, "It is the unique parts that we need to study now."[6] Though he was talking about the justification of a ludic perspective, his argument for freedom from the fetters of imported theories still holds: In order to properly understand digital games, and also in order to become an independent discipline, Game Studies must progress from theories of the second order to theories of the third order, from exaptive to adaptive abstractions—to genuine theories of digital games.

All along, a prime goal in the establishment of Game Studies has been the provision of a common ground, that is, a common terminology as well as accepted methods of research and shared perspectives with regard to subject matter. To achieve this, it is essential to integrate the specialized knowledge of game design theory. As the different histories of literary studies, theater studies, and film studies have shown us, genuine theories of aesthetic artifacts have always been developed through intensive engagement with the respective medium and its most important artifacts.

---

6 Juul, Jesper: "Games Telling Stories? A Brief Note on Games and Narratives," *Game Studies* July 1, 2001; http://www.gamestudies.org/0101/juul-gts/

Adaptative Approaches

The current situation—the coexistence of game design theories of the first order and social science and humanistic theories of the second order—suggests that Game Studies is only an emerging field of study. However, the imminent transition to theories of the third order should allow us to define and establish the analysis of digital games as a discipline. A historical example for the formation of a new discipline following the advent of a new medium is, as mentioned above, film studies. In the early 1960s, the first genuine film theories (theories of the third order) established a disciplinary common ground including terminology, methods of research, and shared perspectives. A similar, agreed upon[7] coherence concerning the boundaries of the discipline, about what is in and out, must be found for Game Studies as well.[8]

However, the orientation to the practices and procedures of the studies of older—analog—media should have its limits. For one, most established disciplines set a rather bad example when it comes to connecting and mediating academic research and scholarship with the aesthetic practices. Their discourses—their perspectives, their terminology—are not only very different from the discourses of the arts, but often oblivious to or even almost hostile towards creative production.[9] As a young, still developing discipline, Game Studies has the chance to avoid these mistakes. [10] Relying on knowledge accumulated in game design theory, we can integrate artistic perspectives into the new discipline from the beginning. The analysis of digital games would thus include the consideration of both "their logic as artifacts, things that have been produced" (Theodor W. Adorno)[11] and the 'logic of their production, things that are being produced.'

---

7   Such an agreement is always provisional, of course.
8   The development of schools of thought that is still awaited in Game Studies—see Mäyrä: *An Introduction to Game Studies*, loc. 206—would probably not be detrimental to such coherence.
9   See Freyermuth: "Angewandte Medienwissenschaften."
10 See also: "In other parts of the academy, study and practice are sadly closed off from one another. Film Production is often divorced from Film Study, Art Studio from Art History, Writing from Literature. Such divisions weaken both sides. Because of the power of digitale media itself, [...] we have an opportunity to avoid the divisions in Digital Media programs." (Janet Murray et al.: "Asking What Is Possible," p. 67)
11 Adorno, Theodor W.: "Valéry's Deviations" (*1960), in: Adorno, Theodor W./Rolf Tiedemann. *Notes to Literature*. vol. 1, New York: Columbia University Press 1991, pp. 137-173, here p. 138.

The motto informing games education at the Georgia Institute of Technology summarizes such an approach:

"If the Game Production programs rally around the cry 'You play games, now learn to make them'; and if the Game Studies programs declare, 'You play games, now learn to study them,' then we might respond, 'You must make games to study them, and you must study games to make them.'"[12]

The second opportunity for Game Studies to distinguish itself from older disciplines results from the fact that digital technology opens up new potentials for research as well as for teaching. Frans Mäyrä once remarked, "deep down, science and scholarship are much like games."[13] However:

"[R]ather than just playing a ready-made game, the work of a scholar is actually much more like that of a game designer, who must develop and implement a systematic structure for new ideas and then see how the creation is 'played with' by members of the academic community."[14]

Apart from the use of digital games for the transfer of knowledge, which Game Studies has an obligation to incorporate into its own teaching, it is up to game scholars to make creative and productive use of the observed parallel between academic research and game design. James Paul Gee recently proposed that the emerging field of New Digital Media Learning (NDML) should 'playfully force' the creation of so-called "worked examples," meaning exemplary research works around which disciplines are centered:

"Rather than waiting for the natural process to take its course, we could create 'play exemplars' that we could use as tools for thought and debate.[15] [...] Thus, it would be like a

---

12 Murray et al: "Asking What Is Possible," p. 60.
13 Mäyrä: *An Introduction to Game Studies*, loc. 100. See also Henry Jenkins: "Games follow something akin to the scientific process." (Jenkins, Henry: Confronting the Challenges of Participatory Culture: Media Education for the 21st Century, The John D. and Catherine T. MacArthur Foundation Reports on Digital Media and Learning, Cambridge, MA: The MIT Press 2009, p. 24; http://mitpress.mit.edu/sites/default/files/titles/free_download/9780262513623_Confronting_the_Challenges.pdf)
14 Mäyrä: Game Studies, loc. 106.
15 Gee, James Paul: *New Digital Media and Learning as an Emerging Area and 'Worked Examples' as One way Forward*, The John D. and Catherine T. MacArthur Founda-

game.[16] [...] Maybe this game would work to accelerate the growth of a new area, but it would be a fine enough outcome if it merely served to create collaboration and the emergence of common ground through interaction and debate, and not just through the fiats of funders and established disciplinary journals."[17]

Gee's proposal, to simulate and advance academic research as a form of pervasive game or alternate reality game, could guide Game Studies—especially if it defines itself through the integration of game design theory as an academic and artistic discipline, rather than merely as an academic one. It must be remembered: While reliable academic procedures and practices of research were established during the 19th century, artistic research—which had flourished in early modernity—was increasingly marginalized.

The dual-reason for this seems to be obvious in hindsight. For one, artistic research from the Renaissance to the Enlightenment hardly published its results and, thereby, failed with regard to verifiability. Its raison d'être was not the research itself, but rather the aesthetic production that was then based on it and which was, of course, 'published.' Second and more importantly, artistic study, by its very nature, could not follow the industrial standards that established themselves with the industrialization of academic and commercial research: detailed planning, Taylorization in execution, and reliable standardization in its presentation.

On the contrary, the hallmarks of artistic research were and still are unconventional and aesthetically willful, experimental arrangements that allow for chance, i.e., experiments that feature open results, creative dabbling, and stabbing in the dark. Artistic research also requires presentations of results, which fulfill not only academic-functional but also artistic-aesthetic criteria, i.e., provide sensory pleasure. Numerous parallels to gaming lie at hand. Tracy Fullerton has worked them out from the perspective of game design theory:

"Play as a process of experimentation—pushing boundaries and trying new things—is an area of common ground for artists and scientists, as well as children. [...] Play is recognized as a way of achieving innovation and creativity because it helps us see things differently or achieve unexpected results."[18]

---

tion Reports on Digital Media and Learning, Cambridge, Mass.: The MIT Press 2010, loc. 385.
16 Ibid., loc. 422.
17 Ibid., loc. 438.
18 Fullerton: *Game Design Workshop*, loc. 2887.

Today, artistic and academic investigation and research call for gamified approaches, whether in accordance with Gee's proposal or of some other variation. And which discipline, if not Game Studies, could and should attempt to realize the integration of academic and artistic methods and procedures, of theoretical and practical perspectives and research goals?

The current variations of Game Studies, whether shaped by the social sciences or the humanities, should therefore actively work at overcoming their distance from game design and its theories, particularly by lending consideration to the perspective of artistic production during teaching and by making the insights of game design theory useful for research. The thoughts of Egenfeldt-Nielsen et al. are still relevant today:

"At present, video game studies may have more questions than answers, more doubts than certainties. The rules are still being formed; the orthodoxies have not yet been established. And for the curious researcher, there are many worlds in need of exploration. Of course, this is part of why the field is so thrilling. In other words, the discipline welcomes you; there is much to be done."

4 Perspectives of Research 1: Digital Games

Five areas of study seem to be of particular note for the development of theories of the third order as well as for the constitution of Game Studies as an institutional discipline. These five areas have in common that they all combine artistic-technical practice in the development of digital games with media-historical and media-aesthetic reflection. In sketching these areas of study, I will follow the tetrad of game design described by Jesse Schell[1] and will then come to the overarching problem of the positioning of games in the context of the evolving digital media dispositif.

MECHANICS

The *mechanics* of a digital game demarcate its inherent borders, that which is technically possible in regard to action and narrative. Parallels can be drawn, from a media-technological perspective, to operating systems, and from a media-aesthetic perspective, to the genre conventions of other media. A promising Game Studies research field is, therefore, the relationship of game mechanics, as they are often coded into engines, to game genres. The categorizations of genres that are circulating in popular media are often contradictory and thereby reveal their own arbitrariness. So far, Game studies has not found convincing genre definitions either.[2]

---

1   See for Jesse Schell's tetrad p. 162ff.
2   Fgenfeldt Nielsen et al. suggest a genre classification according to the qualities of required player interactions and thereby arrive at the four-way division into *Action Games* (motor skills, hand-eye-coordination), *Adventure Games* (logical thinking, patience), *Strategy Games* (calculating numerous variables such as the behavior of other players, in the case of *continuous-time strategy games* with reaction speed) as well as

From the discussion of genres in literature and film we know that a decisive measure of artistic quality lies in the freedom and originality to select, combine, modify, adapt or exapt, break up and reconstitute, parody and destroy genre conventions, and in turn the genre expectations of the readers or viewers. Unlike in literature or film, the genres of which are primarily aesthetic constructions, game genres are based largely on coded mechanics. This interdependence of code and aesthetics is media-specific for digital games.

Marshall McLuhan once elaborated on his assertion that the medium is the message with the note that media differ in regard to "scale or pace or pattern."[3] Game mechanics contain precisely these qualities—they convey its "message," as Brenda Romero writes:

"Why is it important to make games with meaning in their mechanics? Why is the mechanic the message? For me, pure mechanic is pure player. There is nothing else—no story, no cut scene, no text, no outside influence—to accept responsibility for what has happened. The player followed the rules, and the result and resultant meaning is theirs alone."[4]

In Game Studies, genre theory must not only have mechanics as a central category for understanding of both the production and the reception of digital games—it should also reflect on its unique overdetermination in the tension that lies between media aesthetics and media technology.

Story

Henry Jenkins noted that the debate on storytelling in games rests largely on a lack of media specific differentiation of the transmedia term 'narration.'[5] Story-

---

Process-Oriented Games (understanding of systems and their manipulation). See ibid., loc. 1229ff.—An overview concerning the competing and inconclusive definitions of game genres that existed around the turn of the century is provided by Pias, Claus: *Computer-Spiel-Welten*, Munich: Sequenzia 2002, p. 4, note 4. There has been little evolution in the situation as it was described over a decade ago.

3   McLuhan: *Understanding Media*, loc. 164: "For the 'message' of any medium or technology is the change of scale or pace or pattern that it introduces into human affairs."
4   Cited from Fullerton: *Game Design Workshop*, loc. 2548.
5   Jenkins: "Game Design as Narrative Architecture."

telling is radically different in every analog-linear medium—literature, theater, film—and in every media-specific genre—the novel or short-story, drama or one-act play, feature films or shorts. With the expansion of storytelling from analog linearity to digital non- or multi-linearity, different narrative qualities arise once again. In order to understand these, Jenkins calls attention to spatiality as an essential aspect of storytelling in games; game designers don't tell stories, they design worlds with alternative courses of action.[6] Therefore, research towards a theory of interactive-nonlinear storytelling must focus on two things: (1) the specific possibilities to manipulate time and space in multi-linear narrations[7] and (2) the structural qualities of interactive action spaces and storylines that branch and emerge.[8]

AESTHETICS

Since the early industrial age, the relationship between (audio-)visual representation and reality has been the fodder for much discussion. In the context of imitative painterly realism, authenticity refers to genuineness of origin, i.e., to authorship. In the context of photorealism and its technical reproduction, authenticity refers to the genuineness of the content of the image, i.e., to the medium and its integrity. With digital games this complex issue of authenticity reconfigures itself in novel ways. The reason for this lies in two features of digital game image production: digital games are becoming increasingly "photorealistic" and digital game visuals are moving ever closer to "reality."

The first feature is produced by the specific audiovisual qualities of the medium: A central characteristic of the emerging digital media dispositif is hyper-realistic—non-indexical—image production. Of its three variations—hybridiza-

---

6   Ibid., p. 121.
7   As they were already tested in analog theme-park installations and the experience spaces of entertainment architecture, See for example Freyermuth, Gundolf S.: "Holodeck heute," *c't—magazin für computertechnik*, August 30, 1999, 72-77 http://freyermuth.com/reprints/archiv2008/reprintJMar2008/Holodeck_heute.html; and "Vegas, Virtuelle Stadt," *Telepolis*, March 9, 2000; http://freyermuth.com/reprints/Archiv2011/reprint_Sep_Dez_2011.html/vegas.html
8   See also Egenfeldt-Nielsen et al.: *Understanding Video Games*, loc. 327: "What does it mean, for instance, when a person's self-expression moves away from linear representations, such as books and films, and they find more meaning in interactive, non-linear systems where outcomes depend on player choices?"

tion, animation, and real-time rendering—the last one constitutes the special potential of digital games for simulation and 3D-world building.[9] Currently, the range of available means and possibilities for design and expression are growing exponentially. To take account of this in artistic production (in suitable and creative ways) presents a special aesthetic challenge that requires experimental testing and interdisciplinary research—especially as numerous points of intersection link digital games to other areas of artistic production (particularly to film) as well as to various modes of image production in the sciences and commercial endeavors.

For the past few years, digital games have not only generated photorealistic worlds and life forms which have no equivalent in reality; they have also penetrated ever further into everyday reality itself. Whereas analog and even early digital games seemed to exist outside of everyday life—in Huizinga's "magic circle"[10]—, they are now beginning to turn reality into a magic circle, through digital networking and mobilization. With mobile games, alternate reality games, and augmented reality games, the once strict separation of game and reality has been replaced by a "membrane [that] is actually quite porous," as Edward Castronova writes.[11]

A theory of the authenticity of digital games, which Game Studies has yet to develop, must focus on this twofold "realism effect": on the one hand, the assertion of a simulative hyperrealism in games; on the other hand, the superimposition and augmentation of reality through digital games, their mechanics, their narration, their aesthetics, and their technological interfaces.

TECHNOLOGY

In Schell's tetrad, the term 'technology' is taken to mean "any materials and interactions that make your game possible"—from the playing pieces or dice of

---

9   See Freyermuth: "Der Big Bang digitaler Bildlichkeit," p. 294.—In parallel with this improvement in audiovisual realism there were also a multitude of experiments in game development with non-realistic imagery, for instance in the traditions of the avant-garde movements of the 19th and 20th century (Impressionism, Cubism, Futurism, Surrealism, Abstract Art) and of popular culture (comic strips, graphic novels). See also p. 84, note 26.

10 Huizinga: *Homo Ludens*.

11 Castronova: *Synthetic Worlds*, p. 147.

analog board games to the high tech of digital games.[12] For their design as well as their use, technical interfaces have always been an essential component, the conduit to all playful interactions.[13] Chris Crawford once compared digital interactivity—the communication between player and game—with a continuous dialogue which occurs in distinctive cyclical steps, comparable to a conversation between Fred and Joe:

"Step One: Fred listens to what Joe has to say. [...] Step Two: Fred thinks about what Joe said. [...] Step Three: Fred expresses his response back to Joe. [...] Now the tables are turned; the ball is in Joe's court. Joe must listen to what Fred says; Joe must think about it and develop a reaction; then he must express his reaction back to Fred. This process goes back and forth until the participants terminate it."[14]

Until recently, listening and responding on the part of a game had been understood as purely metaphorical. Presently, however, a new turn is underway; the traditional *Graphical User Interface* (GUI) is competing against so-called *Natural User Interfaces* (NUIs). With the implementation of these easier and 'natural' methods of interaction—through gesture, touch, and speech control—a new and even more immersive way of using digital games is emerging.[15] A theory of interaction with digital games as a central desideratum of Game Studies has to recognize the interrelationship between interface and agency in its historical dependence from media aesthetic interests as well as contemporary media technological constraints.

---

12 Schell: *The Art of Game Design*, loc. 123.
13 See for example the short history of exergame interfaces in Ian Bogost's "The Prehistory of Exergaming." (Bogost: *Persuasive Games*, loc. 3525ff.)
14 Chris Crawford presented his basic ideas first in 1989 at the Game Developers Conference that he had founded. See the video recording: http://www.erasmatazz.com/personal/videos/fundamentals-of-interactivi.html. He is quoted here after a print version that was published four years later: Crawford, Chris: "Fundamentals of Interactivity". *The Journal of Computer Game Design* 7 (1993/94); http://www.erasmatazz.com/library/the-journal-of-computer/jcgd-volume-7/fundamentals-of-interactivi.html
15 For immersion in the digital transmedium see Freyermuth: "From Analog to Digital Image Space: Towards a Historical Theory of Immersion,," in: Dogramaci, Burcu/ Liptay, Fabienne (ed.), *Immersion in the Arts and Media*, Amsterdam: Rodopi [to be published in 2015].

TRANSMEDIA

With the transition from industrial to digital culture, the borders previously set by technology between media begin to fade.[16] What during analog times was separated through the incompatibility of different storage and distribution media—film, television, radio, as well as print with its medial variations of book, newspaper, magazine—is now fusing in production, distribution, and reception; among each other as well as with new, digital forms of expression and representation, which are—like digital games—already structured transmedially themselves.[17] Fictional 'worlds' come into existence both within individual transmedia works as well as between them.[18] Therefore, transmediality can be identified in two ways, both in general and in regard to digital games:

- intensive transmediality, the creation of a fiction or non-fiction container comprising several media, i.e., transcending the traditional media-borders within itself—for instance in digital games of the GTA-series (since 1997) or WORLD OF WARCRAFT (since 2004); and
- extensive transmediality, the diverse representation of one and the same material over and beyond a multitude of media—for instance in the science-fiction franchises STAR TREK (since 1965/66) and STAR WARS (since 1997).

Digital games operate transmedially within themselves in that they utilize both a variety of media for their own design[19] as well as incorporate complete works of other media, from paintings to radio shows and all the way to motion pictures.[20] Furthermore, digital games also integrate, both artistically and economically, into extensive transmedial contexts.[21] In this respect, it is central for Game Studies

---

16 See Freyermuth: "Der Big Bang digitaler Bildlichkeit," p. 312ff.
17 See Juul: *Half-Real*, loc. 99: "[G]ames are therefore transmedial in the same way that storytelling is transmedial."
18 See for worldbuilding p. 169ff.
19 Striking in comparison to film and also television is the role of the written word. No other audiovisual medium contains comparable amounts of text. Gamers have to be good and fast readers as, in many popular genres, their survival depends on their reading skills. See Freyermuth "Lesen wird in vielen Computerspielen zu einer Überlebensfähigkeit."
20 See Schell: *The Art of Game Design*, loc. 1326-29.
21 A significant aspect is the semi-continuation of play in forums, wikis, video portals, etc., as it helps to form communities and produces paratexts. Focusing on learning ef-

to develop a theoretical conception of digital games as 'transmedial total works of arts' and to determine their position in the evolving digital media dispositif between the poles of intensive and extensive transmediality.

All in all, the development of genuine theories of digital games (theories of the third order) relies on five areas of particular note:

- the interdependency between genre and mechanics,
- the question of the narrative manipulation of space and time,
- the issue of audiovisual authenticity,
- the relationship between interface and agency,
- the question of transmediality and the position of digital games within the digital media dispositif.

---

fects in internet communication, André Czauderna studied the mechanisms of such semi-continuation of play in a Pokémon forum: Czauderna, André: *Lernen als soziale Praxis im Internet: Objektiv hermeneutische Rekonstruktionen aus einem Forum zum Videospiel Pokémon*, Wiesbaden: Springer 2014.

5 Perspectives of Research 2: Serious Games

Digital games research has always revolved around attempts to define what a game is.[1] The variations of games that are not 'just' for entertainment, but are meant to transfer knowledge or skills as well, have been a part of these efforts. The specific object in this case was not simply to found the term 'serious games.' Rather, many other terms were proposed as possible alternatives, such as "persuasive games,"[2] "applied games,"[3] or "games for change."[4]

However important such attempts at defining or re-defining 'serious games' with regard to cultural or academic policies might be,[5] from the perspective of aesthetic theory they seem to be bound to pre-modern poetics in their search for ahistorical normativity, and thereby equally backwards and futile.[6]

Two of the more important aspects for the transfer of knowledge in digital games are:

---

1 Compare the systematic compilations by Salen/Zimmerman: *Rules of Play*, loc. 1270 and Schell: *The Art of Game Design*, loc. 1078.
2 Bogost, Ian: *Persuasive Games*. Bogost also speaks of "videogames with an agenda." (In: Murray et al: "Asking What Is Possible," p. 62)
3 Breitlauch, Linda: "Spielfreude als erfolgreiche Lern- und Therapiemethode," in: Inderst, Rudolf Thomas/Just, Peter (ed.), *Build 'em Up—Shoot 'em Down: Körperlichkeit in digitalen Spielen*, Glückstadt: Hülsbusch 2013, pp. 179-191.
4 See http://www.gamesforchange.org sowie http://www.g4ceurope.eu
5 See for example Egenfeldt-Nielsen et al.: *Understanding Video Games*, loc. 738: "Defining anything is a highly political project. Define games as narrative and the research grants are likely to end up with departments devoted to film or literature studies. Define games as a subcultural teenage phenomenon and studies of games are less likely to be funded by ministries of culture, to reach the pages of the "serious" press, or to be available in public or research libraries."
6 See Freyermuth: "Game Design und Game Studies."

- The exploration of the fields of study *mechanics, story, aesthetics, technology,* and *transmedia*—as described in the previous chapter—in the context of serious games;
- Placing serious games in the history of digital games as well as in the history of culture and media.

MECHANICS, STORY, AESTHETICS, TECHNOLOGY, TRANSMEDIA

Mechanics. In Game Studies, genre theory entails the investigation of the interdependence of genre aesthetics and mechanics.[7] In the context of serious games, the following research question comes to the fore: To what degree might the 'message' of the game mechanics (which often originate from entertainment games) limit, prefigure, or counteract the possibilities for expression?

Story. Narrative theory of games focuses on the double structure of spatiality and simultaneity in regard to open action spaces and alternative storylines. For serious games the important research question arises: What specific knowledge or what specific forms of knowledge can spatially structured storytelling best prepare for constructive learning processes, especially in comparison with traditional linear textual or audiovisual narratives?

Aesthetics. Unlike the majority of entertainment games, serious games have a simulative or representative relationship with reality and seek to influence real-world behavior. Therefore, serious games are crucial to the theory of digital game authenticity. In regard to their double 'realism effect'—in comparison to the related didactic or documentary forms of expression in literature, theater, and film—we must clarify what parts of them are fact or fiction, documentation or construction. Serious games inherently contain within themselves, as Lisa Gotto

---

7 An open question is also which genres serious games belong to or whether they constitute their own, distinct genre. For exergames, Ian Bogost suggests diverse "rhetorics" (of walking, of agility, of reflexes, of training, of motivation); see Bogost: *Persuasive Games*. Tobias Kopka, on the other hand, identifies exergames as a meta-genre that in principle can make use of the conventions of all game genres. See Kopka, Tobias: "Interface Control Meaning. Eine typologische Gegenstandssichtung des Phänomens Exergames," in: Freyermuth, Gundolf S./Gotto, Lisa/Wallenfels, Fabian (ed.), *Serious Games, Exergames, Exerlearning: Zur Transmedialisierung und Gamification des Wissenstransfers*, Bielefeld: transcript 2013, pp. 265-288.

writes, the historical status of the relationship between audiovisual mediality and reality:

"Serious games are serious also because they do not categorically differentiate between media and reality. They produce and transfer knowledge outside of a fixed order or invariable specifications. Exactly therein lies their media-practical and media-theoretical potential: to be the nucleus of a new dynamic of knowledge generation."[8]

The exact mechanisms, however, of knowledge transfer and knowledge production in the context of serious games and their dual relationship to reality are still to be researched. Various approaches have been attempted. Benjamin Beil, for instance, examined the "deep 'nesting' of entertainment game and serious game,"[9] and Dominik Wessely pursued the "different strategies of knowledge transfer by developers of (serious) games as well as by documentary filmmakers,"[10] concluding: "Game designers and developers are not yet subjected, in their productions, to a comparable pressure to prove their legitimacy as documentary filmmakers who are obliged to the (historical) truth."[11]

Technology. As the transfer of knowledge and learning in general depend on the reduction of the extrinsic load,[12] the design of interaction (limited by available interfaces) contributes significantly to the success of learning. A theory of interaction, located in the tension between media aesthetics and media technology, must be oriented towards determining the aesthetic and practical consequences arising from a reduction in complexity—which is enabled through interface design and crucial to every simulation. Provided that a certain realism of action is retained, the question then remains how reductions of complexity in serious games affect the transfer of knowledge or experiences, i.e., the learning process and the real-world application of what has been learned.

Transmediality. Serious games are more directly embedded in social and cultural processes than entertainment games—processes of learning and training but

---

8 Gotto, Lisa: "Einleitung zum Kapitel 'Serious Games'," in: ibid., pp. 139-143, here p. 143.
9 Beil, Benjamin: "Zwischen Planspiel und Trainingssimulator. Oder: Was man von Computerspielen (nicht) über den Krieg lernen kann," in: ibid., pp. 91-121, here p. 93.
10 Wessely, Dominik: "Fallstudie 1: New Horizon—Das Spiel mit der Geschichte. Historische Narration im Dokumentarfilm und Game," in: ibid., pp. 123-136.
11 Ibid., p. 128.
12 Zorn, Isabel: "Lernen mit digitalen Medien. Zur Gestaltung der Lernszenarien," in: ibid., pp. 49-74, here p. 60.

also of consumerism and the formation of political opinion. Therefore, serious game design and research require an understanding of the structures of extensive transmediality as well as the integration of practical skills and theoretical knowledge. It is here that Game Studies could set an example and work to bridge the schisms between expertise in game design, social sciences, and the humanities in order to bring artistic practice and academic theory together.

GAMIFICATION

For the last decade, *gamification* has been a key concept in bridging game design and Game Studies, digital games, serious games, and knowledge transfer. The term is problematic on two levels: (1) It is weighed down by the high degree of 'hype' and the exaggerated claims and unrealistic expectations of *gamification's* proponents, such as Jesse Schell[13], Gabe Zichermann, and Christopher Cunningham[14]; and (2) the term suffers from a narrow and slightly misleading connotation, which conveys *gamification* as merely the specific application of digital game elements—feedback mechanisms, competition, and reward systems—in areas that have had little affinity for games, such as marketing or education.

The historical phenomenon of replacing—largely unintentionally—industrial processes and values with playful ones, i.e., games, outdates the professionalized appropriation of game elements. Unsurprisingly, this long-lasting transformation began in the context of teaching and learning—when MIT students programmed SPACEWAR! in 1962, the first game that was played on computers.[15] To point: Industrial rationality and drill were displaced by the introduction of 'the playful' through games—both analog and digital. This shift heavily impacted the education and ideals of advanced western regions, and manifested itself in the process of gamification through the application of games. This also brought on a change in both knowledge production and knowledge transfer, between individuals and generations.

In this respect it seems useful to distinguish between gamification of the first and second order:

---

13 See Jesse Schell's popular talk at the *Dice 2010* conference http://www.gamification.org/wiki/Jesse_Schell_DICE
14 Zichermann/Cunningham: *Gamification by Design.*
15 See above p. 59f.

- An *invasive gamification*, which has been driven by a (to a large extent 'naturally' occurring) popularization of analog as well as digital games since the 1960s, as well as the intrusion of games into areas of life previously reserved for other media and practices;
- A *pervasive gamification*, which has—deliberately and professionally—appropriated and exapted elements of digital games for fields and purposes outside the area of games for the past decade.

OPPOSITION TO INDUSTRIALISM

Serious games prove to be a key research area for Game Studies, in part because their emergence over the last decade marks an ongoing change in the history of digital games in particular and digital culture in general. Since the early days of technical and cultural digitalization, its founding principle of virtualization, i.e., the replacement of hardware with software, seems to have affected a creeping loss of 'the real'—*The Murder of the Real*[16]—as well as a gradual abandonment of materiality, discussed in the so-called "disembodiment discourse."[17] Digital games were strongly blamed for both of these overwhelmingly negative terms. The standard accusation—often raised in comparison with 'natural' playing outdoors—was that digital games encouraged children and young adults to withdraw from nature and the public sphere into private fantasy worlds. Digital games—with their sedentary character—seemed to hinder the development of age-appropriate physical competencies and, in extreme cases, cause obesity.[18]

---

16 Baudrillard, Jean: "The Murder of the Real," in: Baudrillard, Jean/Witwer, Julia (ed.), *The Vital Illusion*, New York: Columbia University Press 2000, pp. 59-83. See as well the dromological explanation of the disappearance of reality: Virilio, Paul/Beitchman, Philip: *The Aesthetics of Disappearance*, New York N.Y.: Semiotext(e) 1991.

17 See for example Hayles, N. Katherine: *How We Became Posthuman: Virtual Bodies in Cybernetics, Literature, and Informatics*, Chicago Ill.: University of Chicago Press 1999.

18 The academic and public discussion is too manifold and contradictory to recreate here. A popular and somewhat contemporary account of the obesity-discussion is given by Sanghavi, Darshak: "Are TV and Video Games Making Kids Fat? The Effects of 'Screen Time' on Childhood Obesity," *Slate*, April 13, 2012; http://www.slate.com/articles/health_and_science/medical_examiner/2012/04/are_video_games_making_kids_fat_screen_time_and_childhood_obesity_.html

Serious games, however, and especially exergames and exerlearning games, aim precisely for the opposite effect. They exploit the two certainties of digitalization to their advantage—the loss of contact with reality and the process of disembodiment in dealing with the world of data. In their many variations—from games whose purpose it is to convey educational lessons, to games that attempt to further political enlightenment or try to change aesthetic perception—serious games do not strive to escape reality, but rather shape it positively through the dissemination of knowledge and experiences. Their main goal is to transfer that which is experienced, practiced, and learned by playing outside of reality, in "the magic circle"—generally thought of as escapism—back into reality. By the same token, exergames and exerlearning games turn digital games from a sedentary activity (which virtualizes analog movements and can be played with a few fingers) into a whole body exercise through the use of NUIs.

This process is often situated in social-historical, i.e., ideological contexts. Ian Bogost demonstrates that exergames "reveal the incongruence of work and exercise or leisure, and the prevalence of the ideological structures that push us to work more and move less."[19] Tobias Kopka points to the trend of quantified self-movement and the role of exergames in the "everyday, playful self-control, self-optimization, and self-disciplining."[20] Rolf F. Nohr, working through a historically-based analysis, recognizes the embodiment of digital games as a continuation of what began in early Industrialization: the colonization of the human body through technology by "accommodation, assimilation or immersion."[21]

A contradictory observation should be added to these analyses: with the conception of 'world-improving' utopian and critical games half a century ago—correlating with the shift from the industrial to the postindustrial—digital culture began. The gradual break down of industrial work ethic often reveals itself in the culture of the 1960s as a popularization of the playful: From Eric Berne's bestseller *Games People Play: The Psychology of Human Relationships* (1964)[22] to Joe South's hit song, which it inspired, *Games People Play* (1968), and Clark C. Abt's book *Serious Games* (1970)[23] to the *New Games* movement that Stewart

---

19 Bogost, Ian: *The Expressive Power of Videogames*, Cambridge, MA: MIT Press 2007, loc. 3802.
20 Kopka: "Interface Control Meaning", p. 268.
21 Nohr: "'Rhythmusarbeit': Revisited," p. 379.
22 Berne, Eric: *Games People Play: The Psychology of Human Relationships*, New York: Grove Press 1964.
23 Abt, Clark C.: *Serious Games*, New York: Viking Press 1970.

Brand initiated in the atmosphere of San Francisco's hippie culture and that was popular in the 1970s and early 1980s.[24]

Beside the long held notion that has connected games with the logic of (post-)industrialism, a second tradition started that is still relevant, as it places digital games—and especially serious games, which convey knowledge and promote awareness—in playful contention with Industrialism, its logic as well as its ethics.

---

24 Foundation, New Games/Fluegelman, Andrew: *The New Games Book*, Garden City, N.Y.: Dolphin Books 1976.

Epilog

Epilog

Academization and Aesthetic Production

In discourses of contemporary culture, new media, and new arts gain their importance only after a long delay. Already in the 1950s and 1960s, film had become—economically as well as culturally—a more influential medium than literature, all the while without having found much recognition at universities, in schools, or in the arts and culture sections of many newspapers and magazines. The same holds true today for digital games. The game industry has been growing more quickly than all other branches of audiovisual art and entertainment for quite some time now.[1] Digital games produce larger returns than motion pictures[2], and they are, at least with younger generations, more influential cultural-

---

[1] For growth in the US see for example ESA, Entertainment Software Association: "Essential Facts about the Computer and Video Game Industry," April 2014; http://www.theesa.com/facts/pdfs/ESA_EF_2014.pdf. For growth in Germany see for example N. N.: "Deutscher Markt für digitale Spiele wächst um sechs Prozent," *BIU - Bundesverband interaktive Unterhaltungssoftware*, August 7, 2014; http://www.biu-online.de/de/presse/newsroom/newsroom-detail/datum/2014/08/07/deutscher-markt-fuer-digitale-spiele-waechst-um-sechs-prozent.html

[2] In the US, the video game industry overtook Hollywood almost a decade ago, other countries caught up with this development a few years ago. For the US, see for example Yi, Matthew: "Stacks of New Releases for Hungry Video Game Enthusiasts Mean It's Boom Time for an Industry Now Even Bigger Than Hollywood," *San Francisco Chronicle*, December 18 2004; http://www.sfgate.com/news/article/THEY-GOT-GAME-Stacks-of-new-releases-for-hungry-2663371.php; for the UK, see for example Chatfield, Tom: "Videogames Now Outperform Hollywood Movies," *The Guardian*, December 27 2009; http://www.theguardian.com/technology/gamesblog/2009/sep/27/videogames-hollywood. For Germany see Probst, Maximilian: "Ballern ist nicht alles," *Die Zeit*, December 8 2012; http://www.zeit.de/2012/50/Computerspiele-Medium–Zukunft/komplettansicht

ly. However, public awareness as well as institutions of higher learning are reacting slowly to these developments.

THE CULTURAL RISE OF GAMES

The process of cultural perception clearly follows the model of the industrial media of film and television: economic and social success enables gradual recognition after initial resistance and criticism, which at its core is culturally conservative. This cultural rise is expressed not least by institutional integration:

- *Acceptance into the canon*—see for example (1) the "games canon," a list of video games to be preserved by the Library of Congress established in 2007,[3] (2) the proclamation of "games as cultural treasure" by the German Ministry of Culture in 2008,[4] and (3) the selection of video games by the New York Museum of Modern Art as part of its permanent collection in 2012[5];
- *Official Recognition*—see for example (1) "The Annual Game Developers Choice Awards," presented since 2001 during the Game Developers Conference, (2), the "German Computer Game Prize," jointly awarded by the German government and the game industry[6] since 2009, or (3) the American "Game Awards," backed by Sony, Microsoft, Nintendo, and the largest publishers, which was hosted for the first time in Las Vegas in 2014;[7]

---

3   See Schumann, Heidi: "Is That Just Some Game? No, It's a Cultural Artifact," *New York Times*, March 12 2007; http://www.nytimes.com/2007/03/12/arts/design/12vide.html?_r=0
4   See Zimmermann, Olaf/Schulz, Gabriele: *Streitfall Computerspiele: Computerspiele zwischen kultureller Bildung, Kunstfreiheit und Jugendschutz*, Berlin: Deutscher Kulturrat 2008; http://www.kulturrat.de/dokumente/streitfall-computerspiele.pdf
5   See Hoffman, Brendan: "MoMA Adds Video Games to Its Collection," *New York Times*, November 29 2012; http://artsbeat.blogs.nytimes.com/2012/11/29/moma-adds-video-games-to-its-collection/?_r=0
6   See http://www.deutscher-computerspielpreis.de/5.0.html and http://www.colognegamelab.de
7   N. N.: "Videogame Industry Rallies Around First 'Game Awards'," *Variety*, November 10, 2014; http://variety.com/2014/digital/news/videogame-industry-rallies-around-first-game-awards-exclusive-1201352339/

- *Establishment of relevant educational training and courses*—see for example in the US, (1) Cornell's "Game Design Initiative," which started in 2001 as the first undergraduate program in game design offered at an Ivy League institution,[8] or (2) the game design program at the University of Southern California, which was introduced in 2005 and has earned a number one ranking by the *Princeton Review*;[9] see for example in Germany (3) the bachelor program at the Berlin HTW University of Applied Sciences, offered since 2009[10] and (4) the English language further education masters program at the Cologne Game Lab of the TH Köln—University of Applied Sciences, which was established in 2010.[11]

As the institutional establishment of game design and Game Studies expands, questions arise regarding the process and consequences of such successive academization. In this epilog I will start by sketching the German status quo of current digital games education (*Games Studies and Game Design Education in Germany*). Next, André Czauderna will contribute a description and comparative analysis of game design programs at six other institutions in five countries (*International Game Design Education*). I will then present the structures of artistic-academic instruction at the undergraduate level, through the example of the bachelor program "Digital Games", offered since 2014 at the Cologne Game Lab (*Structure of the Undergraduate Program at CGL*). In conclusion, I will reflect on how the academization of digital games might influence production practices and the aesthetic evolution of this new medium (*Consequences of Academization*).

GAME STUDIES AND DIGITAL GAME DESIGN EDUCATION IN GERMANY

Education concerning digital games at German universities is currently characterized by two circumstances: (1) a roughly 10-year lag time between the estab-

---

8   See http://gdiac.cis.cornell.edu
9   See http://www.princetonreview.com/top-undergraduate-schools-for-video-game-desi gn.aspx, and Stephan, Scott: "USC Maintains Nation's Top Ranking in Game Design," *USC News*, March 11 2014; https://news.usc.edu/59927/usc-maintains-nations-top-rankings-in-game-design/
10 See http://gd-bachelor.htw-berlin.de
11 See http://www.colognegamelab.de

lishment of degree programs in Germany versus programs in Anglo-Saxon as well as Scandinavian and some Asian countries; (2) the strict division between theoretical-academic degree programs, found at universities, and those educational courses oriented towards artistic expression and craftsmanship, found at art colleges, technical universities, and universities of applied sciences. By comparison, US academic Game Studies courses and artistic game design courses, as well as the most influential Game Studies and game design professorships, can be found at leading universities, such as Carnegie Mellon University (CMU, Jesse Schell),[12] New York University (NYU, Eric Zimmerman),[13] or the University of Southern California (USC, Tracy Fullerton).[14]

Moreover, German game-related research and academic education have occurred mostly 'incidentally' until now, i.e., academics of other disciplines research and teach about digital games merely as supplementary material.[15] This

---

12 See http://www.etc.cmu.edu/blog/author/jschell/ and Schell: *The Art of Game Design*.
13 See http://gamecenter.nyu.edu/faculty/eric-zimmerman/ and Salen/Zimmerman: *Rules of Play*.
14 See http://cinema.usc.edu/directories/profile.cfm?id=6513&first=&last=referer%20&title=&did=18&=%2Finteractive%2Ffaculty.cfm&startpage=1&startrow=1 and Fullerton: *Game Design Workshop*.
15 For instance, the media scholar Benjamin Beil (University of Cologne; http://mekuwi.phil-fak.uni-koeln.de/12429.html?&L=1; Beil, Benjamin: *Game Studies: Eine Einführung*, Red guide, Berlin: Lit 2013); the education scholar Johannes Fromme (Otto von Guericke University Magdeburg; https://www.meb.ovgu.de/mitarbeiter/prof-dr-johannes-fromme/; Fromme, Johannes/Unger, Alexander (ed.): *Computer Games and New Media Cultures: A Handbook of Digital Games Studies*, New York: Springer 2012); the film scholar Lisa Gotto (ifs international film school cologne; http://www.filmschule.de/seiten/lehrende-prof-gotto.aspx; Gotto, Lisa: "Type Rider: Typenspiel und digitale Graphie," in: Beil, Benjamin/Freyermuth, Gundolf S./Gotto, Lisa (ed.), *New Game Plus: Perspektiven der Game Studies. Genres – Künste – Diskurse*, Bielefeld: transcript 2015, pp. 115-142); the media scholar Stephan Günzel (btk – University for Art & Design in Berlin; http://www.btk-fh.de/stephan-günzel; Günzel, Stefan: *Egoshooter: Das Raumbild des Computerspiels*, Frankfurt am Main: Campus 2012); the art scholar Thomas Hensel (Pforzheim University of Applied Sciences; https://www.hs-pforzheim.de/De-de/Gestaltung/Studienuebergreifende-Fachgebiete/Designwissenschaften/personen/Seiten/Inhaltseite.aspx; Hensel, Thomas: "Das Computerspiel als Bildmedium," in: GamesCoop (ed.), *Theorien des Computerspiels zur Einführung*, Hamburg: Junius 2012, pp. 128-146.), the communication scholar Christoph Klimmt (Hanover University of Music, Drama and Media; http://www.ijk.hmtm-hannover.de/

situation correlates with the low number of digital games academic conferences held in Germany. The "Clash of Realities" conference is a noteworthy example, which has taken place every two years since 2006 at the TH Köln—University of Applied Sciences and has brought representatives of Game Studies and game design into contact with each other since 2010.[16] Two more examples are the serious games conferences in Darmstadt and Hanover.[17] In contrast, game design conferences reach a much wider audience, particularly the Berlin developer-conference "Quo Vadis" and the Cologne "Game Developers Conference Europe" (GDCE), both with roughly 2,500 attendees per year.[18] Also based in Co-

---

de/institut/personen/prof-dr-christoph-klimmt-direktor/; Klimmt, Christoph: *Computerspielen als Handlung: Dimensionen und Determinanten des Erlebens interaktiver Unterhaltungsangebote*, Cologne: Halem 2006); the media scholar Jochen Koubek (Bayreuth University; http://medienwissenschaft.uni-bayreuth.de/menschen/prof-dr-jochen-koubek/; Koubek, Jochen, et al. (eds.), *Spielkulturen: Funktionen und Bedeutungen des Phänomens Spiel in der Gegenwartskultur und im Alltagsdiskurs*, Glückstadt: Hülsbusch 2013; the media economist Jörg Müller-Lietzkow (University of Paderborn; https://kw.uni-paderborn.de/institute-einrichtungen/mewi/arbeitsschwerpunkte/prof-dr-joerg-mueller-lietzkow/; Müller-Lietzkow, Jörg/Seufert, Wolfgang/Bouncken, Ricarda B.: *Gegenwart und Zukunft der Computer- und Videospielindustrie in Deutschland*, Dornach: Entertainment Media Verlag 2006); the media scholar Rolf F. Nohr (Braunschweig University of Art; http://www.hbk-bs.de/hochschule/personen/rolf-f-nohr/; Nohr, Rolf F.: *Strategie Spielen: Medialität, Geschichte und Politik des Strategiespiels*, Medien ' Welten, Münster u.a.: Lit 2008); the media scholar Claus Pias (Leuphana University of Lüneburg; http://www.leuphana.de/claus-pias.html; Pias, Claus: *Computer-Spiel-Welten*, Munich: Sequenzia 2002); the communication scholar Peter Vorderer (University of Mannheim; http://mkw.uni-mannheim.de/prof_dr_peter_vorderer/prof_dr_peter_vorderer/index.html; Vorderer, Peter: *Playing Video Games: Motives, Responses, and Consequences*, Mahwah, NJ. u.a.: Erlbaum 2006); the communication scholar Jeffrey Wimmer; http://www.tu-ilmenau.de/vwds/team/ehemalige-mitarbeiter/jeffrey-wimmer/; Wimmer, Jeffrey: *Massenphänomen Computerspiele: soziale, kulturelle und wirtschaftliche Aspekte*, Konstanz: UVK Verlagsgesellschaft 2013).

16 See http://www.clashofrealities.com. Starting in 2015, the conference will take place annually.

17 See http://www.serious-games.tu-darmstadt.de/gamedays/index.de.jsp and http://www.nordmedia.de/pages/veranstaltungen/serious_games_conference/

18 See http://qvconf.com/about/quo-vadis/ and http://www.gdconf.com/news/gdc_europe_2013_breaks_attenda.html

logne, "Gamescom" attracts well over 300,000 attendees per year and is "the world's largest gaming event" (measured by exhibition space and number of visitors).[19] These numbers indicate the striking discrepancy between the fascination that digital games inspire in so many (which includes their economic relevance) and the lack of educational offerings at the undergraduate and graduate levels by state universities.

Young people's interest in the field of digital game production has been primarily nurtured by private institutions, including the Games Academy (since 2000, locations in Berlin and Frankfurt),[20] the Mediadesign University of Applied Sciences (since 2014, locations in Berlin, Munich, Düsseldorf),[21] the QANTM Institute (in Germany since 2005, locations incl. Berlin, Cologne, Hamburg, international locations incl. Australia, Singapore, Great Britain, Holland, Austria)[22], as well as the Macromedia University of Applied Sciences (since 2006, location for game design, Stuttgart).[23] These private providers reacted relatively early to the lack of state-funded educational opportunities and quickly addressed an educational shortcoming. However, private providers can be expensive—a Bachelors degree costs several tens-of-thousands of Euros, something Germans are not accustomed to—and they must be profitable in the short-term. Therefore, they strive to meet the current market concerns of their customers with more craft-oriented training.

State-funded education, on the other hand, can operate with a mid- and long-term horizon, concentrating on a solid academic foundation while promoting critical reflection, artistic ambition, and far-reaching economic perspective. This model is based upon theoretical and historical instruction concerning academic-artistic experiments, which encourages intellectual as well as aesthetic risk-taking. The goal should not be limited to merely teaching the status quo; rather it should also enable students to independently react to future technological and aesthetic developments. However, German state-sponsored education in digital games has been heavily influenced by its incidental origins: There have been repeated attempts to integrate Game Studies and game design as a subspecialty of already existing programs, such as computer science, media economics, media, and film studies, as well as various design programs, including interface and interaction design. As of this writing, only two state-funded undergraduate pro-

---

19 See https://en.wikipedia.org/wiki/Gamescom
20 http://www.games-academy.de
21 http://www.mediadesign.de
22 http://de.sae.edu/de/home/
23 http://www.macromedia-fachhochschule.de

grams focus on digital games: the bachelor degree program "Game Design" at the HTW Berlin University of Applied Sciences[24]—which will be analyzed in the following subchapter—and Cologne Game Lab's bachelor degree program "Digital Games" at the TH Köln University of Technology, Arts and Sciences[25] in Cologne—which will be discussed in the subchapter after next.[26]

INTERNATIONAL HIGHER GAME DESIGN EDUCATION: SIX EXAMPLES FROM FIVE COUNTRIES
By André Czauderna[27]

The international field of game design education is in flux. More and more universities offer undergraduate and postgraduate programs in game design and/or game development.[28] This subchapter focuses on Bachelor of (Fine) Arts programs, rather than their Bachelor of Science counterparts or postgraduate programs, and exemplifies concepts from different universities in five countries (Germany, Great Britain, Switzerland, Spain and the United States). Comparing the curricular structures of these programs, the subchapter reconstructs a model of higher game design education that considers not only the creative and technological design and development of digital games, but also their wider aesthetic, historical and cultural contexts and implications.

After a short description of each of the selected programs in the first section of the subchapter, the similarities and differences among the various curricular approaches will be elaborated in the second section. This comparative analysis

---

24 http://gd-bachelor.htw-berlin.de
25 http://www.colognegamelab.de
26 There are also some state-funded graduate programs focusing on digital games; for example, at Hamburg University of Applied Sciences (http://www.gamesmaster-hamburg.de) and at Bayreuth University (http://computerspielwissenschaften.uni-bayreuth.de). Starting in summer 2017, the Cologne Game Lab at TH Köln—University of Applied Sciences will also offer a consecutive Master's program "Digital Games."
27 André Czauderna is an education researcher holding a PhD from Johannes Gutenberg University Mainz. His research interests include learning in video game affinity spaces, the development of creativity, game design education, and didactics in higher education. André works at the Cologne Game Lab of the TH Köln, where he is responsible for the management and development of the study programs.
28 See e.g. Hevga—The Higher Education Video Game Alliance: *Our State of Play. Survey 2014-15*, 2015; http://www.higheredgames.org

of curricular approaches constitutes a reconstruction of a common model of higher game design education based on the following criteria: generalist and specialist education, variety of contents, design over technology, student body diversity, variety of games, learning in collaborative projects, and general education. The subchapter will conclude in the third section by summarizing the model and contextualizing it in relation to the concepts and analyses of Janet Murray, Ian Bogost, Michael Mateas and Michael Nitsche[29] as well as Colleen Macklin and John Sharp.[30]

1. Examples from Germany, Great Britain, Spain, Switzerland, and the United States

The following programs will be described in detail:

- the Game Design BA at HTW Berlin University of Applied Sciences, Germany;
- the Design BA (Major in Game Design) at Zürcher Hochschule der Künste, Switzerland;
- the Game Design and Development Bachelor (Grado Universitario) at ESNE (Escuela Universitaria de Diseño, Innovación y Tecnología), Universidad Camilo José Cela, Spain;
- the Game Design BA at University of the Arts London, Great Britain;
- the Game Design BFA at New York University, USA;
- the Interactive Entertainment BA at University of Southern California, USA.[31]

Game Design BA, HTW Berlin University of Applied Sciences

The Game Design BA at the HTW Berlin was established in 2009.[32] This program, directed by Susanne Brandhorst and Thomas Bremer, is the oldest under-

---

29 Murray, Janet/Bogost, Ian/Mateas, Michael/Nitsche, Michael: "Game Design Education: Integrating Computation and Culture," *Computer*, 39(6), 2006, pp. 43-51.
30 Macklin, Colleen/Sharp, John: "Play, Make, Appreciate: A Games Education Manifesto," talk at the GDC Education Summit 2013; http://www.gdcvault.com. See also: http://playmakeappreciate.tumblr.com
31 All quotes in this section that are not linked to an article or book stem from the respective program's website or online brochure mentioned in the beginning of the respective subsection.
32 http://gd-bachelor.htw-berlin.de

graduate Bachelor's degree program at a German public university[33] which is solely dedicated to the interdisciplinary education of game designers.

The three-and-a-half year program, offered in the German language, includes the following areas of study: Game Art (Environmental Art, Character Art, 3D Art, 2D Art, Lighting Art, etc.); Game System Design (Game Mechanics, Balancing, Monetization, Level Design, etc.); Game Technology (Computer Science, Game Engines, Programming, etc.); Game Producing (Business, Project Management, Product Development, etc.); Game Studies (Theory of Game and Play, Psychology, Social Science, Cultural Science, etc.).

After a first year of basic studies, the approximately 40 students per year (selected through a competitive aptitude test) are invited to develop a specialized individual profile—by selecting project roles and electives—that fulfills the affordances of the gaming industry in a certain area. The following specializations are available: Game System Design, Level Design, and Game Art. Starting at the end of the third year, students must complete an internship of at least 18 weeks.

At HTW Berlin, game development (including its technological aspects) is seen as a design process. Consequently, the course leaders clearly distinguish their program from computer science-centered approaches. Artistic and technical disciplines are perceived as equals, resulting in a holistic approach to game design. In the course of their project-oriented studies, students realize three to four digital games in teams of two to ten people. In spite of a strong focus on game design practice, emphasis is also placed on the theoretical foundations of games with the objective of educating reflective practitioners.

In accordance with Germany's funding system of higher education, HTW Berlin does not charge tuition fees.

Design BA, Zürcher Hochschule der Künste (ZHdK)

Although Game Design at ZHdK is not a stand-alone study program—instead it is part of the three-year Design BA where it can be selected as a major, available since 2010—, its contents are comparable with those of the other programs presented in this subchapter.[34] According to ZHdK's website, the program, taught in Swiss German, aims to teach "conceptual, creative, and technological expertise in the development and implementation of computer-based games." At ZHdK, undergraduate game design education follows a strong generalist approach. Ul-

---

33 In Germany, the majority of (high-level) university education takes place at public universities. There is no significant system of elite private institutions, as in the US, for instance.

34 http://gamedesign.zhdk.ch

rich Götz, director of the game design branch at ZHdK, explains: "Our students leave the university as profoundly trained designers, but also as computer scientists."[35]

At ZHdK, the approximately 15 game design students per year (selected through a competitive aptitude test) encounter the following topics: Design, Interface Design, Game Writing, 3D Modeling and Animation, Scripting and Programming, Sound Design, Production Methods, Game Rules, Game Mechanics, Gameplay, Level Design, Interactive Storytelling, Narration, Drama, Game Logic and Artificial Intelligence, Game Design, Game Analysis, Usability Design, and Game Business. Furthermore, students can participate in research projects and experiments focusing on topics such as Serious Game Design, Interface, and Game Controller Development.

The Design BA at ZHdK costs 720 CHF per semester (i.e., twice a year) plus an additional semester fee of 500 CHF for foreign students (in 2015).

Game Design and Development Bachelor, Escuela Universitaria de Diseño, Innovación y Tecnología (ESNE)

ESNE, a private university school specialized in design, technology, and innovation, offers a four-year Game Design and Development Bachelor program (Grado Universitario).[36] The degree is awarded by the Universidad Camilo José Cela in Madrid, Spain. The language of instruction is Spanish.

ESNE's curriculum reveals an interdisciplinary and generalist approach to game design education covering a wide range of topics from the fields of Game Arts, Game Design, and Game Programming throughout the study program. It differs from the other approaches presented in this subchapter insofar as the curriculum does not include a significant amount of classes in the humanities and social sciences (apart from Art History in the first year).

According to ESNE's website, the school developed its curriculum in close consultation with the industry in order to fulfill their actual needs. On the website, it is also stated that the school intends to qualify its alumni not only for the development of games, but also other types of applications for computers, mobile devices, and online platforms in order to increase their job prospects.

Tuition fees at ESNE are 8,323 EUR per academic year (in 2015/2016).

---

35 Quoted in: Eschbach, Andrea: "Mehr als Ego-Shooter," *Page*, 4/2008 (translation by A.C.).

36 http://www.esne.es/oferta-academica/grados/grado-en-diseno-y-desarrollo-de-videojuegos

Game Design BA, University of the Arts London (UAL)

UAL offers a three-year Game Design BA.[37] On the university's website, course director Roy Caseley places special emphasis on the combination of theory and practice, the diversity of the student body and the high value of collaborative projects with students of other departments, such as Sound Art and Animation.

The program combines a project-oriented "concept-to-game approach"; instruction in technological areas, such as programming and asset manipulation; and Game Studies, the critical reflection on digital games and their players. UAL's philosophy of game design strongly stresses that "the game designer must consider the types of player he wishes to entertain and under which circumstances players will experience a game." Therefore, social sciences and psychology are of high importance within UAL's game curriculum.

According to the university's program description, students will:

- "Critically analyze and discuss theoretical issues in order to understand Games Design within a broad cultural context and the specific context of Games Studies.
- Develop design skills to support a variety of game systems and experiment with original mechanics and player challenges.
- Gain the technical knowledge to develop and evaluate games for a variety of platforms and markets.
- Develop the communication skills to enable effective team working and present game concepts to a variety of audiences.
- Embed research skills necessary to cope with the fast pace of technological change in the games industry to ensure continual professional development.
- Develop the ability to describe games as cultural artifacts with credibility in order to undertake research through post graduate study.
- Ensure students are confident with the concept of play in games design theory and practice in order to critically understand the motive forces inherent in games design."

At UAL, tuition fees are 9,000 GPB for EU citizens and 15,180 GBP for international students (in the academic year 2014/2015).

Game Design BFA, New York University (NYU)

Since January 2015, the Game Center of the Tisch School of the Arts at NYU offers a four-year Game Design BFA—in addition to its already existing Game Design MFA.[38] At the core of the Center's art school approach lies the "explora-

---

37 http://www.arts.ac.uk/lcc/courses/undergraduate/ba-hons-games-design
38 http://gamecenter.nyu.edu

tion of games as a cultural form and game design as creative practice." The program teaches the "fundamentals of game design, game development and critical scholarship" including analog games as well:

"Over the course of four years, you will learn about the theory and practice of making games on and off the computer. This includes everything from the history and scholarship of games to the psychology of player experience to the mathematics of game rules. Our graduates will be the game creators, critics, and scholars that will change the industry and [...] set the world on fire with play."

While at the beginning of their studies students acquire a broad game literacy—"a solid foundation," as stated on the Game Center's website—, students later find a specialization according to their individual interests and talents. Consequently, the Game Center describes its curriculum as "broad and deep, letting [students] focus on game programming, game design, visual design for games, game criticism, or other areas."

The interdisciplinary program includes coursework from seven fields, each field representing a facet of the "complex interdisciplinary endeavor of making and studying games":

- "Primary Areas:
  o Game Studies: Academic, scholarly, and journalistic approaches to games
  o Game Design: Creating the rules of the game and the player experience
  o Game Development: Production processes for creating games

- Production Areas
  o Programming: Interaction, graphics, AI, and other game programming
  o Visual Design: 2D and 3D animation, graphic design, and art direction
  o Audio Design: Music, sound effects, and audio programming
  o Game Business: Marketing, revenue models, and the game industry"

In the final year, "in addition to other advanced-level courses" students have to complete a senior capstone project that "can take a variety of forms, from an individual or group game to a game-related research paper or exhibition."

In the tradition of American liberal arts education, the Game Center offers its BA students a broad general education on top of a more specific game design education:

"A well-rounded education is a cornerstone of the Tisch approach to undergraduate studies. Combining intensive hands-on learning in the creative field of game design, with a world-class education in the liberal arts, students graduating from Tisch are not only prepared to work in their field but are prepared to work in the 21st century as global citizens. With over one-third of the curriculum requirements devoted to writing, humanities, sciences and social sciences, we are making sure that all of the Game Design BFA students explore the intellectual world around them [...]. [Y]ou need a great education to make great games. [...] Games are interdisciplinary by nature, and a great game designer will be one who draws from their life and educational experiences."

In addition, it is assumed that game design education, as it is offered at NYU, imparts a unique "way of thinking about the world":

"If you study history, if you study literature, if you study science and engineering, you're not just studying for a job in that field, you're using that as a structuring element to understand everything else," said Frank Lantz, the director of the Game Center. The undergraduate degree, he said, would help students understand "the significance of game design as not only a potential career but as a way of thinking about the world."[39]

In general, studying in the US is more expensive than it is in Europe. At NYU, tuition fees are ca. 48,000 USD per year.

Interactive Entertainment BA, University of Southern California (USC)

The Interactive Entertainment BA at the Interactive Media & Games Division of the School of Cinematic Arts (SCA) of the University of Southern California (USC) has been voted the best undergraduate game design program in North America for six straight years (from 2010 to 2015) by the Princeton Review.[40] The program is very much shaped by the ideas of Tracy Fullerton who teaches the core game design courses at SCA. Fullerton's textbook *Game Design Workshop: A Playcentric Approach to Creating Innovative Games*,[41] which is mean-

---

39 Suellentrop, Chris: N.Y.U. to Add a Bachelor's Degree in Video Game Design, The New York Times, August 5, 2014; http://artsbeat.blogs.nytimes.com/2014/08/05/n-y-u-to-add-a-bachelors-degree-to-video-game-studies/?_php=true&_type=blogs&smid=p l-share&_r=1
40 http://games.usc.edu
41 Fullerton: *Game Design Workshop*.

while available in its third edition, maps the program's core game design curriculum.

USC's Game faculty includes several renowned game designers, such as Richard Lemarchand (UNCHARTED) and Peter Brinson (The CAT AND THE COUP), as well as influential media scholar Henry Jenkins, who supports the Interactive Entertainment BA as a professor at USC's Annenberg School for Communication and Journalism.

The philosophy of the Interactive Media & Games Division is consistent with the approach of the School of Cinematic Arts as a whole, which believes in "stressing creativity of expression, experimentation and excellence in execution." Similar to NYU's Game Design BFA, the Interactive Entertainment BA offers a combination of a liberal arts education and the specialization in a vocation, i.e., game design (or one of its branches). In line with this approach, students participate in USC's general education program that

"provides a coherent, integrated introduction to the breadth of knowledge you will need to consider yourself (and to be considered by other people) a generally well-educated person. This program requires six courses in different categories, plus writing, foreign language and diversity requirements, which comprise the USC Core."

Students in the Interactive Entertainment BA mix pre-professional courses at the USC Dornsife College of Letters, Arts and Sciences (including the general education requirements) and courses in the main subject, chosen from the curriculum of the School of Cinematic Arts. The study requires a total of 128 units, including a minimum of 48 units in the major.

Despite its high proportion of general education units, the program otherwise pursues a hands-on approach strongly focused on the practice of game development:

"Students make games at all levels of the program gaining hands-on skills across a range of digital media arts. Hands-on skills are taught within a vibrant community of thought that explores new models of interactivity as well as emerging markets and platforms for playful media. Emphasis is placed on collaboration, teambuilding, innovation and creative leadership."

In addition to the Interactive Entertainment major at the SCA, the following minors can be chosen: Game Animation, Game Audio, Game Design, Game Entrepreneurism, Game User Research, and Game Studies. On top of that, the minors in 2D Art for Games and 3D Art for Games can be selected at USC's Roski School of Art and Design.[42]—The tuition fee is ca. 49,500 USD per year.

2. Comparative Analysis of Curricular Approaches

Comparing the curricular (and—to a lesser extent—the didactic) approaches of the examined study programs, this section will reconstruct a common model of game design education that does not only aim at short-term employability, but also at a sustainable preparation for the labor market of the 21st century (in and beyond the gaming industry) as well as the facilitation of students' intellectual and creative abilities, which are valuable beyond the workplace.

Generalist and Specialist Education

The programs featured in this subchapter—as well as the Digital Games BA at TH Köln that is discussed in the next chapter—pursue an approach to game design education that aims to educate its students as both generalists and specialists. The curricula of all programs imply the assumption that academically educated game professionals should own:

- a basic understanding of the work done in all departments involved in game development as well as its media-theoretical contexts and economic conditions, and
- a specialization in one of the departments, such as Game Design, Game Arts, Game Programming or Game Producing—though the depth and degree of formality of specialization strongly varies between study programs.

An individual student's specialization might include a further, more in depth specialization in a certain sub-field, which is especially true in the domain of Game Arts, where some students specialize as Character Designer, Environment Artist, 2D or 3D Animator, or 3D Modeler at an early stage.

At the end of their studies, graduates are either generalists with an informal specialization in one of the departments involved in game development (e.g.,

---

42 At this point, it should be mentioned that the USC Viterbi School of Engineering, which also belongs to the area of USC Games, offers a B.Sc. in Computer Science (Games). The aim of this program is "to graduate students with a solid grounding in computer science and a cross-disciplinary background in game development."

NYU) or specialists in one of these departments with a solid understanding of the other departments (e.g., TH Köln).

Variety of Contents

In their generalist philosophy, all programs offer an enormous variety of classes, ranging from Figure Drawing to Artificial Intelligence to Publishing. Overall, courses can be classified to the following five core areas of study: Game Design (understood as the design of gameplay, mechanics, and narration); Game Arts (including CG Art, Animation, Sound Design, etc.); Game Programming & Engineering; Producing, Project Management, Business Administration, and Entrepreneurship; and Media & Game Studies (including approaches from the humanities, social sciences, and economics).

Design over Technology

Above all, the described programs target the education of *designers* who create gameplay, mechanics, and narration (Game Designers); interface, characters, and environments (Game Artists); or source code (Game Programmers). In this sense, technology is primarily seen as a means to an end.

In the case that programs are concerned with the education of programmers, they do not aim to educate computer scientists, but creatively trained programmers who work at the intersection of design, arts, and technology—as gameplay programmers, for instance.

In a division of labor between university departments, the training of highly specialized programmers, who are also needed for game development, are left to the general computer science programs and the BSc Game Design/Game Development programs.

To sum up, all programs presented in this subchapter prioritize design over technology.

Student Body Diversity

Although the gaming industry is quite diverse when it comes to categories such as national origin and academic background, its gender diversity is rather low. According to IGDA's Developer Satisfaction Survey 2014, only 22 percent of people working in the gaming industry are females.[43] In light of this fact, the ob-

---

43 Edwards, Kate/Weststar, Johanna/Meloni, Wanda/Pearce, Celia/Legault, Marie-Josée: *Developer Satisfaction Survey 2014. Summary Report*, International Game Developers Association, igda.org. 2014, 9; https://c.ymcdn.com/sites/www.igda.org/resource/colle

served programs set gender diversity as a central goal. HTW Berlin course leaders, for instance, emphasize that the percentage of female students in their Game Design BA is approximately 50 percent.

The trend towards gender balance can be verified by a survey from The Higher Education Video Game Alliance (Hevga):[44]

"The average percentage of women in undergraduate programs is slightly more than 30%, with highest representation reported at 57% women. The average is nearly 33% at the graduate level. By contrast, women made up 17.6% of undergraduate and 28.2% of master's degrees conferred in computer and information sciences, and 17.2% of undergraduate and 22.7% of master's degrees in engineering and engineering technologies."[45]

However, diversity—as a goal of the presented programs—does not only subsume the integration of female students. It is about the inclusion of persons who are not attributable to the core target group of AAA games in general.

This trend towards a diversified student body fits to broader developments such as a changing market of digital games and the opening of the gaming industry to new target groups. Programs assume that a diverse student body—accompanied by the inclusion of new perspectives—helps to think outside the box of traditional game development and contributes to the diversification of game concepts (concerning aesthetics, mechanics and narration). An increase in diversity of digital games (including new innovative forms of games and play), in turn, allows for greater reach to new broad and diverse audiences.[46]

---

ction/9215B88F-2AA3-4471-B44D-B5D58FF25DC7/IGDA_DSS_2014-Summary_R eport.pdf

44 Hevga surveyed 73 colleges and universities from 5 countries and 27 different U.S. states and Canadian provinces.

45 Hevga: *Our State of Play*, 3.

46 In recent years, this philosophy has been represented repeatedly on the Education Summit of the Game Developers Conference in San Francisco. Many presentations and panels pointed to the advantages of diverse teams for the development process (e.g. Macklin/Sharp: "Play, Make, Appreciate"; Isbister, Katherine: "Game Design Education 10+ Years," Talk at the GDC Education Summit 2014; Fernandez-Vara, Clara/Wlochowski, Julia/Gomez, Elaine/Lemoine, Elyse/Kiai, Deirdra 'Squinky': "Increasing Gender Diversity in Game Development Programs," Talk at the GDC Education Summit 2015; http://www.gdcvault.com

Variety of Games

In accordance with the above-mentioned trend towards the diversification of the student body, the programs described in this subchapter not only encourage students to deal with long-established genres (based on well-known aesthetics, mechanics and narrative forms; sold by the AAA industry to the former core audience of digital games), but also support engagement with new genres and game forms, such as serious games, virtual/augmented reality games, indie games, and art games.

It is part of the ethos of academic freedom to devote oneself to games that might not earn money immediately (but require long-term development effort and/or new business models) or are non-commercial per se, but offer aesthetically, mechanically or narratively different concepts than those currently offered by the AAA industry.

Overall, programs intend to promote a broad game literacy based on the engagement with a variety of genres and game forms. Consequently, graduates should be qualified not only for the present and future of AAA development, but also for smaller and newly emerging areas of the gaming industry (such as its serious games sector) as well as for freelancing and development of their own companies. Furthermore, programs envision related creative industries (such as software development, broadcasting, and journalism), other technology industries (such as the automotive and aerospace industries) as well as still undefined fields that require 21st century design and system thinking, as potential fields of work for game designers.[47]

Learning in Collaborative Projects

When it comes to didactics, the programs presented in this subchapter exhibit an art school style project orientation. This implies the notion that learning in game school should not be based on ex-cathedra teaching and top-down instruction. Instead, it relies on constructivist theories of learning, on learning-by-doing, and peer-to-peer learning, among other things.

Learning in projects, as applied in the respective programs, usually rests upon a collaboration of individuals in interdisciplinary teams. This is noteworthy for two reasons. First, according to the theory of situated learning, it is particu-

---

47 This claim is justified by Miguel Sicart (Sicart, Miguel: "Teaching Beyond the Industry," Talk at the GDC Education Summit 2015; http://www.gdcvault.com). Sicart proposes to teach "game design thinking," i.e., to not only train game designers, but "reflective practitioners," who are able to design and to produce "other playful things" or "playable media," in addition to games.

larly promising to learn in "communities of practice."[48] Second, the above-mentioned collaboration in teams is supposed to prepare students for their future everyday work in the gaming industry that heavily relies on the ongoing collaboration in diverse interdisciplinary teams.

General Education

Although programs examined in this subchapter work with the gaming industry and usually consider its needs in curriculum development, they pursue an approach that goes beyond the short-term tailor-made creation of specialists for the gaming industry. Their model of game design education can be clearly differentiated from solely vocational approaches.

Programs' curricula usually entail a set of classes from the humanities, social sciences, and in some cases natural sciences (USC/NYU). In particular, the programs at NYU and USC (and TH Köln) value theoretical perspectives through the comprehensive inclusion of respective professorships and a high ratio of theory classes. NYU and USC programs are part of the tradition of liberal arts education and thus include a broad choice of classes (from anthropology to neuroscience) that are not necessarily linked to game development in an obvious way.

In all cases, programs aim at academic education in general: the facilitation of a broad store of reference knowledge as well as analytical and critical thinking skills; the broadening of students' horizons; and the support of an intellectual and creative mindset, among other things—all of which are assessed as valuable for game development as well as personality and identity development. In this sense, programs prepare students not only for the workplace (in and beyond the gaming industry), but also for life in general during the 21st century.

While a high level of integration of content from the humanities and social sciences is not always immediately appreciated by parts of the gaming industry and future students alike, large portions of the providers of game-related programs queried in the Hevga-Survey (most of them from North America) believe that the traditional liberal arts are "important" or even "very important" for game design education.[49]

This position has already been justified nearly a decade ago by Janet Murray, Ian Bogost, Michael Mateas, and Michael Nitsche who illustrate the usefulness

---

48 Lave, Jean/Wenger, Etienne: *Situated Learning: Legitimate Peripheral Participation*, Cambridge: Cambridge University Press 1991.

49 Hevga: *Our State of Play*, p. 4: "More than three-fourths of respondents indicated that the traditional liberal arts are important to game-related programs and students in the field; nearly 42% say they are very important."

of a liberal arts approach of game design education by referring to the distinction between "predictably useful" and "unpredictably useful":

"Vocationally focused university programs and trade schools have seized upon the opportunity to supply the next set of technically trained personnel for the game industry—but we must still determine who will supply the next set of visionaries and artists.
[...] Fields like business, medicine, and computer science seem practical because they are predictably useful: We can know in advance how to reap immediate gain from them. By contrast, the humanities are unpredictably useful: We cannot know in advance how they might serve us.
As the name suggests, the humanities help us understand what it means to be human, no matter the contingencies of profession, economics, or current affairs. [...] It is this unpredictable usefulness, this postponed fungibility in the humanities that people so often mistake for uselessness.
In large part, education for the game industry is predictably useful. Studios need skilled workers who can write C++ code, model 3D objects, configure massive networks, and perform a host of other practical tasks. [...]
The game industry needs technically competent developers, artists, and designers fundamentally versed in the rich subtleties of human experience. This is perhaps the most promising and valuable collaboration academia could provide the game industry: potential developers, artists, designers, and marketers with a meaningful understanding of the human condition and the ability to express themselves through video games. This collaboration is less about the actual than the possible. As such, it requires a leap of faith, more on the part of industry than academia."[50]

3. Conclusion

All programs presented in this subchapter (as well as the BA Digital Games at TH Köln) combine a vocational higher education and—in varying degrees—a broader academic education including content from the humanities and social sciences. On the one hand programs teach a range of necessary generalist and specialist skills for immediate employability in the gaming industry. On the other hand programs take into account that "if the fit [to the current industry] is too narrow and the program too short-sighted in serving the immediate hiring needs, its graduates might find their skills losing value when the needs of the industry

---

50 Murray/Bogost/Mateas/Nitsche: "Game Design Education," pp. 45-46.

shift in response to new technologies."[51] Thus, programs aim to impart enduring and transferable 21st century knowledge and skills including communication and collaboration competencies as well as an academic and creative mindset and habitus—valuable for a constantly changing work life, but also a fulfilling creative and intellectual life beyond the workplace.

All in all, programs are highly concerned with the short- and long-term employability of their graduates as well as the short- and long-term needs of the gaming industry. Different from pure vocational programs, they pursue an approach of game design education that forms their students as both generalists and specialists—assuming that a combination of generalism and specialism based on an interdisciplinary practical and theoretical game design education will improve employability in general, but even moreso in the long run. A look at job advertisements indeed reveals that the gaming industry does not only require pure specialists (who will be continuously recruited from computer science programs, BSc, and MSc Game Design programs, and a variety of programs in diverse areas such as Visual Effects, Producing, Business Administration, etc.), but also broadly trained generalists with a specialization in one field, a comprehensive game literacy, a range of soft skills, and a well-rounded general education.[52]

Furthermore, programs believe that in the "ludic century"[53] game literacy in combination with a creative mindset and the ability to communicate and collaborate in diverse interdisciplinary and intercultural teams (in addition to other soft skills) will be transferable to other professional fields. Finally, programs are keen on facilitating students' entrepreneurial spirit and competencies.

Beyond the vocational aspects of higher education, programs carry the spirit that Colleen Macklin and John Sharp (both at Parsons School of Design) presented in their "Play, Make, Appreciate: A Games Education Manifesto."[54] Criticizing the hitherto dominant game design and development education models—the engineering model and the art studio model—as too narrow, Macklin and Sharp propose "a broader consideration of games and play in higher education."

---

51 Ibid., p. 43.
52 See e.g. data from Canada in Douglas, Sean/Della Rocca, Jason/Jenson, Jennifer/Kee, Kevin/Rockwell, Geoffrey/Schaeffer, Jonathan/Simon, Bart/Wakkary, Ron: *Computer Games and Canada's Digital Economy: The Role of Universities in Promoting Innovation*. Report to the Social Science Humanities Research Council. Knowledge Synthesis Grants on Canada's Digital Economy, 2010, p. 23; http://circa.ualberta.ca/wp-content/uploads/2010/03/ComputerGamesAndCanadasDigitalEconomy.pdf
53 Zimmerman: "Manifesto for a Ludic Century."
54 Macklin/Sharp: "Play, Make, Appreciate."

They question "game puritanism and the fetishizing of games at the expense of play" and argue for a more holistic approach that does not only emphasize crafts and craft-based skills, but also games and play in a larger cultural context. They argue to disengage game design education from the self-centered culture of insiders, to leave the game-centric point of view, to promote diversity, and to extensively integrate content from the broad field of liberal arts.[55]

STRUCTURE OF AN UNDERGRADUATE PROGRAM FOR GAME DESIGN

Taking the CGL bachelor as an example, I will now outline how an undergraduate program can convey artistic-academic and handcraft-practical knowledge and skills for the conception, development, and production of digital games as well as other nonlinear interactive audiovisions.[56] Every year the CGL accepts 35 to

---

[55] In line with these considerations, Macklin and Sharp even went a step further than the programs presented in this subchapter when they deliberately decided against the introduction of a Game Design major at Parsons—in favor of leaving the undergraduate Game Design education in a broader Design and Technology BFA in order to avoid a loss in diversity of content and student body.—As programs strongly aim at the facilitation of its students' technological, economic, artistic, and cultural creativity, the underlying model of game design education outlined in this subchapter should not only be evaluated in terms of graduate employability, but also in terms of significant innovation in digital games caused by artists and visionaries educated by programs based on this very model. See below *Consequences of Academization*, p. 256ff.

[56] The Cologne Game Lab is an institute of the TH Köln, a state-funded university of technology, arts and sciences in Cologne, Germany. The program was developed by Björn Bartholdy, André Czauderna, Katharina Tillmans, and myself. An essential part of the development process included workshops with representatives of academia and the games industry on curriculum content, necessary specializations and economic perspectives, i.e., employability and entrepreneurship support. One of the results was the decision to teach exclusively in English: To a large extent, games are produced in global networks, they are distributed globally and online, and consumed globally and online. Thus game development requires intercultural competencies, even more so than the production of older audiovisual media. Most game companies—including the major German developers—use English as a working language. English instruction increases the program's attraction for applicants from other cultures, which is abso-

40 undergraduate students after an artistic-academic aptitude test. Seven professors supervise the students and hold courses in the following areas of specialization: *Media and Game Studies, Media Design, Game Design, 3D Animation and Computer Graphics Art for Games, Computer Programming for Games, Sound Design for Games,* and *Economics and Entrepreneurship for Games*. Instruction is also supplemented with lectures from experienced members of the international game industry. This undergraduate program thereby distinguishes itself through its combination of academic and artistic education, which allows for the interconnected creation, application, and research of interactive content.

The teaching goals can be divided into academic knowledge and skills, career-oriented artistic-handcraft skills, as well as (inter-)cultural and ethical competencies. Particular importance is placed on the development of a committed attitude towards one's own artistic-academic efforts, i.e., the development of critical power of judgment in regard to the cultural and social effects resulting from one's own work. In addition, students should be able to identify and capitalize on potential economic opportunities by developing innovative methods and approaches.

Three specializations are offered:

- *Game Arts.* Courses in this specialization convey the fundamentals of designing a digital game's visual and auditory elements. This includes visual representations from the early phase of project development (*Concept Art*), the creation of characters, objects, and whole worlds (*Character Design, Asset Design, World Design*), the animation of two-dimensional and three-dimensional graphic elements (*2D, 3D Animation*) as well as the development of GUIs and NUIs within creative and ergonomic parameters (*Interface Design*).
- *Game Design.* Courses in this specialization impart the fundamentals of ludic and narrative design, i.e., the fundamentals of game mechanics as well as multi- and nonlinear audiovisual narration. In addition, focal areas include the design of systems, the requirements of emergent play, the design of the interaction—especially user interface design—, the creation and administration of game design documents, the analysis of the gaming experience, playtesting, the particular requirements of AAA and indie game development, the special qualities of serious games and game-based learning.

---

lutely necessary for heterogeneous teams, and also provides optimal preparation for the later work experience.

- *Game Programming.* Courses in this specialization cover the IT basics of digital games, i.e., how worlds and the actions taking place in them are simulated through the execution of algorithms. Students learn programming languages, the fundamentals of computer architecture, fundamental mathematics, fundamental programming (algorithms, AI), graphic technologies, front-end technologies (2D/3D graphics, browsers), and back-end technologies (networks, databases, client/server) as well as operating systems and software management. However, the objective is not to train computer programmers in the traditional sense, but gameplay programmers: Creative programmers, trained in design as well, who work at the intersection of aesthetics and technology.

The students of all three specializations receive additional joint instruction in Media Theory and Game Studies as well as in Media Economics and Media Management. The courses of *Media and Game Studies* introduce students to academic work and convey the fundamentals of modern media history. Students learn to pose critical questions concerning the production, usage, and impact of nonlinear audiovisions. Special emphasis is placed on the history and theories of games, the history of audiovisual media and arts (theater, film, television, games, transmedia), and on the cultural aspects of digitalization. Within *Media and Game Studies*, the separate field of *Media Economics* addresses aspects of economic activity and protocol in digital media production and distribution, especially entrepreneurship and project management.

CGL's undergraduate course offerings strive toward a convergence of media theory and media practice by offering historical and theoretical knowledge as well as orientation knowledge relevant for practical artistic work. In both lectures and seminars, students learn theoretical concepts as well as the history of the arts, culture, and media. These lessons are then applied to medial production. Accordingly, undergraduate courses are characterized by trans-disciplinary historical and theoretical instruction and a high proportion of practical project-based work; the aim being to achieve an equilibrium between artistic-academic and technological-economic orientation. This balance is reinforced by the division of the semesters: The first half offers theoretical seminars, the content of which is applied to practical exercises and smaller projects. The knowledge and skills acquired in the first half of the semester are subsequently applied in the context of greater collaborative projects in the second half.[57]

---

57 Exceptions are the fifth and the seventh semesters; see below.

These respective tasks focus on structural archetypes of digital games (ludic games, narrative games, adaptations, casual games, serious games, etc.). The goal is first to conceptualize and then to realize playable prototypes or 'vertical slices'—high-quality realizations of a single moment in a game, demonstrating progress in all areas of the project. Reinforcing the knowledge and skills they learned during their practical lessons, students receive the opportunity to explore various ideas, approaches, and procedures in short, iterative cycles, while developing unique strategies for problem solving. This method mirrors the game industry's own way of operating and so familiarizes the students with their future working environment.

The undergraduate program's seven semesters are divided into three phases:

- In the first two semesters students attain fundamental knowledge and basic skills in joint courses regardless of their specializations, i.e., game artists also take part in the introductory lectures, seminars, and practical exercises of the game designers and gameplay programmers, and vice versa. Students' roles in the collaborative projects are flexible, so that they may explore different tasks in game development. This general education should lay a 'common ground' as a basis for future interdisciplinary collaboration.
- Between the third and sixth semester students concentrate on their specializations. While the collaborative projects of the second half of the semester grow more complex and challenging, students take on the roles that correspond to their specialization. A 'mobility window' also falls into this second phase of the degree program. During their fifth semester—in order to expand their cultural horizons, deepen their expertise, and gain independent media practical experience—students have three options: (1) spend a semester abroad (at a partner university), (2) complete an industry internship at home or abroad, or (3) complete a larger, self-conceptualized project.
- In the seventh semester, the bachelor thesis concludes the program. The BA project can be completed individually or collaboratively. It consists of two parts, a game or a playable prototype and an academic study.

After graduating, students are faced with the choice of either continuing their education or finding a job. In the first case, they might apply for a spot in the masters program, "Digital Games", that will be offered by the CGL starting in 2017 or they might—as the English-language degree program has well-prepared them to do so—continue studying abroad. In the second case, students are faced with three possibilities:

1) Seeking work in the German and/or international games industry;
2) Seeking work in one of the numerous related industries which employ digital games (especially serious games or elements of digital games in the context of gamification). Worth considering are fields of basic and further training, the design of teaching materials, research in the natural and social sciences, advertising and marketing, film, television, and transmedia production, journalism, visual arts and curatorial practice in museums and galleries, the automotive and aeronautics industries, and the military.
3) Pursuing entrepreneurial opportunities in the field of digital games—particularly as the indie game scene is booming and government funding and subsidies for game development are being established in Germany.

CONSEQUENCES OF ACADEMIZATION

Whether or not it is intended, the artistic-academic programs of study that are currently emerging will change aesthetic production. These courses form artistic personalities, individuals who would not have produced games at all or at least different ones without this education. Jenova Chen, graduate of the Game Design program of the University of Southern California, co-founder of thatgamecompany and designer of the multiple prize-winning games FLOWER (2009) and JOURNEY (2012), describes the effect of his studies:

"[...] I was able to read and speak about game design in an academic way. This design vocabulary is going to replace 'fun' and 'cool,' allowing you to see deeper into video games. Video games are so new that the theories and rules applied in this field usually come from elsewhere. I learned theories from film, screenwriting, and psychology, and I came up with my own rules out of them. If I hadn't gone to grad school, I probably would have never touched those areas."[58]

To help foresee the mid- and long-term consequences arising from the academization of game development, present film culture offers itself as a model, i.e., the

---

58 Quoted from Fullerton: *Game Design Workshop*, loc. 5066.

relationship between commercial film production, academic film studies at universities, and artistic-academic instruction at film schools.[59]

In the filmmaking countries of the Western, democratic world, academic film studies, as well as the first artistic-academic study courses at film schools, arose only in the 1960s, when film was already more than half a century old.[60] The consequences for film as an art form and as an industry were drastic and long-term. The so-called *film school generation*, the first cohort of graduates from American film schools—among them George Lucas, Francis Ford Coppola, Paul Schrader, Martin Scorsese, Robert Zemeckis—became known as "New Hollywood" because they were revolutionizing the industry; first in the Sixties and Seventies through artistic renewal, then in the Eighties through economic renewal with blockbuster cinema—as aesthetically questionable as this may have been. Something comparable happened in West Germany. Among the first graduates of the two first West German film schools were Wim Wenders and Bernd Eichinger in Munich, and Wolfgang Petersen in Berlin. Their work also stands for an artistic and economic evolutionary push that helped to define German cinema and beyond for a half-century.

One essential force behind this historical break, which the first academically educated filmmakers were responsible for, was likely an advanced film literacy that they acquired over the course of their academic studies—in contrast to the older generation of filmmakers who were primarily craftsmen. The term 'literacy' means more than simply 'alphabetization' or 'education.' Rather, it also denotes the ability to confidently navigate a complex and culturally influenced medial system and to recognize connections in meaning and context independently through critical analysis and interpretation. Originally this skill pertained only to

---

59 Another example would be the spread of creative writing programs in the US—from 52 in 1975 to more than 350 in 2004, if we include undergraduate degree programs even to over 700, according to Mark McGurl's study *The Program Era: Postwar Fiction and the Rise of Creative Writing* (Cambridge, Mass.: Harvard University Press 2009, loc. 506). McGurl investigates "how, why, and to what end has the writing program reorganized U.S. literary production in the postwar period." (Ibid., loc. 557) Some of his findings can be applied to film school education as well.—For this observation, I have Sylke Rene Meyer to thank.

60 Almost 40 years after the talkies, almost 70 years after the first silent movies.—Where not economic but political interests determined development, film schools were founded earlier: for example in the communist USSR of the 1920s, in fascist Italy of the 1930s, in the national-socialist occupied France of the 1940s, in the communist GDR of the early 1950s.

systems of writing and speaking. In the meantime, the term 'literacy' has come to encompass all symbolic-medial systems that make up cultures, whether they rest on letters, numbers, still images, or moving pictures—including digital games.

The goal of artistic-academic digital games research and education must, therefore, be *game literacy*: the transfer of historical and theoretical foundational knowledge and sophisticated hermeneutical competencies necessary to understand games in their cultural-historical context as well as their contemporary aesthetic impact. If and when this is accomplished, i.e., with the transition from handcraft, industry-internal schooling to artistic-academic higher education, similar effects can be hoped for just as they once pertained to film: an artistic as well as economic evolutionary push, followed by a maturing of the medium. This process should also precipitate a new self-awareness, an evolved self-judgment, and self-valuation for all those who deal with digital games.

For the future course of this development, the three points I stressed in the main sections of this introduction will undoubtedly be decisive:

1) The historical and theoretical insight into the double alterity of digital games and, at the same time, an artistic and practical awareness of their otherness in relation to analog games as well as older audiovisual media;
2) The necessity of the continued technological and aesthetic development of virtual design and especially game design into a central cultural technology of the 21st century, which could have an impact far beyond games; for instance from the design of linear audiovisions to the design of social and political processes;
3) The necessity for overcoming the schisms of Game Studies, especially through the integration of academic-theoretical and artistic-practical perspectives in teaching as well as research.

Sources

LITERATURE

Aarseth, Espen J.: *Cybertext: Perspectives on Ergodic Literature*, Baltimore Md.: Johns Hopkins University Press 1997.

Adams, Ernest: "Postmodernism and the Three Types of Immersion," in: *Gamasutra*, July 9, 2004; http://www.designersnotebook.com/Columns/063_Post modernism/063_postmodernism.htm

Adorno, Theodor W.: "Valéry's Deviations" (*1960), in: Adorno, Theodor W./ Rolf Tiedemann. *Notes to Literature*. vol 1, New York: Columbia University Press 1991, pp. 137-173.

Adorno, Theodor W./Dahrendorf, Ralf/Habermas, Jürgen/Popper, Karl R.: *Der Positivismusstreit in der deutschen Soziologie*, Darmstadt: Luchterhand 1976.

Alberti, Leon Battista: *On Painting*. Translated with Introduction and Notes by John R. Spencer, New Haven: Yale University Press 1970 (*1956); http://www.noteaccess.com/Texts/Alberti/

Allgaier, Joachim: "Verschmelzen Computerspiel und Film? Perspektiven der Medienkonvergenz am Beispiel digitaler Spiele," *Telepolis*, February 15, 2009; http://www.heise.de/tp/r4/artikel/29/29536/1.html

Arnheim, Rudolf: *Film as Art*, London: Faber 1969 {*1932}.

Ault, Susanne: "Blu-ray/videogame Discs to be released for PS3," Video Business, March 3, 2009; http://www.videobusiness.com/article/CA6636623.htm l?desc=topstory

Avedon, Elliott M./Brian Sutton-Smith: *The Study of Games*, New York: J. Wiley 1971.

Baer, Ralph H.: "Foreword," in: Mark J. P. Wolf (ed.), *The Medium of the Video Game*, Austin: University of Texas Press 2002, pp. ix-xvi.

Bateson, Gregory: "A Theory of Play and Fantasy," in: Gregory Bateson (ed.), *Steps to an Ecology of Mind: Collected Essays in Anthropology, Psychiatry,*

Evolution, and Epistemology, San Francisco: Chandler Pub. Co. 1972, pp. 138-148.

Baudrillard, Jean: *Simulacra and Simulation*, Ann Arbor: University of Michigan Press 1994 (*1981).

———: "The Murder of the Real," in: Jean Baudrillard/Julia Witwer (ed.), *The Vital Illusion*, New York: Columbia University Press 2000, pp. 59-83.

Baudrillard, Jean/Guillaume, Marc: *Radical Alterity*, Los Angeles, CA; Cambridge, Mass.; London: Semiotext(e); Distributed by the MIT Press 2008.

Baudrillard, Jean/Lotringer, Sylvère: *The Ecstasy of Communication*, Brooklyn N.Y.: Autonomedia 1988.

Bazin, André/Gray, Hugh: *What Is Cinema?*, Berkeley: University of California Press 1967 (*1958-1962).

Beck, Kent/Beedle, Mike/Bennekum, Arie van/Cockburn, Alistair/Cunningham, Ward/Fowler, Martin/Grenning, James/Highsmith, Jim/Hunt, Andrew/Jeffries, Ron/Kern, Jon/Marick, Brian/Martin, Robert C./Mellor, Steve/Schwaber, Ken/Sutherland, Jeff/ Thomas, Dave: "Manifesto for Agile Software Development," 2001; http://agilemanifesto.org

Beil, Benjamin: *Avatarbilder: Zur Bildlichkeit des zeitgenössischen Computerspiels*, Bielefeld: transcript 2012.

———: *Game Studies: Eine Einführung*, Red guide, Berlin: Lit 2013.

———: "Zwischen Planspiel und Trainingssimulator. Oder: Was man von Computerspielen (nicht) über den Krieg lernen kann," in: Freyermuth, Gundolf S./Gotto, Lisa/Wallenfels, Fabian (ed.), *Serious Games, Exergames, Exerlearning: Zur Transmedialisierung und Gamification des Wissenstransfers*, Bielefeld: transcript 2013, pp. 91-121.

Beil, Benjamin/Bonner, Marc/Hensel, Thomas (ed.), *Computer | Spiel | Bilder*, Glückstadt: vwh Verlag Werner Hülsbusch, 2014.

Beil, Benjamin/Freyermuth, Gundolf S./Gotto, Lisa: "Vorwort," in: (ed.), *New Game Plus: Perspektiven der Game Studies. Genres – Künste – Diskurse*, Bielefeld: transcript 2015, pp. 7-24.

Benjamin, Walter: "Little History of Photography," in: Benjamin, Walter, *et al. Selected Writings*. 4 vols, Cambridge, Mass.: Belknap Press 1996, vol. 2, part 2, pp. 507-530.

———: *The Work of Art in the Age of its Technological Reproducibility, and Other Writings on Media*. Cambridge, Mass.: Belknap Press of Harvard University Press 2008.

Berents, Catharina: *Kleine Geschichte des Design: Von Gottfried Semper bis Philippe Starck*, Munich: C.H. Beck 2011.

Bergo, Bettina: "Emmanuel Levinas," *Stanford Encyclopedia of Philosophy*, August 3, 2011; http://plato.stanford.edu/entries/levinas/

Berlin, Leslie: "Kicking Reality of a Notch," *The New York Times*, July 12, 2009; http://www.nytimes.com/2009/07/12/business/12proto.html?_r=1&partner=rss&emc=rss

Berlinger, Yehuda: "The History of the New Games Foundation: Play Hard. Play Fair. Nobody Hurt," Yehuda: Gaming, Technology, Philosophy, and Life, February 14, 2008; http://jergames.blogspot.com/2008/02/history-ofnew-games-foundation.html

Berne, Eric: *Games People Play: The Psychology of Human Relationships*, New York: Grove Press 1964.

BIU, Bundesverband Interaktive Unterhaltungssoftware: "Games Report 2011," 2011; http://www.biu-online.de/fileadmin/user_upload/pdf/games_report_2011.pdf

———: "Altersverteilung," 2014; http://www.biu-online.de/de/fakten/reichweiten/altersverteilung.html

———: "Mehr als jedes dritte Spiel wird als Download gekauft," October 20, 2014; http://www.biu-online.de/de/presse/newsroom/newsroom-detail/datum/2014/10/20/mehr-als-jedes-dritte-spiel-wird-als-download-gekauft.html

———: "Spieler in Deutschland," 2014; http://www.biu-online.de/de/fakten/reichweiten/spieler-in-deutschland.html

———: "Deutscher Markt für digitale Spiele wächst um sechs Prozent," August 7, 2014; http://www.biu-online.de/de/presse/newsroom/newsroom-detail/datum/2014/08/07/deutscher-markt-fuer-digitale-spiele-waechst-um-sechs-prozent.html

———: "Die deutsche Gamesbranche 2013," 2014; http://www.biu-online.de/de/fakten/marktzahlen-2013/die-deutsche-gamesbranche-2013.html

———: "Hintergrund: Computer- und Videospiele in Deutschland: Kreativbranche mit Wachstum- und Innovationspotential," 2014; http://www.biu-online.de/de/presse/newsroom/themendossier-computer-und-videospiele-in-deutschland.html

Bjork, Staffan/ Holopainen, Jussi: *Patterns in Game Design*, Hingham, Mass.: Charles River Media 2005.

Bloch, Ernst. "Nonsynchronism and the Obligation to its Dialectics," *New German Critique* 11, 1977 (*1932).

Bogost, Ian: *Persuasive Games: The Expressive Power of Videogames*, Cambridge, MA: MIT Press 2007.

Bolz, Norbert: *Bang Design: Design-Manifest des 21. Jahrhunderts*, Hamburg: Trendbüro 2006.

Borges, Jorge Luis: "On Exactitude in Science," in: Borges, Jorge Luis/Hurley, Andrew (ed.), *Collected Fictions*, London, New York: Allen Lane The Penguin Press 1999, pp. 325.

Box Office Mojo: "Top Single Day Grosses" http://boxofficemojo.com/alltime/ days/?page=open&p=.htm

Brand, Stewart: "Spacewar: Fanatic Life and Symbolic Death Among the Computer Bums," *Rolling Stone*, December 7, 1972; http://www.wheels.org/ spacewar/stone/rolling_stone.html

Bredekamp, Horst: "*Kunstkammer*, Play-Palace, Shadow Theatre: Three Thought Loci by Gottfried Wilhelm Leibniz," in: Schramm, Helmar, et al. *Collection, Laboratory, Theater: Scenes of Knowledge in the 17thCcentury*. Berlin, New York: Walter de Gruyter 2005, pp. 266-283.

Breitlauch, Linda: "Spielfreude als erfolgreiche Lern- und Therapiemethode," in: Inderst, Rudolf Thomas/Just, Peter (ed.), *Build 'em Up – Shoot 'em Down: Körperlichkeit in digitalen Spielen*, Glückstadt: Hülsbusch 2013, pp. 179-191.

Brinkemper, Peter V.: "Paradoxien der Enträumlichung. Zur Philosophie des 3D-Films," *Glanz und Elend. Literatur und Zeitkritik*, 2012; http://www.glan zundelend.de/Artikel/abc/s/starwars.htm

Brown, Scott: "Q&A: Hobbit Director Guillermo del Toro on the Future of Film," *Wired*, June 2009; http://www.wired.com/entertainment/hollywood/ magazine/17-06/mf_deltoro?currentPage=all

Butler, Judith: *Bodies that Matter: On the Discursive Limits of 'Sex,'* Abingdon, Oxon; New York, NY: Routledge 2011 (*1993).

Butler, Mark: *Would you like to play a game? Die Kultur des Computerspielens*, Berlin: Kulturverlag Kadmos 2007.

Caillois, Roger: *Man, Play and Games*, Urbana: University of Illinois Press 2001 (*1958).

Cain, James M.: *The Postman Always Rings Twice*, New York: A. A. Knopf 1934.

Campbell, Colin: "How League of Legends is Upending the Video Game Business," October 24, 2014; http://www.polygon.com/2014/10/24/7061573/ho w-league-of-legends-is-upending-the-video-game-business

Campbell-Kelly, Martin/Aspray, William: *Computer: A History of the Information Machine*, New York: Basic Books 1996.

Carlson, David E.: "David Carlson's Virtual World, The Online Timeline," http://iml.jou.ufl.edu/carlson/timeline.shtml

Carroll, Lewis: *Sylvia and Bruno Concluded*, London, New York: Macmillan 1893; http://archive.org/stream/sylviebrunoconcl00carriala/sylviebrunoconcl 00carriala_djvu.txt

Cashmore, Pete: "FarmVille Surpasses 80 Million Users," *Mashable*, February 20, 2010; http://mashable.com/2010/02/20/farmville-80-million-users/
Castronova, Edward: "Virtual Worlds: A First-Hand Account of Market and Society on the Cyberian Frontier," in: CESifo Working Paper Series 618, December 2001; http://papers.ssrn.com/sol3/papers.cfm?abstract_id=294828
———: *Synthetic Worlds: The Business and Culture of Online Games*, Chicago: University of Chicago Press 2005.
———: *Exodus to the Virtual World: How Online Fun is Changing Reality*, New York: Palgrave Macmillan 2007.
Chandler, Raymond: *The Big Sleep*, New York: A. A. Knopf 1939.
Chaplin, Heather: "Will The 21st Century Be Defined By Games?," *Kotaku*, September 12, 2013; http://www.kotaku.com.au/2013/09/will-the-21st-centurybe-defined-by-games/
Chase, Linda: *Hyperrealism*, London: Academy Editions 1975.
Chatfield, Tom: Fun Inc.: *Why Games are the Twenty-First Century's Most Serious Business*, London: Virgin (Kindle edition) 2010.
———: "Bridging the Gap," *Prospect*, December 2011; http://www.prospectmagazine.co.uk/arts-and-books/bridging-the-gap
Christie, Agatha: *And Then There Were None*, New York: St. Martin's Griffin 2004 (*1939)
Colleen/Sharp, John: "Play, Make, Appreciate: A Games Education Manifesto," Talk at the GDC Education Summit 2013; http://www.gdcvault.com
Corliss, Richard: "Prisoners Wins the Weekend, but It's No 'Grand Theft Auto V'," *Time*, September 22, 2013; http://entertainment.time.com/2013/09/22/prisoners-wins-the-weekend-but-its-no-grand-theft-auto-v/
Coupland, Douglas: *Marshall McLuhan: You Know Nothing of My Work!*, New York: Atlas (Kindle edition) 2010.
Crabtree, Sheigh: "Video Games Grow Up," *The Hollywood Reporter*, April 7, 2006; http://www.allbusiness.com/services/motion-pictures/4899000-1.html
Crawford, Chris: *The Art of Computer Game Design*, Berkeley, Calif.: Osborne/McGraw-Hill 1984.
———: "Fundamentals of Interactivity," *The Journal of Computer Game Design* 7, 1993/94; http://www.erasmatazz.com/library/the-journal-of-computer/jcgd-volume-7/fundamentals-of-interactivi.html
———: "The Phylogeny of Play," March 1, 2010; http://www.erasmatazz.com/library/science/the-phylogeny-of-play.html
Crecente, Brian: "Convergence, Smergence ... Hollywood Director Paul W.S. Anderson Believes Games and Movies Should Remain Separate," *Kotaku*, September 3, 2010; http://kotaku.com/327820/convergence-smergenceholly

wood-director-paul-ws-anderson-believes-games-and-movies-shouldremain-separate

Czauderna, André: *Lernen als soziale Praxis im Internet: Objektiv hermeneutische Rekonstruktionen aus einem Forum zum Videospiel Pokémon*, Wiesbaden: Springer 2014.

De Campo, Alberto/Hentschel, Ulrike/King, Dorothee/ Kufus, Axel (ed.): *Play: Test*, Revolver: Berlin 2013.

Deleuze, Gilles: "Leibniz," Les Cours de Gilles Deleuze – webdeleuze.com, April 15, 1980; http://www.webdeleuze.com/php/texte.php?cle=50&groupe=Leibniz&langue=2

Derrida, Jacques: *Mémoires: for Paul de Man*, New York: Columbia University Press 1986.

Deterding, Sebastian/Dixon, Dan/Khaled, Rilla/Nacke, Lennart E.: "Gamification: Toward a Definition," *CHI 2011 Gamification Workshop Proceedings*, 2011; http://hci.usask.ca/publications/view.php?id=219

Deutsches Filminstitut: "50 Jahre Kino in Deutschland," 2000; http://www.deutsches-filminstitut.de/hdf/cont_k_12.html

Dixon, Wheeler Winston: "Twenty-Five Reasons Why It's All Over," in: Lewis, Jon (ed.), *The End of Cinema as We Know It: American Film in the Nineties*, New York: New York University Press. 2001, pp. 356-366.

———: "Vanishing Point: The Last Days of Film," *Senses of Cinema* 43, 2007; http://www.sensesofcinema.com/2007/feature-articles/last-days-film.

Donovan, Tristan: *Replay: The History of Video Games*, Lewes, East Sussex: Yellow Ant (Kindle edition) 2010.

Dos Passos, John: *Manhattan Transfer*, Boston: Houghton Mifflin Co. 2000 (*1925).

Douglas, Sean/Della Rocca, Jason/Jenson, Jennifer/Kee, Kevin/Rockwell, Geoffrey/Schaeffer, Jonathan/Simon, Bart/Wakkary, Ron: *Computer Games and Canada's Digital Economy: The Role of Universities in Promoting Innovation*. Report to the Social Science Humanities Research Council. Knowledge Synthesis Grants on Canada's Digital Economy, 2010, p. 23; http://circa.ualberta.ca/wp-content/uploads/2010/03/ComputerGamesAndCanadasDigitalEconomy.pdf

Dresser, Christopher: *Principles of Decorative Design*, London, New York: Cassell, Petter 1873; http://www.gutenberg.org/ebooks/39749

Drucker, Peter F.: *Post-Capitalist Society*, New York: HarperBusiness 1993.

Dunnigan, James F.: *The Complete Wargames Handbook: How to Play, Design, and Find Them*, New York, N.Y.: Morrow 1992; http://www.strategypage.com/wargames-handbook/chapter/contents.aspx

Dyson, George: *Turing's Cathedral: The Origins of the Digital Universe*, New York: Vintage Books (Kindle edition) 2012.

Ebert, Roger/Siskel, Gene/Scorsese, Martin/Spielberg, Steven/Lucas, George: *The Future of the Movies*, Kansas City Mo.: Andrews and McMeel 1991.

Eco, Umberto. *Travels in Hyper Reality: Essays*. San Diego: Harcourt Brace Jovanovich 1986 (*1975).

Edwards, Kate/Weststar, Johanna/Meloni, Wanda/Pearce, Celia/Legault, Marie-Josée: *Developer Satisfaction Survey 2014. Summary Report*, International Game Developers Association, igda.org. 2014, 9; https://c.ymcdn.com/sites/www.igda.org/resource/collection/9215B88F-2AA3-4471-B44D-B5D58FF2 5DC7/IGDA_DSS_2014-Summary_Report.pdf

Egenfeldt-Nielsen, Simon: "Die ersten zehn Jahre der Serious Games-Bewegung. Zehn Lektionen," in: Freyermuth, Gundolf S./Gotto, Lisa/Wallenfels, Fabian (ed.), *Serious Games, Exergames, Exerlearning: Zur Transmedialisierung und Gamification des Wissenstransfers*, Bielefeld: transcript 2013, pp. 145-163.

Egenfeldt-Nielsen, Simon/Smith, Jonas Heide/Tosca, Susana Pajares: *Understanding Video Games: The Essential Introduction*, New York: Routledge (Kindle edition) 2008.

Eisenstein, Sergei/Jay Leyda. *Film Essays and a Lecture*. Princeton, N.J.: Princeton University Press 1982.

Electronic Arts: "Unternehmenspräsentation September 12, 2009," http://www.presse.electronic-arts.de/publish/page204218419835234.php3?1=1&aid=41& spieleid=

Elsaesser, Thomas: "The 'Return' of 3-D: On Some of the Logics and Genealogies of the Image in the Twenty-First Century", in: *Critical Inquiry* 39 (Winter 2013), pp. 240-241.

———: "Die 'Rückkehr' der 3D-Bilder. Zur Logik und Genealogie des Bildes im 21. Jahrhundert," in: Freyermuth, Gundolf S./Gotto, Lisa (ed.), *Bildwerte: Visualität in der digitalen Medienkultur*, Bielefeld: transcript 2013, pp. 25-67.

Ermi, Laura/Frans Mäyrä: "Fundamental Components of the Gameplay Experience. Analysing Immersion," *DiGRA Conference 2005*, pp. 7-8; http://www.digra.org/dl/db/06276.41516.pdf

ESA, Entertainment Software Association: "Essential Facts about the Computer and Video Game Industry 2011," http://www.theesa.com/facts/ pdfs/ESA _EF_2011.pdf

———: "Essential Facts about the Computer and Video Game Industry 2014," http://www.theesa.com/wp-content/uploads/2014/10/ESA_EF_2014.pdf

———: "Essential Facts about the Computer and Video Game Industry 2015," http://www.theesa.com/wp-content/uploads/2015/04/ESA-Essential-Facts-2015.pdf

Eschbach, Andrea: "Mehr als Ego-Shooter," *Page*, 4/2008.

Fallan, Kjetil: *Design History: Understanding Theory and Method*, New York: Berg Publishers 2010.

Fassler, Manfred: *Was ist Kommunikation?*, Munich: Wilhelm Fink Verlag 1997.

Fernandez-Vara, Clara/Wlochowski, Julia/Gomez, Elaine/Lemoine, Elyse/Kiai, Deirdra "Squinky": "Increasing Gender Diversity in Game Development Programs," Talk at the GDC Education Summit 2015; http://www.gdcvaul t.com.

Fleischmann, Monika: "Die Spur des Betrachters im Bild," in: Peter Weibel/ Zentrum für Kunst und Medientechnologie (Karlsruhe) (ed.), *Vom Tafelbild zum globalen Datenraum: neue Möglichkeiten der Bildproduktion und bildgebenden Verfahren*, Ostfildern-Ruit: Hatje Cantz Edition ZKM 2001, pp. 138-149.

Fondaumière, Guillaume de: "Berlinale Keynotes: Rethinking Content," March 1, 2007; http://www.youtube.com/watch?v=zEQrQb7cSrc&hd=1

Frasca, Gonzalo: "Ludology Meets Narratology: Similitude and Differences Between (Video) Games and Narrative," ludology.org (Finnish original 1999); http://www.ludology.org/articles/ludology.htm

Freyermuth, Gundolf S.: "Freizeitpark im Fernsehsessel," *c't – magazin für computertechnik*, September 13, 1999; http://www.heise.de/kiosk/

———: "Holodeck heute," *c't – magazin für computertechnik*, August 30, 1999, pp. 72-77; http://freyermuth.com/reprints/archiv2008/reprintJMar2008/Holo

———: "Die Zukunft des Kinos: Synthetische Realitäten / The Future of Cinema: Synthetic Realities," in: Prinzler, Hans Helmut/Jacobsen, Wolfgang/Sudendorf, Werner (ed.), *Filmmuseum Berlin*, Berlin: Nicolaische Verlagsbuchhandlung 2000, pp. 315-382 (English/German).

———: "Vegas, Virtuelle Stadt," *Telepolis*, March 9, 2000; http://www.hei se.de/tp/artikel/3/3488/1.html

———: "Der Tod des Tonfilms – Revisited," in: Polzer, Joachim, (ed.), *Weltwunder der Kinematographie – Beiträge zu einer Kulturgeschichte der Filmtechnik. Aufstieg und Untergang des Tonfilms / Die Zukunft des Kinos: 24p?*, Potsdam: Polzer 2002, pp. 17-33.

———: "Der große Kommunikator. Soziale Konsequenzen von 'media merging' und Transmedialisierung," in: Siever, Torsten/Schlobinski, Peter/

Runkehl, Jens (ed.), *Websprache.net. Sprache und Kommunikation im Internet*, Berlin, New York: Walter de Gruyter 2005, pp. 15-45.

―――: "Cinema Revisited. Vor und nach dem Kino – Audiovisualität in der Neuzeit," in: Kloock, Daniela (ed.), *Zukunft Kino*, Marburg: Schüren 2007, pp. 15-40.

―――: "Offene Geheimnisse. Die Ausbildung der Open-Source-Praxis im 20. Jahrhundert," in: Lutterbeck, Bernd/Bärwolff, Matthias/Gehring, Robert A. (ed.), *Open Source Jahrbuch 20: Zwischen freier Software und Gesellschaftsmodell*, Berlin: Lehmanns Media 2007, pp. 17-57.

―――: "Prinzip Weltenbau. Digitale Spiele & Film: Konkurrenz, Kooperation, Komplementarität," *Film-Dienst*, May 7, 2009, pp. 6-10.

―――: "Spiel // Film. Prolegomena zu einer Theorie digitaler Audiovisualität," in: Kaminski, Winfred/Lorber, Martin (ed.), *Clash of Realities 2010: Computerspiele: Medien und mehr ...*, Munich: kopaed 2010, pp. 27-46.

―――: "Das Boot. Ein Meilenstein der Film- und Fernsehgeschichte," *Schnitt. Das Filmmagazin*, July 2011; http://www.schnitt.de/211,0063,01 deck_heu te.html

―――: "Ursprünge der Indie-Praxis. Zur Prähistorie unabhängigen Game Designs," in: Kaminski, Winfred/Lorber, Martin (ed.), *Gamebased Learning. Clash of Realities 2012*, Munich: kopaed 2012, pp. 313-326.

―――: "Angewandte Medienwissenschaften. Integration künstlerischer und wissenschaftlicher Perspektiven in Lehre und Forschung," in: Ottersbach, Beatrice/Schadt, Thomas (ed.), *Filmlehren. Ein undogmatischer Leitfaden für Studierende*, Berlin: Bertz + Fischer 2013, pp. 263-278.

―――: "Der Big Bang digitaler Bildlichkeit: Zwölf Thesen und zwei Fragen," in: Freyermuth, Gundolf S./Gotto, Lisa (ed.), *Bildwerte: Visualität in der digitalen Medienkultur*, Bielefeld: transcript 2013, pp. 287-333.

―――: "NetzWerke. Kommunikative Vernetzung als Basis audiovisuellen Erzählens," in: Wolf, Philipp (ed.), *Medieninnovationen: Internet, Serious Games, TV*, Leipzig: Leipziger Universitätsverlag 2013, pp. 105-150.

―――: "Transmedia-Welten. Zehn Thesen," in: Hörisch, Jochen/Kammann, Uwe (ed.), Organisierte Phantasie: *Medienwelten im 21. Jahrhundert – 30 Positionen*, Paderborn: Fink u.a. 2014, pp. 137-147.

―――: "'Lesen wird in vielen Computerspielen zu einer Überlebensfähigkeit'," in: Böhm, Thomas (ed.), *New Level: Computerspiele und Literatur*, Berlin: Metrolit 2014, pp. 115-144.

―――: "Vom Drama zum Game. Elemente einer historischen Theorie audiovisuellen Erzählens," in: Kaminski, Winfred/Lorber, Martin (ed.), *Clash of*

Realities 2014: Computerspiele: Spielwelt-Weltspiel: Narration, Interaktion und Kooperation im Computerspiel, Munich: kopaed 2014, pp. 29-37.

——: "Game Design und Game Studies," in: Sachs-Hombach, Klaus/Thon, Jan-Noël (ed.), *Game Studies. Aktuelle Ansätze der Computerspielforschung*, Köln: Herbert von Halem 2015.

——: "From Analog to Digital Image Space: Towards a Historical Theory of Immersion," in: Dogramaci, Burcu/Liptay, Fabienne (ed.), *Immersion in the Arts and Media*, Amsterdam: Rodopi [to be published 2015].

Freyermuth, Gundolf S./Gotto, Lisa/Wallenfels, Fabian (ed.), *Serious Games, Exergames, Exerlearning: Zur Transmedialisierung und Gamification des Wissenstransfers*, Bielefeld: transcript, 2013.

Friedberg, Anne: *Window Shopping: Cinema and the Postmodern*, Berkeley: University of California Press 1993.

——: *The Virtual Window: From Alberti to Microsoft*, Cambridge, Mass.: MIT Press 2006.

Friedewald, Michael: *Der Computer als Werkzeug und Medium: Die geistigen und technischen Wurzeln des Personal Computers*, Berlin: GNT-Verlag 1999.

Fromme, Johannes/Unger, Alexander (ed.): *Computer Games and New Media Cultures: A Handbook of Digital Games Studies*, New York: Springer 2012.

Fullerton, Tracy. *Game Design Workshop: A Playcentric Approach to Creating Innovative Games*. Boca Raton: CRC Press/Taylor & Francis (Kindle edition) 2014.

Furtwängler, Frank: "Im Spiel unbegrenzter Möglichkeiten. Zu den Ambiguitäten der Videospielforschung und -industrie," in: Distelmeyer, Jan/Hanke, Christine/Mersch, Dieter (ed.), *Game over!?: Perspektiven des Computerspiels*, Bielefeld: transcript 2008, pp. 59-72.

Gadamer, Hans-Georg: "The Relevance of the Beautiful. Art as Play, Symbol and Festival", in: *The Relevance of the Beautiful and Other Essays*, Cambridge University Press 1986.

GamesCoop: *Theorien des Computerspiels zur Einführung*, Hamburg: Junius 2012.

Ganguin, Sonja/Hoblitz, Anna: "Serious Games – Ernstes Spielen. Über das Problem von Spielen, Lernen und Wissenstransfer," in: Freyermuth, Gundolf S./Gotto, Lisa/Wallenfels, Fabian (ed.), *Serious Games, Exergames, Exerlearning: Zur Transmedialisierung und Gamification des Wissenstransfers*, Bielefeld: transcript 2013, pp. 165-183.

Gee, James Paul: *What Video Games Have to Teach Us About Learning and Literacy*, New York: Palgrave Macmillan 2003.

———: *New Digital Media and Learning as an Emerging Area and 'Worked Examples' as One way Forward*, The John D. and Catherine T. MacArthur Foundation Reports on Digital Media and Learning, Cambridge, Mass.: The MIT Press 2010.

Gibson, William: "Talk of the Nation, The Science in Science Fiction (Interview with William Gibson, [Quote starting min. 11:50])," National Public Radio, November 30, 1999; http://www.npr.org/templates/story/story.php?storyId=1067220

Goffman, Erving: *The Presentation of Self in Everyday Life*, Edinburgh: University of Edinburgh, Social Sciences Research Centre 1956.

Goldblatt, David: *The Ball is Round: A Global History of Football*, New York: Riverhead Books (Kindle edition) 2008.

Gottdiener, Mark: *The Theming of America: Dreams, Visions, and Commercial Spaces*, Boulder, Colo.: Westview Press 1997.

Gotto, Lisa: "Einleitung zum Kapitel 'Serious Games'," in: Freyermuth, Gundolf S./Gotto, Lisa/Wallenfels, Fabian (ed.), *Serious Games, Exergames, Exerlearning: Zur Transmedialisierung und Gamification des Wissenstransfers*, Bielefeld: transcript 2013, pp. 139-143.

———: "Type Rider: Typenspiel und digitale Graphie," in: Beil, Benjamin/Freyermuth, Gundolf S./Gotto, Lisa (ed.), New Game Plus: Perspektiven der Game Studies. Genres – Künste – Diskurse, Bielefeld: transcript 2015, pp. 115-142.

Gould, Stephen Jay/Vrba, Elizabeth S.: "Exaptation: A Missing Term in the Science of Form," in: *Paleobiology* 6, 1 (1982): pp. 4-15.

Grieves, Kevin: "On This Day in History: First Live Radio Broadcast of a Soccer Match, 1927," *The Modern Historian*, January 22, 2009; http://modernhistorian.blogspot.de/2009/01/on-this-day-in-history-first-live-radio.html

Grubb, Jeff: "King: 93M Daily Candy Crush Saga Players, 500M Installs, and $568M Profit in 2013," *VentureBeat*, February 18, 2014; http://venturebeat.com/2014/02/18/candy-crush-saga-publisher-king-bythe-numbers-inforgraphic/

Guggenheim, Michael: "The Long History of Prototypes," *limn Number Zero: Prototyping Prototyping*; http://limn.it/the-long-history-of-prototypes/

Guinness Buch der Rekorde, Hamburg: Guinness Verlag GmbH 2001.

Günzel, Stefan: "Von der Zeit zum Raum. Geschichte und Ästhetik des Computerspielmediums," *Rabbiteye – Zeitschrift für Filmforschung*, 2010, pp. 90-108; http://www.rabbiteye.de/2010/2/guenzel_computerspielmedium.pdf

———: *Egoshooter: Das Raumbild des Computerspiels*, Frankfurt a.M.: Campus 2012.

———: "Spiel-bildliche Abhandlung: Tractatus ludico-imaginarius," in: Beil, Benjamin/Bonner, Marc/Hensel, Thomas (ed.), *Computer | Spiel | Bilder*, Glückstadt: vwh Verlag Werner Hülsbusch 2014, pp. 21-24.

Ha, Anthony: "Zynga's Pincus Says FarmVille Has Passed $1B In Total Player Purchases," *TechCrunch*, February 5, 2013; http://techcrunch.com/2013/02/05/farmville-1-billion/

Hart, Hugh: "Virtual Sets Move Hollywood Closer to Holodeck," *Wired*, March 27, 2009; http://www.wired.com/underwire/2009/03/filmmakers-use/

Hartmann, Tilo: "Gewaltspiele und Aggression. Aktuelle Forschung und Implikationen," in: Kaminski, Winfred/Lorber, Martin (ed.), *Computerspiele und soziale Wirklichkeit*, Munich: kopaed 2006, pp. 81-99.

Hauser, Arnold: *The Social History of Art*, 4 vols London, New York: Routledge 1999 (*1951).

Hayles, N. Katherine: *How We Became Posthuman: Virtual Bodies in Cybernetics, Literature, and Informatics*, Chicago Ill.: University of Chicago Press 1999.

Hegel, Georg Wilhelm Friedrich: *Lectures on the History of Philosophy, vol 2: Plato and the Platonists*, Lincoln: University of Nebraska Press 1995.

Hensel, Thomas: "Das Computerspiel als Bildmedium," in: GamesCoop (ed.), *Theorien des Computerspiels zur Einführung*, Hamburg: Junius 2012, pp. 128-146.

———: "Uncharted. Überlegungen zur Bildlichkeit des Computerspiels," in: Freyermuth, Gundolf S./Gotto, Lisa (ed.), *Bildwerte: Visualität in der digitalen Medienkultur*, Bielefeld: transcript 2013, pp. 209-235.

Herodotus/Macaulay, G.C.: *The History of Herodotus*, London, New York: Macmillan and Co. 1890; http://www.sacred-texts.com/cla/hh/index.htm

Hevga—The Higher Education Video Game Alliance: *Our State of Play. Survey 2014-15*, 2015; http://www.higheredgames.org

Hilgers, Philipp von: "Vom Einbruch des Spiels in der Epoche der Vernunft," in: Bredekamp, Horst/Schneider, Pablo (ed.), *Visuelle Argumentationen: die Mysterien der Repräsentation und die Berechenbarkeit der Welt*, Munich: Fink 2006, pp. 205-224.

Hinman, Lawrence M.: "Nietzsche's Philosophy of Play," in: *Philosophy Today* 18, Summer 1974, pp. 106-123.

Höltgen, Stefan: "Phallische Heldin in Paris. Das sieht nach seltsamen Experimenten aus: 'Tomb Raider' als Hybrid zwischen Spiel und Film," *Telepolis*, December 2, 2006; http://www.heise.de/tp/r4/artikel/24/24090/1.html

Huizinga, Johan. *Homo Ludens: A Study of the Play Element in Culture*. Boston: Beacon Press (Kindle edition) 1955 (*1938).

Hunicke, Robin/Leblanc, Marc/Zubek, Robert: "MDA: A Formal Approach to Game Design and Game Research," *Proceedings of the Challenges in Games AI Workshop, Nineteenth National Conference of Artificial Intelligence*, 2004; http://www.zubek.net/robert//publications/MDA.pdf

Illek, Christian P.: "Gaming in Deutschland," *Bitkom*, August 13, 2013; http://www.bitkom.org/files/documents/BITKOM_Praesentation_Gaming_PK_1308 13(1).pdf

Isbister, Katherine: "Game Design Education 10+ Years," Talk at the GDC Education Summit 2014; http://www.gdcvault.com

Jenkins, Henry: "Transmedia Storytelling: Moving Characters From Books to Films to Video Games Can Make Them Stronger and More Compelling," *Technology Review*, January 15, 2003; http://www.technologyreview.com/news/401760/transmedia-storytelling/

———: "Game Design as Narrative Architecture," in: Wardrip-Fruin, Noah/Harrigan, Pat (ed.), *First Person: New Media as Story, Performance, and Game*, Cambridge, Mass.: MIT Press 2004, pp. 119-129.

———: *Confronting the Challenges of Participatory Culture: Media Education for the 21st Century*, The John D. and Catherine T. MacArthur Foundation Reports on Digital Media and Learning, Cambridge, MA: The MIT Press 2009; http://mitpress.mit.edu/sites/default/files/titles/free_download/9780262 513623_Confronting_the_Challenges.pdf

Jusko, Jill: "Milestone Reached," *Industry Week*, August 2002; http://www.industryweek.com/

Juul, Jesper: "A Clash Between Game and Narrative: A Thesis on Computer Games and Interactive Fiction," 1999; http://www.jesperjuul.net/thesis/

———: "Games Telling Stories? A Brief Note on Games and Narratives," *Game Studies*, 1. July 2001; http://www.gamestudies.org/0101/juul-gts/

———: *Half-Real: Video Games Between Real Rules and Fictional Worlds*, Cambridge, Mass.: MIT Press (Kindle edition) 2005.

———: *A Casual Revolution: Reinventing Video Games and Their Players*, Cambridge, MA: MIT Press 2009.

Kelly, Kevin: "The Next 5,000 Days of the Web," December 2007; http://www.ted.com/talks/kevin_kelly_on_the_next_5_000_days_of_the_web/transcript?language=en

———: "Window on the World," in: N. N., "13 of the Brightest Tech Minds Sound Off on the Rise of the Tablet," *Wired*, April 2010; http://www.wired.com/magazine/2010/03/ff_tablet_essays/all/1

Kent, Steve L.: *The Ultimate History of Video Games: From Pong to Pokémon and Beyond: The Story Behind the Craze That Touched Our Lives and Changed the World*, Roseville, Calif.: Prima Pub. 2001.

Kickstarter: "Stats," November 28, 2014; https://www.kickstarter.com/help/stats?ref=footer

Klimmt, Christoph: *Computerspielen als Handlung: Dimensionen und Determinanten des Erlebens interaktiver Unterhaltungsangebote*, Köln: Halem 2006.

Koch, Cameron: "Free-to-Play Games Continue to Dominate the MMO Game Marketplace," *Techtimes*, October 24, 2014; http://www.techtimes.com/articles/18666/20141024/free-to-play-games-continue-to-dominate-the-digitalvideo-game-marketplace.htm

Kohler, Chris: "What Beowulf Means For The Convergence Of Movies And Games," *Wired*, November 19, 2007; http://www.wired.com/gamelife/2007/11/what-beowulf-me/

Kopka, Tobias: "Interface Control Meaning: Eine typologische Gegenstandssichtung des Phänomens Exergames," in: Freyermuth, Gundolf S./Gotto, Lisa/ Wallenfels, Fabian (ed.), *Serious Games, Exergames, Exerlearning: Zur Transmedialisierung und Gamification des Wissenstransfers*, Bielefeld: transcript 2013, pp. 265-288.

Koubek, Jochen/Mosel, Michael/Werning, Stefan (eds.), *Spielkulturen: Funktionen und Bedeutungen des Phänomens Spiel in der Gegenwartskultur und im Alltagsdiskurs*, Glückstadt: Hülsbusch 2013.

Kracauer, Siegfried: *Theory of Film: The Redemption of Physical Reality*, New York: Oxford University Press 1960.

Krämer, Sybille: "Ist Schillers Spielkonzept unzeitgemäß? Zum Zusammenhang von Spiel und Differenz in den Briefen 'Über die ästhetische Erziehung des Menschen,'" in: Bürger, Jan (ed.), *Friedrich Schiller: Dichter, Denker, Vor- und Gegenbild*, Göttingen: Wallstein-Verlag 2007, pp. 158-171.

———: "Operative Bildlichkeit. Von der 'Grammatologie' zu einer 'Diagrammatologie'? Reflexionen über erkennendes 'Sehen,'" in: Hessler, Martina/ Mersch, Dieter (ed.), *Logik des Bildlichen: zur Kritik der ikonischen Vernunft*, Bielefeld: transcript 2009, pp. 94-123.

Lämmert, Eberhard: "Germanistik – eine deutsche Wissenschaft," in: Lämmert, Eberhard/Killy, Walther/Conrady, Karl Otto/Polenz, Peter von (ed.), *Germanistik – eine deutsche Wissenschaft*, Frankfurt a.M.: Suhrkamp 1967, pp. 7-41.

Landow, George P.: *Hypertext: The Convergence of Contemporary Critical Theory and Technology*, Baltimore: Johns Hopkins University Press 1992.

Laurel, Brenda: *Computers as Theatre*, Reading Mass.: Addison-Wesley Pub. Co. 1993.
Lauro, Christina: "MMO Mechanics: Procedural Generation is the Future," in: *Massively by joystiq*, February 26, 2014; http://massively.joystiq.com/2014/02/26/mmo-mechanics-procedural-generation-is-the-future/
Lave, Jean/Wenger, Etienne: *Situated Learning: Legitimate Peripheral Participation*, Cambridge: Cambridge University Press 1991.
Leibniz, Gottfried Wilhelm: "Zufällige Gedanken von der Erfindung nützlicher Spiele aus dessen mündlicher Unterredung aufgezeichnet von F. F. F.," in: Leibniz, Gottfried Wilhelm/Guhrauer, Gottschalk E. (ed.), *Leibnitz's deutsche Schriften*, Berlin: Veit 1840, pp. 491-493.
Leonhardt, David: "John Tukey, 85, Statistician; Coined the Word 'Software,'" *The New York Times*, July 28, 2000; http://www.nytimes.com/2000/07/28/us/john-tukey-85-statistician-coined-the-word-software.html
Lessing, Gotthold Ephraim/Ellen Frothingham. *Laocoon. An Essay upon the Limits of Painting and Poetry*. Boston: Roberts brothers 1874 (*1766); https://archive.org/details/laocoonessayupon00lessrich
Lévinas, Emmanuel: "The Philosopher and Death," in: (ed.), *Alterity and Transcendence*, New York: Columbia University Press 1999, pp. 153-168.
Lewis, Helen: "Why Are We still so Bad at Talking about Video Games?," *New Statesman*, November 20, 2012; http://www.newstatesman.com/culture/2012/11/why-are-we-still-so-bad-talking-about-video-games
Licklider, J. C. R.: "Man-Computer Symbiosis," *IRE Transactions on Human Factors in Electronics HFE-1* (1960) 4-11; http://www.memex.org/licklider.pdf
Loemker, Leroy E.: "Introduction: Leibniz as Philosopher," in: Leibniz, Gottfried Wilhelm/Loemker, Leroy E. (ed.), *Philosophical Papers and Letters*, Dordrecht, Holland ; Boston: D. Reidel Pub. Co. 1976, pp. 1-69.
Long, Neil: "Two Billion Downloads? We're Just Getting Started, Says Angry Birds Creator Rovio," January 23, 2014; http://www.edge-online.com/features/two-billion-downloads-were-just-getting-started-says-angry-birdscreator-rovio/
Ludes, Peter/Hörisch, Jochen: *Einführung in die Medienwissenschaft: Entwicklungen und Theorien*, Berlin: Erich Schmidt Verlag 2003.
Luhmann, Niklas. *The Reality of the Mass Media*, Stanford, Calif.: Stanford University Press 2000
Manovich, Lev: "Database as a Symbolic Form," *Millenium Film Journal*, Fall 1999; http://www.mfj-online.org/journalPages/MFJ34/Manovich_Database_FrameSet.html

———: *The Language of New Media*, Cambridge Mass.: MIT Press 2000.

Marcuse, Herbert: *Eros and Civilization: Philosophical Inquiry Into Freud*, Boston: Beacon Press 1955

Mäyrä, Frans: *An Introduction to Game Studies*, London: SAGE (Kindle edition) 2008.

McGonigal, Jane: *Reality Is Broken: Why Games Make Us Better and How They Can Change the World*, New York: Penguin Press (Kindle edition) 2011.

McLuhan, Marshall: *Understanding Media: The Extensions of Man*, Berkeley: Gingko Press (Kindle edition) 2013 (*1964).

Mead, George Herbert/Morris, Charles W.: *Mind, Self & Society From the Standpoint of a Social Behaviorist*, Chicago, Ill.: The University of Chicago Press 1934; https://www.brocku.ca/MeadProject/Mead/pubs2/mindself/Mead_1934_toc.html

Mechner, Jordan: "The Sands of Time: Crafting a Video Game Story," *Electronic Book Review*, 2008; http://www.electronicbookreview.com/thread/first person/pop-friendly

Mersch, Dieter: "Logik und Medialität des Computerspiels. Eine medientheoretische Analyse," in: Distelmeyer, Jan/Hanke, Christine/Mersch, Dieter (ed.), *Game over!?: Perspektiven des Computerspiels*, Bielefeld: transcript 2008, pp. 19-41.

Metzger, Nils: "Können Pixel Kunst sein?," *Neue Zürcher Zeitung*, April 19, 2013; http://www.nzz.ch/aktuell/feuilleton/literatur-und-kunst/koennen-pixel-kunst-sein-1.18067546

Motion Picture Association of America: "Theatrical Market Statistics 2014"; http://www.mpaa.org/wp-content/uploads/2015/03/MPAA-Theatrical-Market-Statistics-2014.pdf

Müller-Lietzkow, Jörg/Seufert, Wolfgang/Bouncken, Ricarda B.: *Gegenwart und Zukunft der Computer- und Videospielindustrie in Deutschland*, Dornach: Entertainment Media Verlag 2006.

Murray, Janet Horowitz: *Hamlet on the Holodeck: The Future of Narrative in Cyberspace*, New York: Free Press 1997.

Murray, Janet/Bogost, Ian/Mateas, Michael/Nitsche, Michael: »Asking What Is Possible: The Georgia Tech Approach To Game Research and Education," in: *International Digital Media and Arts Association Journal* 2, no. 1 (Spring 2005), pp. 59-68.

Murray, Janet/Bogost, Ian/Mateas, Michael/Nitsche, Michael: "Game design education: Integrating Computation and Culture," *Computer*, 39(6), 2006, pp. 43-51.

Murray, Janet H./Jenkins, Henry: "Before the Holodeck: Translating Star Trek into Digital Media," in: Smith, Greg M. (ed.), *On a Silver Platter: CDROMs and the Promises of a New Technology*, New York: New York University Press 1999, pp. 35-57.

N. N.: "Happened on This Day – 16 September," *news.BBC*, September 16, 2002; http://news.bbc.co.uk/sport2/hi/funny_old_game/2260280.stm

N. N.: "EA SPORTS FIFA Soccer Franchise Sales Top 100 Million Units Lifetime," Business Wire, 4. November 2010; http://www.businesswire.com/news/home/20101104006782/en#.VH8zdIs2JVo

N. N.: *Star Citizen Wiki*, November 2014; http://starcitizen.wikia.com/wiki/Star_Citizen

N. N.: "Germany Yearly Chart: The Year's Top-Selling Game at Retail Ranked by Unit Sales – 2013," *VGChartz*, 2014; http://www.vgchartz.com/yearly/2013/Germany/

N. N.: "Infographic: The German Games Market," Newzoo: Games Market Research, January 6, 2014; http://www.newzoo.com/infographics/infographic german-games-market/

N. N.: "Most Successful Crowdfunding Campaigns," *CrowdfundingBlog*, October 29, 2014; http://www.crowdfundingblog.com/most-successfulcrowdfunding-projects/

N. N.: "USA Yearly Chart: The Year's Top-Selling Game at Retail Ranked by Unit Sales – 2013," VGChartz, 2014; http://www.vgchartz.com/yearly/2013/USA/

N. N.: "Crown Soccer Special," *The International Arcade Museum at Museum of the Game*; http://www.arcade-museum.com/game_detail.php?game_id=16047

N. N.: "Gronk! Flash! Zap! Video Games Are Blitzing The World," *Time*, January 18, 1982; http://content.time.com/time/covers/0,16641,19820118,00.html

N. N.: "Milliardster PC verkauft," in: *Heise Newsticker*, July 1, 2002; http://www.heise.de/newsticker/meldung/Milliardster-PC-verkauft-67490.html

N. N.: MarketLine Industry Profile: Global Movies & Entertainment, April 2015, www.marketline.com

N. N.: "Modern Warfare 2 Biggest Entertainment Launch Ever," *Guiness World Records*, 2010; http://community.guinnessworldrecords.com/_Call-of-Duty-Modern-Warfare-2-Most-Successful-Entertainment-Launch-of-All-Time/BLOG/2308082/7691.html

N. N.: "The Future Has Arrived—It's Just Not Evenly Distributed Yet. William Gibson? Anonymous? Apocryphal?," *Quote Investigator*, January 24, 2012; http://quoteinvestigator.com/2012/01/24/future-has-arrived/

N. N.: "Global Games Market Will Reach $102.9 Billion in 2017," *newzoo: Games Market Research*, May 15, 2014; http://www.newzoo.com/insights/global-games-market-will-reach-102-9-billion-2017-2/#H778PRVRTcsr5wy1.99

N. N.: "Mit 2,66 Milliarden Euro ist Deutschland größter Gamesmarkt in Europa – Newzoo und G.A.M.E Bundesverband legen Marktzahlen für 2013 vor," March 17, 2014; http://game-bundesverband.de/de/mit-266-milliarden-euro-ist-deutschland-groster-gamesmarkt-in-europa-newzoo-und-g-a-m-e-bundesverband-legen-marktzahlen-fur-2013-vor/

N. N.: "'Spacewar!,'" in: Parish, Jeremy (ed.), *The Essential 50 Archives, 1UP.com*; http://www.1upp.com/features/essential-50-part-1-spacewar

Neuenfeld, Jörg: *Alles ist Spiel: zur Geschichte der Auseinandersetzung mit einer Utopie der Moderne*, Würzburg: Königshausen & Neumann 2005.

Neumann, John von: "First Draft of a Report on the EDVAC," 1945; http://www.virtualtravelog.net/wp/wp-content/media/2003-08-TheFirstDraft.pdf

New Games Foundation/Fluegelman, Andrew: *The New Games Book*, Garden City, N.Y.: Dolphin Books 1976.

Nietzsche, Friedrich. *Birth of Tragedy*, Arlington, VA: Richer Resources Publications 2009 (*1872); http://records.viu.ca/~johnstoi/Nietzsche/tragedy_all.htm

Nohr, Rolf F.: *Strategie Spielen: Medialität, Geschichte und Politik des Strategiespiels*, Medien'Welten, Münster u.a.: Lit 2008.

———: "'Rhythmusarbeit': Revisited," in: Freyermuth, Gundolf S./Gotto, Lisa/Wallenfels, Fabian (ed.), *Serious Games, Exergames, Exerlearning: Zur Transmedialisierung und Gamification des Wissenstransfers*, Bielefeld: transcript 2013, pp. 351-386.

Norman, Donald A.: *Emotional Design: Why We Love (Or Hate) Everyday Things*, New York: Basic Books 2004.

Ostrowska, Dorota/Roberts, Graham: *European Cinemas in the Television Age*, Edinburgh University Press 2007.

Parkin, Simon: "30 Years Later, One Man Is Still Trying To Fix Video Games," *Kotaku*, December 27, 2013; http://kotaku.com/30-years-later-one-mansstill-trying-to-fix-video-gam-1490377821

Pautz, Michelle: "The Decline in Average Weekly Cinema Attendance: 1930-2000," *Issues in Political Economy*, 2002, Vol. 11; http://org.elon.edu/ipe/pautz2.pdf

Pias, Claus: *Computer-Spiel-Welten*, Munich: Sequenzia 2002.

Prensky, Marc: *Digital Game-Based Learning*, New York: McGraw-Hill 2001.

―――: *'Don't Bother Me Mom, I'm Learning!': How Computer and Video Games Are Preparing Your Kids for Twenty-First Century Success and How You Can Help!*, St. Paul, Minn.: Paragon House 2006.

Probst, Maximilian: "Ballern ist nicht alles," *Die Zeit*, December 8, 2012; http://www.zeit.de/2012/50/Computerspiele-Medium-Zukunft/komplettansicht

Pross, Harry: *Medienforschung: Film, Funk, Presse, Fernsehen*, Darmstadt: Habel 1972.

Pudovkin, Vsevolod Illarionovich, et al. *Selected Essays*. London; New York: Seagull Books 2006.

Reich, Robert B.: *The Work of Nations: Preparing Ourselves for 21st-Century Capitalism*, New York: A.A. Knopf 1991.

Reynolds, Jack: "Jacques Derrida (1930-2004)," *Internet Encyclopedia of Philosophy – A Peer-Reviewed Academic Source*; http://www.iepp.utm.edu/derrida/

Ritterfeld, Ute/Cody, Michael J./Vorderer, Peter: *Serious Games: Mechanisms and Effects*, New York: Routledge 2009.

Rojas, Peter: "Hollywood: the People's Cut. The Fans are Now Editing Hollywood Blockbusters," *The Guardian*, July 24, 2002; http://www.theguardian.com/film/2002/jul/25/internet.technology

Rolfe, J. M./Staples, K. J.: *Flight Simulation*, Cambridge und New York: Cambridge University Press 1986.

Rose, Frank: *The Art of Immersion: How the Digital Generation is Remaking Hollywood, Madison Avenue, and the Way We Tell Stories*, New York: W.W. Norton & Co. (Kindle edition) 2011.

Rubin, Peter: "The Inside Story of Oculus Rift and How Virtual Reality Became Reality," *Wired*, May 20, 2014; http://www.wired.com/2014/05/oculus-rift-4/

Rupley, Sebastian: "One Billion PCs Shipped," *PC Magazine*, July 3, 2002; http://www.pcmag.com/article2/0,4149,340368,00.asphttp://www.pcmag.com/article2/0,4149,340368,00.asp

Ryan, Marie-Laure: *Narrative as Virtual Reality: Immersion and Interactivity in Literature and Electronic Media*, Baltimore: Johns Hopkins University Press 2001.

Salen, Katie/Zimmerman, Eric: *Rules of Play: Game Design Fundamentals*, Cambridge, Mass.: MIT Press (Kindle edition) 2003.

―――: *The Game Design Reader: A Rules of Play Anthology*, Cambridge, Mass.: MIT Press 2006.

Sanghavi, Darshak: "Are TV and Video Games Making Kids Fat? The Effects of 'Screen Time' on Childhood Obesity," *Slate*, April 13, 2012; http://ww

w.slate.com/articles/health_and_science/medical_examiner/2012/04/are_vide o_games_making_kids_fat_screen_time_and_childhood_obesity_.html

Scheler, Max/Manfred S. Frings. *The Human Place in the Cosmos.* Evanston, Ill.: Northwestern University Press 2009 (*1928).

Schell, Jesse: *The Art of Game Design: A Book of Lenses*, Amsterdam und Boston: Elsevier/Morgan Kaufmann (Kindle edition) 2008.

———: "Die Zukunft des Erzählens: Wie das Medium die Geschichten formt," in: Beil, Benjamin/Freyermuth, Gundolf S./Gotto, Lisa (ed.), New Game Plus: Perspektiven der Game Studies. Genres – Künste – Diskurse, Bielefeld: transcript 2014, pp. 357-374.

Schiller, Friedrich: "Letters on the Aesthetical Education of Man," http://www.gutenberg.org/files/6798/6798-h/6798-h.htm

———: "To My Friends" (1802); http://www.readbookonline.net/readOnLine/20462/

Schlegel, Friedrich/von Behler, Ernst/Anstett, Jean Jacques/Eichner, Hans: Kritische *Friedrich-Schlegel-Ausgabe: Erste Abteilung: Kritische Neuausgabe*, vol. 2, Munich, Paderborn, Wien: F. Schöningh 1967.

Schwingeler, Stephan: "It's All About Connecting the Dots: Raum und Perspektive im Computerspiel," in: Beil, Benjamin/Bonner, Marc/Hensel, Thomas (ed.), *Computer | Spiel | Bilder*, Glückstadt: vwh Verlag Werner Hülsbusch 2014, pp. 25-58.

———: *Kunstwerk Computerspiel – digitale Spiele als künstlerisches Material: Eine bildwissenschaftliche und medientheoretische Analyse*, Bielefeld: transcript 2014.

Semper, Gottfried: *Der Stil in den technischen und tektonischen Künsten, oder, Praktische Aesthetik: ein Handbuch für Techniker, Künstler und Kunstfreunde*, Frankfurt a.M.: Verlag für Kunst und Wissenschaft 1860; http://digi.ub.uni-heidelberg.de/diglit/semper1863/0001

Shakespeare, William: "As You Like It," in: First Folio, 1623; http://internetshakespeare.uvic.ca/Library/Texts/AYL/F1/default/;jsessionid=13C1507FF23EB7C013571D7117075DF1

Shannon, Claude Elwood: "A Mathematical Theory of Communication," *The Bell System Technical Journal*, vol. 27, July/October 1948, pp. 379-423, 623- 656. Online reprinted with corrections from The Bell System Technical Journal; http://cm.bell-labs.com/cm/ms/what/shannonday/paper.html

Sicart, Miguel: "Teaching Beyond the Industry," Talk at the GDC Education Summit 2015; http://www.gdcvault.com

Simmel, Georg. *The Philosophy of Money.* Abingdon, Oxon; New York: Routledge 2011 (*1900).

Slovin, Rochelle: "Hot Circuits: Reflections on the 1989 Video Game Exhibition of the American Museum of the Moving Image," in: Mark J. P. Wolf (ed.), *The Medium of the Video Game*, Austin: University of Texas Press 2002, pp. 137-154.
Smith, E. E.: First Lensman, Reading, Pa.: Fantasy Press 1950.
———: Gray Lensman, Reading, Pa.: Fantasy Press 1951.
———: Second Stage Lensmen, Reading, Pa.: Fantasy Press 1953.
———: Children of the Lens, Reading, Pa.: Fantasy Press 1954.
Spencer, Herbert: *The Principles of Psychology*, London u.a.: Williams and Norgate 1855-1880; http://archive.org/details/principlesofpsyc022412mbp
Spitzenorganisation der Filmwirtschaft,: "Filmbesuch 1925-2009," 2010; http://www.spio.de/index.asp?SeitID=381
Sterling, Bruce: *Shaping Things*, Cambridge, Mass.: MIT Press 2005.
Stone, Allucquere Rosanne: *The War of Desire and Technology at the Close of the Mechanical Age*, Cambridge, Mass.: MIT Press 1995.
Suellentrop, Chris: N.Y.U. to Add a Bachelor's Degree in Video Game Design, *The New York Times*, August 5, 2014; http://artsbeat.blogs.nytimes.com/2014/08/05/n-y-u-to-add-a-bachelors-degree-to-video-game-studies/?_php=true&_type=blogs&smid=pl-share&_r=1
Sullivan, Steve/Williams, Chris: "The New Force at Lucasfilm," *BusinessWeek*, March 27, 2006; http://www.businessweek.com/print/innovate/content/mar2006/id20060327_719255.htm
Sutton-Smith, Brian: *The Ambiguity of Play*, Cambridge, Mass.: Harvard University Press 1997.
Tanz, Jason: "The Curse of Cow Clicker: How a Cheeky Satire Became a Videogame Hit," *Wired*, December 20, 2011; http://archive.wired.com/magazine/2011/12/ff_cowclicker/all/
Tucker, Greg: "Interactive Entertainment Industry Matures," *Patriot News-Harrisburg PA*, June 7, 1998, www.nexis.com
Turing, Alan: "On Computable Numbers, with an Application to the Entscheidungsproblem," in: *Proceedings of the London Mathematical Society* ser. 2. vol. 42, 1936-7, pp. 230-265; corrections, Ibid, vol 43, 1937, pp. 544-546; http://www.abelard.org/turpap2/tp2-ie.asp
Turkle, Sherry: *Life on the Screen: Identity in the Age of the Internet*, New York: Simon & Schuster 1995.
———: *Alone Together: Why We Expect More From Technology and Less From Each Other*, New York: Basic Books 2011.

Von Neumann, John/Morgenstern, Oskar: *Theory of Games and Economic Behavior*, Princeton: Princeton University Press 1944; https://archive.org/detai ls/theoryofgamesand030098mbp

Vorderer, Peter: *Playing Video Games: Motives, Responses, and Consequences*, Mahwah, NJ. u.a.: Erlbaum 2006.

Walker, Trey: "The Sims Overtakes Myst," *Gamespot*, 2002; http://www.ga mespot.com/articles/the-sims-overtakes-myst/1100-2857556/

Walther, Bo Kampmann: "Cinematography and Ludology: In Search of a Lucidography," 2004; http://www.brown.edu/Research/dichtung-digital/2004/1/ Walther/index.htm

Wardrip-Fruin, Noah: *Expressive Processing: Digital Fictions, Computer Games, and Software Studies*, Cambridge, MA: The MIT Press 2009.

Wessely, Dominik: "Fallstudie 1: NEW HORIZON – Das Spiel mit der Geschichte. Historische Narration im Dokumentarfilm und Game," in: Freyermuth, Gundolf S./Gotto, Lisa/Wallenfels, Fabian (ed.), *Serious Games, Exergames, Exerlearning: Zur Transmedialisierung und Gamification des Wissenstransfers*, Bielefeld: transcript 2013, pp. 123-136.

Wikipedia: "Stichwort 'Arcade game,'" http://en.wikipedia.org/wiki/List_of_hig hestgrossing_arcade_games#List_of_highestgrossing_arcade_video_games

Williams, Dmitri: "Bridging the Methodological Divide in Game Research," in: Simulation and Gaming 36, December 4, 2005, pp. 1-17; http://www.dmitri williams.com/GameMethods.pdf

Wimmer, Jeffrey: *Massenphänomen Computerspiele: soziale, kulturelle und wirtschaftliche Aspekte*, Konstanz: UVK Verlagsgesellschaft 2013.

Wolf, Mark J. P.: *The Medium of the Video Game*, Austin: University of Texas Press 2002.

———: "The Video Game as a Medium," in: Wolf, Mark J. P. (ed.), *The Medium of the Video Game*, Austin: University of Texas Press 2002, pp. 13-33.

Zagal, José P./Bruckman, Amy: "The Game Ontology Project: Supporting Learning While Contributing Authentically to Game Studies," *CLS 08 Proceedings of the 8th International Conference for the Learning Sciences*, 2014, pp. 499-506; http://www.fi.uu.nl/en/icls2008/283/paper283.pdf

Zichermann, Gabe/Cunningham, Christopher: *Gamification by Design: Implementing Game Mechanics in Web and Mobile Apps*, Sebastopol, Calif.: O'Reilly Media 2011.

Zielinski, Siegfried: *Audiovisions: Cinema and Television as Entr'actes in History*, Amsterdam: Amsterdam University Press 1999.

Zimmerman, Eric: "Manifesto for a Ludic Century," *Kotaku*, September 9, 2013; http://kotaku.com/manifesto-the-21st-century-will-be-defined-by-games-127 5355204

———: "How I Teach Game Design. Lesson 1: The Game Design Process," *Gamasutra*, October 19, 2013; http://www.gamasutra.com/blogs/EricZimmer man/20131019/202710/How_I_Teach_Game_Design_Lesson_1_The_Game _Design_Process.php

Zimmermann, Olaf/Schulz, Gabriele: *Streitfall Computerspiele: Computerspiele zwischen kultureller Bildung, Kunstfreiheit und Jugendschutz*, Berlin: Deutscher Kulturrat 2008; http://www.kulturrat.de/dokumente/streitfallcom puterspiele.pdf

Zorn, Isabel: "Lernen mit digitalen Medien. Zur Gestaltung der Lernszenarien," in: Freyermuth, Gundolf S./Gotto, Lisa/Wallenfels, Fabian (ed.), *Serious Games, Exergames, Exerlearning: Zur Transmedialisierung und Gamification des Wissenstransfers*, Bielefeld: transcript 2013, pp. 49-74.

FILMOGRAPHY

A SCANNER DARKLY (USA 2006, D: Richard Linklater)
ARCADE (USA 1993, D: Albert Pyun)
AVATAR (USA/UK 2009, D: James Cameron)
BABEL (USA/F/MEX 2006, D: Alejandro González Iñárritus)
BEOWULF (USA 2007)
DAS BOOT (D 1981, D: Wolfgang Petersen)
EDGE OF TOMORROW (USA 2014, D: Doug Liman)
ENCOUNTER AT FARPOINT (USA 1987, D: Corey Allen)
ENEMY OF THE STATE (USA 1998, D: Tony Scott)
EXISTENZ (USA 1999, D: David Cronenberg)
FINAL FANTASY: THE SPIRITS WITHIN (USA 2001, D: Hironobu Sakaguchi)
GAMER (USA 2009, D: Mark Neveldine/Brian Taylor)
GERTIE THE DINOSAUR (USA 1914, D: Winsor McCay)
GROUNDHOG DAY (USA 1993, D: Harold Ramis)
HARRY POTTER AND THE DEATHLY HALLOWS PART 2 (UK/USA 2011, D: David Yates)
HELLBOY (USA 2004, D: Guillermo del Toro)
HOW I MET YOUR MOTHER (USA 2005 – 2014, P: Carter Bays/ Craig Thomas)
INCEPTION (USA 2010, D: Christopher Nolan)
INDIANA JONES (USA 1981, D: Steven Spielberg)

IRRÉVERSIBLE (FR 2002, D: Gaspar Noé)
JAMES BOND FILM DR. NO (UK 1962, D: TERENCE YOUNG)
LADY IN THE LAKE (USA 1947, D: Robert Montgomery)
LOLA RENNT (D 1998, Tom Tykwer)
MARVEL'S THE AVENGERS (USA 2012, D: Joss Whedon)
MULHOLLAND DRIVE (USA 2001, D: David Lynch)
PAN'S LABYRINTH (ESP/MEX 2006, D: Guillermo del Toro)
PULP FICTION (USA 1994, D: Quentin Tarantino)
RENAISSANCE (FR 2006, D:Christian Volckmann)
RESIDENT EVIL (D, UK, FR 2002, D: Paul W. S. Anderson)
SIN CITY (USA 2005, D: Frank Miller/ Robert Rodriguez)
SLIDING DOORS (UK/USA 1998, D: Peter Howitt)
SPEED RACER (USA 2008, D: Andy and Lana Wachowski)
STAR TREK: THE NEXT GENERATION (USA 1987-1994, P: Gene Roddenberry)
STAR WARS (USA 1977, D: George Lucas)
STAR WARS: EPISODE I: THE PHANTOM MENACE (USA 1999, D: George Lucas)
STRANGE DAYS (USA 1995, D: Kathryn Bigelow)
SUPER MARIO BROS. (USA 1993, D: Rocky Morton/Annabel Jankel)
MARVEL'S THE AVENGERS (USA 2012, D: Joss Whedon)
MAX PAYNE (USA/CA 2008, D: John Moore)
MEMENTO (USA 2000, D: Christopher Nolen)
MINORITY REPORT (USA 2002, D: Steven Spielberg)
THE DARK KNIGHT RISES (UK/USA 2012, D: Christopher Nolan)
THE LAST STARFIGHTER (USA 1984, D: Nick Castle)
THE MATRIX (USA 1999, D: Andy and Lana Wachowski)
THE POLAR EXPRESS (USA 2004, D: Robert Zemeckis)
THE THIRTEENTH FLOOR (USA 1999, D: Josef Rusnak)
TIMECODE (USA 2000, D: Mike Figgis)
TRON (USA 1982, D: Steven Lisberger)
WAKING LIFE (USA 2001, D: Richard Linklater)
WATCHMEN (USA/UK/CA 2009, D: Zack Snyder))
WING COMMANDER (USA/LUX 1999, D: Chris Roberts)

GAMOGRAPHY

ADVENTURELAND (Adventure International 1978, O: Adventure International)
ALAN WAKE (Microsoft Game Studios 2010, O: Remedy Entertainment)
ANGRY BIRDS (Chillingo 2009, O: Rovio Entertainment)

ANSTOSS – DER FUßBALLMANAGER (Ascaron 1993-2006, O: Ascaron)
ASSASSIN'S CREED (Ubisoft 2008, O: Ubisoft Montreal)
ASHERON'S CALL (Microsoft 1998, O: Turbine Entertainment)
ASTEROIDS (Atari 1979, O: Atari)
AVATAR (Plato 1977, O: Jim Schwaiger)
BALDUR'S GATE (BioWare 1998, O: Interplay Entertainment)
BALANCE OF POWER (Mindscape 1985, O: Chris Crawford)
BATTLEZONE (Atari 1980, O: Atari)
BEYOND: TWO SOULS (Sony Computer Entertainment 2013, O: Quantic Dream)
BIOSHOCK (2K Games 2007, O: 2K Boston/2K Australia/2K Marin)
BLACK & WHITE (EA Games 2001, O: Lionhead Studios)
BRAID (Valve 2008, O: Number None, Inc./Microsoft Game Studios)
BREAKOUT (Atari 1976, O: Atari)
CALL OF DUTY: BLACK OPS (Activision 2010, O: Treyarch)
CALL OF DUTY: MODERN WARFARE 2 (Activision 2009, O: Infinity Ward)
CANDY CRUSH SAGA (King 2012)
CIVILIZATION (MicroProse 1991, O: MicroProse)
COLOSSAL CAVE ADVENTURE (CRL 1972, O: William Crowther/Don Woods)
COMPUTER SPACE (Nutting Associates 1971, O: Nutting Associates)
COW CLICKER (Ian Bogost 2010)
CROSSFIRE (Neowiz Games 2007, O: SmileGate)
CROWN SOCCER SPECIAL (Taito 1967)
CRYSIS 2 (Electronic Arts 2011, O: Crytek/Crytek UK)
CRYSIS 3 (Electronic Arts 2013, O: Crytek)
DEUS EX (Eidos Interactive 2000, O: Ion Storm)
DIABLO III (Blizzard Entertainment 2012, O: Blizzard Entertainment)
DONKEY KONG (Nintendo 1981, O: Nintendo)
DOOM (id Software 1993, O: id Software)
DOOM II (GT Interactive 1994, O: id Software)
DUNGEON (Don Daglow 1975/76)
DUNGEONS & DRAGONS
DUNGEON FIGHTER Online (Neople 2005, O: Neople)
EASTERN FRONT (1941) (APX/Atari inc. 1981, O: Chris Crawford)
ELITE: DANGEROUS (Frontier Developments 2014, O: David Braben)
ENDGAME (Google Niantic Labs 2015, in development)
EVERQUEST (SonyOnline 1999)
EVERQUEST NEXT (Sony Online 2015, in development)
FABLE (Microsoft Game Studios 2004, O: Big Blue Box/Lionhead Studios)
FAHRENHEIT (Atari SA 2005, O: Quantic Dream)

FARMVILLE (Zynga 2009)
FIFA (Electronic Arts seit 1993, O: Electronic Arts)
FIFA 14 (Electronic Arts 2013, O: EA Canada)
FINAL FANTASY (Squaresoft/Squareenix seit 1987, O:Squaresoft/Squareenix)
FLIGHT SIMULATOR (SubLogic 1978, O: SubLogic)
FLOW (Sony Computer Entertainment 2006, O: thatgamecompany)
FLOWER (Sony Computer Entertainment 2009, O: Thatgamecompany/Bluepoint Games)
GRAND THEFT AUTO V (Rockstar Games 2013, O: Rockstar North)
HABITAT (Quantum Link/ Fujitsu 1985, O: Lucasfilm Games)
HALF-LIFE (Sierra Entertainment 1998, O: Valve)
HARRY POTTER AND THE PHILOSOPHER'S STONE (Electronic Arts 2001, O: KnowWonder)
HEAVY RAIN (Sony Computer Entertainment 2010, O: Quantic Dream)
INDIANA JONES AND THE LAST CRUSADE: THE GRAPHIC ADVENTURE (Lucasfilm Games 1989, O: Lucasfilm Games)
INGRESS (Niantic Labs 2012)
IT CAME FROM THE DESERT (Cinemaware 1989, O: Cinemaware)
JOURNEY (Sony Computer Entertainment 2012, O: Thatgamecompany)
KING'S QUEST-Serie (Sierra Entertainment 1984-1998, O: Sierra Entertainment)
LABYRINTH (Activision 1986, O: Lucasfilm Games)
LEAGUE OF LEGENDS (Riot Games seit 2009, O: Riot Games)
MADDEN FOOTBALL (Electronic Arts seit 1988, O: Electronic Arts)
MADDEN NFL 25 (EA Sports 2013, O: EA Tiburon)
MAJESTIC (Electronic Arts 2001)
MANIAC MANSION (Lucasfilm Games 1987, O: Lucasfilm Games)
MARIO BROS. (Nintendo 1983, O: Nintendo)
MAX PAYNE (Gathering of Developers 2001, O: Remedy Entertainment)
MAZE WAR (Steve Colley 1974)
MICROSOFT FLIGHT SIMULATOR (Microsoft seit 1982, O: SubLogic)
MIGHTY NO. 9 (Comcept 2015, in development)
MYST (Brøderbund 1993, O: Cyan)
MYSTERY HOUSE (On-Line Systems 1979/80, O: Roberta und Ken Williams)
NIGHT DRIVER (Micronetics 1976, O: Atari)
NIM (Herbert Koppel, Eugene Grant and Howard Bailer 1952)
NO MAN'S SKY (Hello Games 2015, in development)
NOUGHTS AND CROSSES (A. S. Douglas 1952)
PAC-MAN (Midway Games 1980, O: Namco)
PIRATES! (MicroProse 1987, O: Sid Meier/MicroProse)

PONG (Atari 1972, O: Atari)
POPULOUS (Electronic Arts 1989, O: Bullfrog Productions)
PRINCE OF PERSIA: THE SANDS OF TIME (Ubisoft, SCEJ 2003, O: Ubisoft Montreal)
PRO EVOLUTION SOCCER (Konami 2001, O: Konami Computer Entertainment Tokyo)
PROJECT ETERNITY (Paradox Interactive 2015, in development. O: Obsidian Entertainment)
QUAKE (GT Interactive 1996, O: id Software)
SIM CITY (Electronic Arts 1989, O: Maxis)
SPACE INVADERS (Midway Games 1978, O: Taito)
SPACE WAR (Atari 1978, O: Atari)
SPACEWAR! (Steve Russell 1961)
SPASIM (Jim Bowery 1974)
STAR CITIZEN (Cloud Imperium Games 2015, in development)
STAR TREK (Mike Mayfield 1971)
STAR WARS: REBEL ASSAULT (LucasArts 1993, O: LucasArts)
STRANGLEHOLD (Midway Games 2007, O: Midway Chicago/Tiger Hill Entertainment)
SUPER MARIO BROS. (Nintendo 1985, O: Nintendo)
TANKTICS (Chris Crawford 1978)
TENNIS FOR TWO (William Higinbotham 1958)
THE BEAST (Microsoft 2001, O: Sean Stewart,/Elan Lee/Pete Fenlon)
THE CAT AND THE COUP (Steam 2011, O: Peter Brinson/Kurosh ValaNejad)
THE HITCHHIKER'S GUIDE TO THE GALAXY (Infocom 1984, O: Infocom)
THE KING OF CHICAGO (Cinemaware 1986, O: Cinemaware)
THE LEGEND OF ZELDA (Nintendo 1986, O: Nintendo EAD)
THE SECRET OF MONKEY ISLAND (LucasArts 1990, O: Lucasfilm Games)
THE SIMS (Electronic Arts 2000, O: Maxis)
TITANFALL (Electronic Arts 2014, O: Respawn Entertainment)
TOMB RAIDER: THE ACTION ADVENTURE (Eidos Interactive/Bright Entertainment 2008, O: Little Worlds Studio)
TORMENT: TIDES OF NUMENERA (inXile Entertainment 2015, in development)
TV SPORTS: FOOTBALL (Cinemaware 1989, O: Cinemaware)
ULTIMA ONLINE (Electronic Arts 1997, O: Origen)
ULTIMA III: EXODUS (Origin Systems 1983, O: Richard Garriott)
ULTIMA UNDERWORLD: THE STYGIAN ABYSS (Origin Systems 1992, O: Blue Sky Productions)

UNCHARTED 3: DRAKES DECEPTION (Sony Computer Entertainment 2011, O: Naughty Dog)
WING COMMANDER (Origin Systems 1990, O: Origin Systems)
WING COMMANDER II: VENGEANCE OF THE KILRATHI (Origin Systems 1991, O: Origin Systems)
WING COMMANDER III: HEART OF THE TIGER (Origin Systems 1994, O: Origin Systems)
WING COMMANDER IV: THE PRICE OF FREEDOM (Electronic Arts 1996, O: Origin Systems)
WING COMMANDER V: PROPHECY (Electronic Arts 1997, O: Origin Systems)
WING COMMANDER: ACADEMY (Origin Systems 1993, O: Origin Systems)
WING COMMANDER: ARMADA (Electronic Arts 1994, O: Origin Systems)
WING COMMANDER: PRIVATEER (Electronic Arts 1993, O: Origin Systems)
WING COMMANDER: SECRET OPS (Electronic Arts 1998, O: Origin Systems)
WOLFENSTEIN 3D (Apogee Software 1992, O: id Software)
WORLD OF WARCRAFT (Blizzard 2004)
World Series Baseball (Sega 1994, O: Blue Sky Software)
ZORK (Infocom 1977, O: Infocom)